DAWN LANGMAN undertook a mainstream speech and acting training in Australia, followed by seven years of performing and teaching at secondary and tertiary levels. Her quest for an integrated approach that includes the spiritual dimension led her to train with Maisie Jones at the London School of Speech Formation in the method developed by Rudolf and Marie Steiner. She then taught for ten years at Emerson College in Sussex. Following this, Dawn trained in Michael Chekhov's acting technique with Ted Pugh and Fern Sloan of the Actors Ensemble in New York. Returning to Australia, she founded the School of the Living Word, where for eight years she continued to research the integration of Speech Formation with Chekhov's technique. She currently teaches this methodology at the Drama Centre, Flinders University, South Australia.

In the same series:

The Art of Speech, Body – Soul – Spirit – Word, A Practical and Spiritual Guide (forthcoming 2014)

The Integrated Actor, Body – Soul – Spirit – Word, A Practical and Spiritual Guide (forthcoming 2015)

THE ART OF ACTING

Body – Soul – Spirit – Word

A Practical and Spiritual Guide

DAWN LANGMAN

Artwork by Raphaela Mazzone

TEMPLE LODGE

First published in Great Britain in 2014 by Temple Lodge Publishing,
Hillside House, The Square
Forest Row, RH18 5ES

E-mail: office@templelodge.com

www.templelodge.com

Unless otherwise acknowledged, all epigraphs are taken from *The Bhagavad Gita*, the holy Hindu scripture that is part of the ancient Sanskrit epic *The Mahabharata*

A catalogue record for this book is available from the British Library

ISBN 978 1 906999 59 9

Cover by Morgan Creative
Typeset by DP Photosetting, Neath, West Glamorgan
Printed and bound in the UK by 4edge Limited, Essex

For Ted Pugh and Fern Sloan,
who taught me Chekhov's work in this spirit.

Contents

Acknowledgements 1

Preface 3

THE CONTEXT

Michael Chekhov — a brief introduction 9

Why a spiritual path for the actor? 11

Understanding the nature of the actor and the artist 18

Terms of reference 40

THE PRACTICE

Chapter 1 – The Psycho-Physical Principle 55

Awakening our body as a sensing organ 55
The body as sensing organ explorations 1–3 56

The four qualities-of-movement 57
MOULDING — *Qualities-of-movement explorations 1–6* 57
FLOATING — *Qualities-of-movement explorations 7–10* 60
FLYING — *Qualities-of-movement explorations 11–14* 63
RADIATING — *Qualities-of-movement explorations 15–19* 64
Transitions – Qualities-of-movement explorations 20–23 66
The four temperaments – Four temperaments explorations 1–2 71

Chapter 2 – Body 75

Inhabiting the body 75

Counter tensions — *Counter tensions explorations 1–5* 77

Impulse and sustaining 84
Impulse – *Impulse explorations 1–5* 84
Sustaining – *Sustaining explorations 1–4* 86
Sustaining and commitment 87

Space 89

Expansion and contraction — *Expansion & contraction explorations 1–27*   90

Time   104
Tempo — fast and slow — *Tempo explorations 1–3*   104
The dynamics of staccato and legato — *Staccato & legato explorations 1–2*   106
Interplay of tempo and dynamic — *Tempo & dynamic explorations 1–13*   107

Layering — *Layering explorations 1–3*   116

Gravity and levity — *Gravity & levity explorations 1–7*   118
The 'Three Sisters' — falling, lifting and balancing — *Gravity & levity
    explorations 8–9*   122

Ancient Greek gymnastics   124
RUNNING — *Greek gymnastics explorations 1–3*   124
LEAPING — *Greek gymnastics explorations 4–5*   125
WRESTLING — *Greek gymnastics explorations 6–9*   126
DISCUS — *Greek gymnastics explorations 10–11*   128
JAVELIN — *Greek gymnastics explorations 12–13*   132

Chapter 3 — Soul   135

The threefold nature of our soul-life   135
THE THREE CENTRES: THINKING, FEELING AND WILLING   135
THE FEELING CENTRE AND THE HEART (HEART-CENTRE) — *Heart-centre explorations 1–6*   136
THE WILL CENTRE IN THE BELLY (WILL-CENTRE) — *Will-centre explorations 1–5*   140
THE THINKING CENTRE IN THE HEAD (HEAD-CENTRE) — *Head-centre explorations 1–5*   146
TRANSITIONS BETWEEN THE THREE CENTRES — *3-centres explorations 1–2*   153
THE THREE CENTRES AND THE CHAKRAS   155

Imaginary-centres — *Imaginary-centres explorations 1–6*   159

Animals — *Animals explorations 1–2*   168

Feelings or emotions   174

Qualities and sensations — *Quality & sensation explorations 1–5*   176

Atmosphere — *Atmosphere explorations 1–8*   179

Incorporating objects: stick, ball & veil — *Incorporating objects
    explorations 1–7*   184

The Sphinx   189

Right and left: understanding and emotion — *Right & left explorations 1–3*   192

The 12 senses   194

Bridge to chapter 4   200

Chapter 4 — Spirit   201

Spirit and the creation of character   201

Objectives   206

Psychological gesture   207
Gesture — *PG exploration 1*   207
Archetypal-gesture — *PG explorations 2–13*   209
PG in scene work — *PG explorations 14–18*   216

Imaginary body, bizarre body — *Imaginary-body explorations 1–2*   220

Imaginary centres — *Imaginary centres explorations 1–2*   224

Further thoughts about the Self or spirit of the character   226

Visualization and incorporation — *Visualization & incorporation explorations 1–3*   227

Archetypes — *Archetypes explorations 1–3*   230

Chapter 5 — Art and Chekhov's 'Four Brothers'   233

The Four brothers   233
THE SENSE OF EASE — *Four brothers explorations 1–2*   234
THE SENSE OF FORM — *Four brothers explorations 3–8*   235
THE SENSE OF BEAUTY — *Four brothers explorations 9–13*   237
THE SENSE OF THE WHOLE — *Four brothers explorations 14–19*   241
VARIATIONS — *Four brothers explorations 20–22*   244

Chapter 6 — Performance and the Threshold   246

Artistic sensibility and 'stage-fright'   246

Steiner and the threshold   248
Implications for the actor   248
Crossing the threshold — *Threshold explorations 1–2*   249
Presence or possession — *Presence explorations 1–8*   251

An actor's relationships   258
Actor to character   258
Actor to actor   258
Ensemble — *Ensemble explorations 1–10*   259
Character to character — *Character-to-character explorations 1–5*   263
Actor to audience — *Actor-to-audience exploration 1*   264
De-roling — *De-roling explorations 1–2*   264

Epilogue — Dionysus and the New Epidaurus   267
A new Epidaurus   267
Baby Dionysus   268
Dionysus comes of age   271
St John the Baptist/Dionysus   273
Our Western theatre lineage   275

Bridge to Book 2 — *The Art of Speech*   280

APPENDICES

Appendix A — Hamlet speech   283

Appendix B — Michael Chekhov's original preface for *To the Actor*   284

Appendix C — An autobiographical note   288

**Appendix D — Colleagues working with Chekhov in the context of
Anthroposophy and Speech Formation**   298

Bibliography   300

Additional reading   301

Original artworks that serve as a basis for Raphaela Mazzone's illustrations   302

Notes   304

Table of illustrations

Figure 1 – Isis enfolds us in her wings

Figure 2 – The monster sphinx

Figure 3 – The Pharaoh faces Osiris

Figure 4 – Anubis leads the human soul

Figure 5 – Nike of Samothrace

Figure 6 – Counter-tensions 1

Figure 7 – Counter-tensions 2

Figure 8 – Counter-tensions 3

Figure 9 – The discus thrower

Figure 10 – The spear thrower

Figure 11 – The spear thrower

Figure 12 – The heart-centre of Apollo

Figure 13 – Heart-centre based on the figure of Apollo

Figure 14 – Will-centre based on a warrior 1

Figure 15 – Will-centre based on a warrior 2

Figure 16 – Head-centre based on the charioteer

Figure 17 – 'I see' 1

Figure 18 – 'I see' 2

Figure 19 – Head-centre connected to the stars

Figure 20 – The Charioteer

Figure 21 – Head-centre connected to the stars

Figure 22 – The 7 chakras in relationship to the 3 centres

Figure 23 – Undefended heart 1 – 'I embrace the earth'

Figure 24 – Undefended heart 2 – 'I embrace the heavens'

Figure 25 – Undefended heart 3 – 'I embrace humanity'

Figure 26 – Defended heart 1

Figure 27 – Defended heart 2

Figure 28 – Da Vinci: human being in a circle

Figure 29 – Van Gogh's 'Boots with laces'

Figure 30 – Hermes/Mercury and Baby Dionysus

Figure 31 – Bacchus/John the Baptist

Figure 32 – Priests enact the trope within the Easter mass

Figure 33 – Our Western lineage

Figure 34 – Wheat sprouting from the body of Osiris

Figure 35 – Demeter bestows upon Triptolemus an ear of grain

Acknowledgements

Throughout my life, stars lit up my path reminding me of what I half-remembered: great individuals whose lives have touched mine. Some I have been blessed to work with here on earth and some inspire and work with me from other realms. All have confirmed: a spiritual path for the actor is there for those who wish to find it.

I thank them: my beloved parents who worked unceasingly to provide me with opportunities to fulfil my potential that they did not have themselves; Joanna Priest and Musgrave Horner, who nurtured my instinctive sense of the spiritual dimensions of art with their own; Rudolf Steiner, who shaped that instinctive sense into a sure pathway based on a deeper knowing of the human being as the Word made flesh; Maisie Jones, whose selfless devotion to that Word has provided the foundation for my life's work; Michael Chekhov, whose profound study of Steiner enabled him to penetrate his own genius with consciousness and reveal the art of the actor as spiritual lawfulness; Ted Pugh and Fern Sloan, who taught me Chekhov's work in this spirit; Mechthild Harkness and Sophia Walsh, other pioneers in the work of Speech Formation in the English language who have inspired me.

I thank the students who have woven their destinies with mine, who have shared in exploration and development of the work, and whose reactions to my unconscious patterns have been the mirror in which I have seen myself. I thank them for their courage, honesty and love.

I thank Perry Hart who through her sister art of music, honoured me with an artistic partnership in which we shared the same quest for the spirit and in which, through her encouragement and nurturing belief in me, I matured as an artist.

I thank Rosalba Clemente, whose inspiring colleagueship, support and recognition of my work have opened up a further chapter in its evolution I could never have predicted.

These and many others have enabled me to develop my own contribution to a path of training for the actor arising from the knowledge that the same wondrous realities, eternally creating and expressing in the greater universe, are at work in the human being. Art can cause these depths in us to resonate. What in us can move and speak, express, is that same divine spirit which can never be content until it is conscious of itself, in all its manifestations, as the embodiment of love.

I thank William, whose generosity throughout the years has made my work possible, and Patricia for her faithful support and friendship through the years.

For the creation of this book specifically, thanks to the following friends and colleagues whose encouragement and feedback have given me invaluable assistance in various development stages of the text: Marjolein Baars, Rosalba Clemente, Lindsay

Dearlove, Michael Elsworth, Dr Jane Gilmer, Sarah Kane, Michele Langman, Julie Le Gal Brodeur, Sarah Lohrey, Luciano Maycott, Dr Alduino Mazzone, Fern Sloan, Katerina Vlachou.

And for the tireless enthusiasm and efforts of my editor, Clare Strahan, without whose support the books would never have reached completion.

Preface

I write for those who resonate with a sense that theatre and the art of acting spring from a spiritual dimension that the mainstream of our western culture, even now, is reluctant to admit. I first remember performing in grade three at primary school; a simple, naïve play — something about roundheads and cavaliers — I have vague flashes of forgetting lines. I don't know whether I was seen then as 'gifted' and would not have known or cared what that meant. What I have never forgotten is the excitement of participating in something bigger than everyday reality; some magic that attracted everything and everyone into its sphere. Mothers sewed for weeks for the event. The routines of normal life, lessons and classroom culture completely gave way for the occasion.

I am reminded of this by the moment in the film *Shakespeare in Love* when the actors are gripped by their sense of participation in the birth of *Romeo and Juliet* and the privilege to be part of some grand intensity of life that is not an escape from everyday reality but a glimpse into what is really always there behind appearances; the extra-ordinary to which our ordinary lives aspire and which makes them meaningful and bearable. Of the incredible gift to be stretched into those intensities by a great script, feel them pour through one's own being and be received by an audience who, for a moment, share in those intensities, then pour their gratitude towards the actors who have opened up to them a path to a greater and deeper appreciation of their own humanity.

Over the years, students, friends and colleagues have asked me to write about the practical and esoteric aspects of my work to integrate *Michael Chekhov's acting technique* with Rudolf and Marie Steiner's *Art of Speech Formation*. The following interpretations and descriptions of Chekhov's work arise from my experience as a student, teacher and performer exploring a technique, arising as much from an oral tradition handed on by those who worked with him as from anything that can be found in books.[1]

A century has passed since Steiner blessed us with his insights into human con-sciousness and indications for the renewal of each branch of human work and knowledge. The methodologies that inspired those who lived a hundred years ago and passed that treasure on, have needed to evolve to meet the needs of human beings now — whose expanding sensibilities urgently require the healthy path advised by Steiner. In that same hundred years, mainstream theatre practice has focused on ways to access 'truthful emotion'. Depth of soul has been cultivated without a conscious understanding of the spirit. In contrast, research in the context of Rudolf Steiner's work has focused on the spirit, often at the soul's expense. The path suggested in these books brings soul and spirit into balance.

Chekhov understood his work was a contribution to the *theatre of the future*. His is not the only one. In the Roy Hart theatre and in Eugenio Barba's Odin Teatret, I have glimpsed the growing edge of theatre practice that would consciously embrace the spirit. The success of Tony Kushner's *Angels in America* indicates that when artistic genius renders its vision in dramatic form, the mainstream context is ready to receive works that pierce the veil and explore not only layers of our soul but also dimensions of the spirit. As these increasingly reveal themselves within our everyday realities, our culture will increasingly demand and produce the texts and works and actors that bear witness to them. Many of the suggestions Steiner made to actors in the *Speech and Drama* lectures have not been implemented yet because a methodology that honours body, soul and spirit has needed to evolve. Chekhov's psycho-physical approach is one key to such a methodology, and naturally extends into the voice if that is encouraged – creating a bridge to a holistic experience of Speech Formation.[2]

This approach signifies nothing less than the transformation of an ancient path.

For many centuries humanity endured and accepted the split between our conscious striving for perfection, projected onto work and religious practice, and the unconscious patterns that block our path. Those who survived the brutal centuries were constituted to ignore their vulnerability, suppress these patterns and by sheer will push through to achieve their goals. Yet although many still choose to subject themselves to regimes of cruelty, there is a growing wave of those who are 'not so strong as our grandparents used to be' and whose apparent 'weakness', from the perspective of that old paradigm, forces them to seek a different way; one which works to integrate what is normally regarded as 'the work' with personal, social, physical and psycho-spiritual health.

In the modern age, our culture moves away from a paradigm based upon suppression in order to 'get on with the work' to a new one based on the necessity for transformation of the shadow, both personal and group; recognition that this transformation cannot be excluded from the work but *is* our work; and that which we have formerly regarded as the work provides the form within which we can meet, and find pathways to transform, these patterns in ourselves.

It seems clear to me that a new order is emerging in which an ideal is not more precious or important than a human being; in which abuse and cruel judgement perpetrated in the name of that ideal will be exposed as a delusion. My teachers and colleagues have been, without exception, caring and humane. The level of abuse I refer to is a layer that exists in the unconscious levels of ourselves and the vessels that contain our culture, and is only rarely consciously intended. At an individual level, it manifests in willingness to harm oneself in the pursuit of ideals. In the traditions of our arts and sports and religious practice, abuse to the body/soul is accepted as the norm, the price to be paid in the pursuit of excellence.

When I took on the responsibility to form a Speech and Drama training, I saw the opportunity to take some first steps to create a culture in which healing work could be included. I became a student in the methodology of psychodrama. Within a safely guided process I was able, under supervision, to increasingly integrate processes of personal development with the training of my students' Speech and acting skills. Although I could not go beyond a certain point in this, I was confirmed in the vision of a future process; one in which the emotional struggles we artists undergo in mastering our art could be recognized as necessary to the work and part of it.

I believe a sustainable approach to acting includes the cultivation of a sense of *true identity*. Not the fragile ego dependent on others' recognition, but that spiritual Self within that is unassailable and indestructible and which allows actors to healthily negotiate the vast ocean of the many selves to which they are susceptible. What I mean by this 'Self' is articulated in the three connected books of this series.[3]

In Bertolt Brecht's play, *Mother Courage*, the characters have largely lost touch with their humanity, brutalized by years of unthinkable conditions in the Thirty Years' War. Only one remains in touch with her human spirit: Kattrin, abused by a soldier in childhood, and who cannot speak. Kattrin gives her life to save the nearby village, beating a drum to warn the villagers that soldiers are approaching.

It is an image for our time. Humanity wrestles with abuse that would obliterate the spirit's voice from our culture. This work bears witness to the certainty that as theatre continues to evolve, the human spirit will find its voice again.

A performance-training methodology in which means and end are not split from each other is one that embodies a new stage in our understanding of what love can mean. Its starting point is trust that *love is at our centre,* embracing what we are and supporting us to grow into all we may become. Chekhov's methodology, in combination with the Art of Speech Formation, has offered me the chance to explore the art of acting in this greater context.

Chekhov said, 'We are all babies in this long tremendous way.'[4] I have managed to take a few first steps and been astonished in the classroom, in rehearsals, in performance, by what happens when these two streams of work come together. A student in New York, granted such a glimpse, expressed it thus: 'It blows my mind!'

Having retired from active work to write these books, in 2012, I was surprised to be invited to teach this integrated Speech methodology to acting students at the Drama Centre at Flinders University in South Australia. It took so many years to find and bring together all the pieces of the puzzle. Now I can feel in the commitment and energy with which the students plunge into the process, that the truth of Steiner's research into Speech, integrated with the tools of Chekhov's methodology, is self-evident to them. The resulting richness language offers them, grants access to aspects of themselves that they have longed to know and integrate with their artistic journey.

These moments confirm for me that this work can make a contribution to an art of theatre that evolves along with the evolving human Self.

Dawn Langman
Adelaide 2013

THE CONTEXT

Michael Chekhov – a brief introduction

Michael Chekhov (1891–1955) was acknowledged as a master actor and teacher of his art within the mainstream of commercial film and theatre. He attempted to make conscious the unconscious processes comprising his genius, and sought confirmation of his research by studying the way that other great artists worked. Thus, he could identify the elements and processes by which we learn to practise art consciously.

How do we make audiences recognize themselves within a work of art; for their perception to be shifted, to cause them to be deeply moved, whether to tears or laughter? What is it that we do – and how can we better do it? From his observations in relation to these questions, Chekhov created an objective path of training for the actor that reached beyond the polishing of talent to become a healing path of inner development and transformation.

For those who searched consciously for this, working with Chekhov showed them how their path to be an actor was also a path to the spirit. At the time Chekhov was developing his work and finding language to articulate it, he could not publicly express what he had to say in this regard. In the mainstream context in which his destiny had placed him, it would not have been appropriate to speak directly of the spiritual source of his work. For this reason, the original preface to Chekhov's own book, *To the Actor*, was not published at that time.[*] Those, however, who asked specifically to understand that source, he answered.

We live now, half a century later, in a time when it is commonplace to speak directly concerning matters once considered occult. I am one of an increasing number who have needed to make these levels conscious in myself and in my work. This book is the result of exploring the basic exercises Chekhov gave, in the spiritual context within which they originate.

Like the great artists he draws on for his inspiration, Michael Chekhov has bequeathed to us a body of work which can be understood at many levels. His ideas may be grasped simply as tools that work in practice, or appreciated for their rich psychology, or as revelations of a deeper understanding of the spirit.

The validity of exploring Chekhov's work in relation to the work of Rudolf Steiner is justified by Chekhov's own acknowledgement. In a conversation with the actors who trained with him at Dartington Hall in England, Chekhov was recorded to have spoken thus:

> I am very proud that I belong to that movement. (Rudolf Steiner's Anthroposophy.) But I will never impose on our students anything of Anthroposophy … First of all, freedom …

---

[*] A transcript of Chekhov's original preface can be found as Appendix B.

Neither can I say that I am working in the theatre, just the same, for instance, as Reinhardt[*] is — whom I admire very much. I will never go his way because I believe in another way, which is what Dr Steiner has given to me as a far distant light ... If you will take Dr Steiner's method ... you will see there a cosmic gesture. If you will take what I call my 'Method' (it is not actually mine, but it is my effort to adjust our profession to things which I believe enough in,) it is a great cosmic spirit which we have to absorb ... We are all babies in this long tremendous way ...[5]

---

[*] Max Reinhardt (1873–1943) was an Austrian actor and director, recognized for his genius in the creation of a stylised visual imagery. This integrated the use of space with architectural and choreographic elements aimed to sweep the spectator into an experience of the drama, far transcending realism or the drama's literary source. On leaving Russia in 1928, Chekhov collaborated on several productions with Reinhardt.

Why a spiritual path for the actor?

Textbooks on the history of theatre state that the origin of drama was sacred ritual and that the first actors were the priests of their community. Is there a way of understanding this connection which is helpful to the actor of today?

We stand in the wings, waiting for our cues, calming our nerves with distractions; jokes, alcohol, cigarettes, mobile phones and internet connections, stories of past triumphs or disasters made delicious in the telling. We are about to embark on a journey that most actors find mysterious and challenging, many terrifying – some leave their own body to become someone else, some invite that someone else to enter them. Perhaps that someone else, that character, has experiences that in our own daily life we would not dare to face; emotions we may have learned to 'put the lid on'. If we allow ourselves to feel the violence or primal power the character demands, will we be torn to pieces or stay whole?

Who is there to guide us on this journey? Who has there ever been, as we walk into the judgement hall, exposed now, with no skin to keep us separate? We wait on the verdict of the audience or critics – was it 'good' or 'bad'? We have done our best, given our all, and poured our life-blood on the stage.

Why do actors subject themselves to this, day after day, night after night? When the moment comes, will our hearts be strong enough?

It's a form of dying. The Ancient Egyptians described it in great detail: how to leave the body and set out on that journey for which nothing in everyday existence has prepared us. Will I remember who I am? Will I recognize myself when I am not contained within my skin? How will I know which of the thoughts and feelings I experience, belong to me?

How does the *Egyptian Book of the Dead* describe such things? This text reminds us there was a time when guides travelled with us.

> *The First Priest speaks*: I come to you, you High Work Masters who have your dwelling in the heavens, on earth and in the world of souls.
> I bring to you this human soul.
> She has done no deed that would provoke the distaste of the Gods.
> Grant that she may live among you, day by day.
>
> *The Soul of the Dead speaks*: Let me appear before thy face Osiris,
> At the altar of the Lord of Truth.
> Allow me to come and go in the soul world.
> My heart is with me in the house of hearts.
> I understand with my heart.

Figure 1 – ISIS enfolds us in her wings

I am master over my heart.
I am master over my hands.
I am master over my legs.
I have the power to perform what my Ka (spirit) desires.
My soul shall not be prisoner to my body at the gates of Amentet.

The priests make cutting gestures across the eyes and the mouth and address the soul of the dead as Osiris – one who has overcome death.

Priests together: Hail Osiris! Thy mouth has been opened.
Thy two eyes have been opened ...
Thou shalt walk, thou shalt talk
And thy body shall be with the great Company of the Gods.

The Soul of the Dead speaks: Apep, fiend who feeds upon the weak,
May I never collapse before thee.
May thy poison never enter my members,
For my members are as the members of Ra (the Sun).
The power which surroundeth me
is the power which is in the gods forever ...
Let not the spirit-self be taken from me,
that dwells within my heart.
May I receive my Name
in the house of the Most High.
May I remember my name in the House of Fire,
In the night when the years shall be numbered ...

The Second Priest speaks: I come to you, Ye Work Masters, who have your dwelling in the world of souls,
I bring you this human soul.
Grant unto her food and drink and air that she may breathe,
And a home in the fields of peace
as is meet for a servant of Horus...

The Goddess Isis speaks: I come to thee to protect thee.
I give thee air for thy breathing.
Breathe the North wind that cometh from the God Tem.
It is I who have moulded your lungs.
I lead thee to the divine life ...
I make thy word to be truth before the goddess Nut.
I give thee power to worthily stand before the Gods ...

The Soul of the Dead speaks: Whatever God I meet upon my way His Name I shall be able to name ...

No evil shall befall me in this land or in this hall of Maat
For I know the names of the gods within . . .

All parts of the Door speak: Thou knowest us. Enter thou in.

Thus speaks the Floor of the hall: Tread not upon me.

Says the Dead: Why not, when indeed I am pure?

Says the Floor: Because not yet hast thou spoken the name of thy feet which would walk upon me. Tell it to me.

The Dead speaks: Garment of the God Menu is the name of my right foot. Lock of hair of the Goddess Nephthys is my left foot.

Says the Floor: Walk on for thou knowest us . . .

The Guardian speaks: Knowest thou the name of this door?

The soul of the dead speaks: Opener of Shu is the name of this door.

Guardian: Knowest thou the name of this lintel and this threshold?

The Soul of the Dead speaks: Lord of Truth upon his two feet is the name of the lintel. Lord of Strength, the binder of cattle,
is the name of the threshold.

Guardian: Pass, for thou knowest, Osiris . . .

The Soul of the Dead speaks: No evil shall befall me in this land and in this Hall of Maat,
For I know the names of the gods within . . .

This text reminds us of the true names of earthly things, connecting our memories of them with their reality: 'This step is the foot of the goddess . . .', 'This lintel is the . . .'. Our guides were beside us when our hearts were weighed in the balance against the feather of truth; to advocate on our behalf should they be found too heavy, weighed down, dense with unpurified emotion; if the great work of ourselves, the 'magnum opus'[*] were to know the judgement, 'less than perfect' and we should be devoured by the monster waiting there; the distorted Sphinx, whose features mirror our own monstrous distortions.

---

[*] The 'great work' was the term used by alchemists to mean that aspect of human evolution that must be completed by our own conscious work to transform the raw material bestowed on us by nature. This was the occult understanding of the quest to turn lead into gold.

Figure 3 – The Pharaoh faces Osiris

Head of a crocodile: bony thinking, without warmth or blood, which makes the clever, facile, glib interpretation. Breast of a lion, beast of prey: emotions that tear the soul to pieces, a performance that is self-indulgent. Limbs of a hippopotamus: the will, sunk in mud of its own lethargy – incapable of action, it has lost the discipline to practise and wants rewards without the work, yet lurking underneath the reeds and sensing threat, is sudden to attack.

But if my guide has led me truly, I walk safely past the beast, enter the great hall and stand before Him face to face – the god, Osiris – recognize, in Him, the indestructible core of my own being – my Self, Osiris, I AM.[*]

And around me Isis folds her wings.

The parallel between the actor's journey and the journey of the soul after death is not arbitrary or coincidental. The details, as recorded in Egyptian texts, also formed the steps of a path trod by neophytes on the journey of initiation. There, under guidance of the Hierophant, pupils prepared to make this very journey, while alive; to leave their earthly bodies in the 'temple sleep' and undergo what soul and spirit only normally experienced after death. But now they would be guided to return again into their bodies, bringing back the memory of those realities that lie beyond our earthly senses.

Perhaps drama has its roots in temple rituals and the first actors were priests because their training prepared them for the terrors and ordeals of *life outside the body* – which could not be survived by the unprepared. As drama (and theatre) evolved over the centuries, it separated from its sacred origins. Nevertheless, many actors of today find themselves adrift in the deeper mysteries intrinsic to their art, and long to reconnect their creativity to them.

We see the god Anubis in the well-known image on papyrus in the British Museum. He holds her hand, so firmly and confidently, as he leads the human soul to have her heart weighed in the balance. Rudolf Steiner and Michael Chekhov are two who walk beside us and lead us safely through the perils of this path. They help us rightly name the beings and the levels we encounter on our way and find the heart-strength that enables us to stand up whole and human in our art; to know that even as we probe the darker depths, we need not abandon our humanity.

Communication in our time provides an expanding, mutually fructifying soil of theatre practice, shared by actors and practitioners around the world and so the reader may recognise material not exclusively developed first by Chekhov. Where this is the case, it is because Chekhov's legacy is as much a way of understanding process as any specific exercises that he gave. Ideas from other sources are viewed through the

---

[*] See Figure 3 *The Pharaoh faces Osiris* on page 15, and Figure 4 *Anubis leads the human soul* on page 17.

Figure 4 – ANUBIS leads the human soul

Chekhov lens, fashioned out of questions such as: when I work, would it make a difference to know the 'true name' of my foot, my hand, my breath, the threshold that I cross? To experience the aspects of my soul and body that I train, or the space I work in, as expressions of divine creation? To know again the 'High Work Masters' who inspire us?[*] By attempting to translate those ancient certainties into forms compatible with an actor's consciousness today, I hope to contribute to an understanding of the art of acting in its sacred role as bearer of the new mysteries.

---

[*] See pages 11–14 for an excerpt of *The Egyptian Book of the Dead.*

Understanding the nature of the actor and the artist

I have known actors and artists whose lives demonstrate emotional maturity and balance. Some have struggled with their demons to achieve this balance, some have been blessed with childhoods that nurtured and did not undermine it, demonstrating that an artist does not need to be unbalanced to create. In any case, the next chapter may help you understand yourself, or some of those you teach or work with. In it, we explore how creativity, artistic sensibility, emotional dysfunction and the necessity to cultivate what Steiner calls healthy supersensible cognition, relate to the journey of the actor, and the connection of all of these to evolving human consciousness.

LET'S! is a simple game, played by actors to warm up. Let's be chickens! *Yes, let's!* Let's lay an egg! *Yes, let's!* Let's eat an ice cream! *Yes, let's!* Let's be the ice cream! *Yes, let's!* Let's be a helicopter … etc. We return to the consciousness of childhood before the rational mind interferes and calls out, *No! That is not possible!*

In childhood, we know we can be anything: a choo choo train, a lion, tiger, spider, tree. There are no boundaries. A chair can just as easily become the horse on which we ride as the broom our magic staff. We have power to manifest what we need and, its purpose over, make it disappear again. This capacity is natural in children. We learn by imitating; playing out things and actions and people who surround us, not perceiving yet that they are separate from ourselves.

This unconscious capacity to imitate remains until experiences teach the child to form clear boundaries between itself and its environment. Until then its entire organism functions as a 'sensitive membrane' receptive even to the subtlest stimuli. Those who are gifted to be actors retain that sensitivity as adults and are able either to consciously recreate this 'childlike condition' or, for reasons of their destiny, do not in the natural course of their development form such clear boundaries of self. The latter are likely to struggle to find balance unless they find a way to manage the condition that enables them to act, but makes it hard to live. Chekhov coined the term *sensitive membrane* to describe the specific form artistic sensibility must take for an actor whose body/soul gestalt must be their instrument.

The biographies of many actors record the difficulties of those for whom the sensitive membrane is both gift and curse. The retention of their childlike ability to experience themselves within the other, and the other in themselves, is what makes them actors. Yet this very gift makes it difficult, even impossible, to function in a world in which survival of the self demands firm boundaries.

Someone has a gift to play an instrument, or sing, paint, sculpt, act, etc., but to become an artist requires a combination of conditions: *artistic sensibility* along with gifts specific to that art and commitment to develop skills that communicate that sensitivity to others. The challenge to become a healthy human being faces everyone. The form this challenge takes for those with 'artistic sensitivity' and the talent to express it through the art of acting, is to cultivate *consciously* that sensitive membrane they retained unconsciously, and develop healthy boundaries that make it possible to distinguish between self and world without a loss of sensitivity. This is the goal of Chekhov's training for an actor.

Artistic sensibility, creativity and dysfunction

Great works of art reveal experiences otherwise imperceptible to ordinary consciousness. The paintings of Van Gogh, for example, or Turner's later works, reveal the forces and energies at work behind material appearances. Other levels of perception such as those possessed by poets, novelists and dramatists reveal dynamics of the soul — the emotions and thoughts that drive us and form a subtext to behaviour. Still others are attuned to realities of spirit that also stream into existence. These last sound through great music or Shakespeare's language, into which they weave a *super-text*. This capacity, to perceive behind the surface of physical perception which 'normal' consciousness refers to as reality, is *artistic sensibility*. What those possessing it perceive, is what demands to be expressed.

The capacity for supersensible perception is connected to our creativity; it is the doorway that grants access to the invisible realm where the causes that create effects in the world of outer form have their source. The materialist dismisses such perceptions as 'mere imagination'. Yet, only those at home in the realm of unseen causes can make the creative leaps which manifest in a new creation in the realm of form — that proves those unseen causes valid. Arthur Koestler describes this view of creativity in his book, *The Act of Creation*, observing that it is equally the root of scientific progress as of art.

Biographies of many artists, particularly great ones, reveal a fine line between their genius or gift, and behaviour which might be termed dysfunctional, even pathological. Some endure, sometimes end their lives in, episodes labelled as insanity. Such torment is judged to be a tragic price that artists have to pay for the extraordinary gifts that, after all, are what allow them to perceive dimensions of reality that lie beyond the experience of so-called 'normal' people.

William Blake understood the necessity to cultivate, consciously, the ability to live in both 'worlds' at once. Nevertheless, even his most loyal patrons and supporters reported incidents indicating that the boundary between his genius and what the world perceived as 'madness' was often difficult to establish and maintain.

The acceptance of the idea that extra-ordinary perception is in some way dependent on imbalance or pathology, that dysfunction is the price that must be paid for that gift, is confirmed by this story of the poet, Rainer Maria Rilke. Rilke refused psychoanalysis with Freud because he feared that probing the unconscious dynamics that fed his springs of inspiration would destroy the source of his poetic genius. For, as he wrote, in his letters: 'if one were to drive out [his] devils', his 'angels by some chance [might] leave as well'.[6]

Many paths and opportunities exist today for human beings seeking wholeness. The age in which we live invites us to move beyond the archetype of artist as a temperamental genius whose challenging, dysfunctional behaviour is justified by their creations and to consider that a healthy psyche and artistic gift could co-exist. We have reached a stage in evolution when artists who seek a way to practise their art that is sustainable, can work towards a healthy integration that includes their gift.

The evolution of human consciousness

The seminal myths of our theatrical tradition contain guidance for the actor. Drama did not evolve out of the temple just to entertain the populace, but to fulfil an important function in the education and spiritual life of the community. Can the actors who performed have been exempt from the necessity to understand what they imparted to the audience? As actors, we think of plays as vehicles for our performances but *Oedipus the King*, for example, can also teach us on our quest for healing.

The legend which is the back-story to Sophocles' play tells how Oedipus, foster child to the king and queen of Corinth and ignorant of his true parentage, flees from Corinth to escape the prophecy that he would kill his father and marry his own mother. On the road to Thebes, a stranger blocks his path. Oedipus knocks him from his chariot, resulting in the stranger's death, and continues on his way.

As Oedipus approaches the city, he is confronted by a monster-sphinx who poses him a riddle. To grasp the full significance of this, we need to understand the nature of the Sphinx. Her many images, embodying imaginations of the lion, bull and eagle, reflect an ancient understanding of humanity. In her benign form, with a human face, she depicts the divine Self of the human being; born out of, yet destined to control and integrate the creative forces of the starry worlds we call the Zodiac. Lacking this divine human Self to mediate, these forces degenerate into a monstrous form that devours its victims. This is the sphinx that confronts Oedipus, demanding that he solve the riddle: what goes on four legs in the morning, two legs in the afternoon and three legs in the evening?

Oedipus is one of the first representatives of the newly evolving power of the human intellect to make an independent judgement based on examination of material phenomena. From the perspective offered by his cleverness, Oedipus recognizes that the answer is the human being; but described only in terms of the material conception of reality which would in time, replace the ancient understanding embodied in the wisdom of the Sphinx. Based solely on the evidence of physical perception, a human life is indeed reduced to what appears between the gates of birth and death.

In the short term, the cleverness of Oedipus saves the city from the monster, which hurls itself from a cliff. Oedipus is hailed as a saviour and the people make him king. But only for a little while does he deliver the salvation that his cleverness had promised. Oedipus gained power and independence through his own intelligence, yet this very quality tempted him into the arrogance the Greeks called *hubris*. Hubris prompted him to throw the stranger from his chariot, believing he had the right to eradicate what he saw as an obstruction on his path.

Like Odysseus, Oedipus stands at the threshold of the coming materialistic age. In many ways, his character embodies those qualities of consciousness that human beings would develop in the next two or three millennia. From these emerged what we call our modern Western civilization. Modern human beings believe their cleverness gives them the right to dominate (makes them kings) and justifies their use of power to conquer and destroy. Thinking that this cleverness can solve any riddles that the monsters who seem to threaten us can pose, we do not see that we become the monster.

The ancient consciousness that preceded intellect is demonstrated by Tiresias, the seer. Blind to the physical world he inhabits other levels of reality. Oedipus mocks Tiresias' clairvoyance as inferior to his own intelligence because it did not find the answer to the sphinx's riddle. Clever intellect on its own, however, was incapable of grasping the subtext and super-text embedded in the prophecy that Oedipus would kill his father and marry his own mother. It thus condemned him to the same literal understanding of the words that had driven his biological parents to have him killed at birth. Just as their consciousness could make no sense of the language of the mysteries, Tiresias could make no sense of a riddle that reduced the mystery of human life to a few paltry attributes. He dwelt within realities not comprehensible to Oedipus, but that would reveal themselves as true.

The hubris shown by Oedipus demonstrates a self constructed out of the experience of separation from the world; an experience generated by the evidence of our senses — that perceive a boundary between the body and the world which it inhabits. Such a 'separated' self survives only as far as it is able to control that world and crush the opposition to its will. Totally identified with the physical body, it interprets the destruction of that body as its 'death'. The Greeks called this self, built out of appearances, the 'persona'.

Sophocles shows us that there is another Self, not bound by laws of time and space. This Self, not subject to the dissolution that the persona fears as death, is committed to the search to find and recognize itSelf. The call to undertake this search went out from mystery centres such as those at Delphi and Eleusis and was expressed in the words: Know Thyself!

One who answered, set out on a journey called *initiation*. It led to knowledge of the Self which cannot be threatened or destroyed, but, because it dwells beyond the veil of physical perception, is only able to reveal itSelf when the obscuring veil of the illusory self and world is torn away. Initiation, then, demanded courage to face exposure of the persona, the illusory self, to its own nothingness. In so doing, the initiate experienced the Self that cannot be destroyed, and overcame the fear of death.

Such is the archetype that lies behind the journey of the tragic hero, whose quest is for self-knowledge, the necessity for which cannot be perceived by a consciousness exclusively identified with matter. It is out of that other consciousness that Tiresias replies to Oedipus in the language of the mysteries. Once again Oedipus fails to understand; still convinced the truth about his own beginnings (the origin of who he *thought* himself to be) can be found only in the details of his physical conception:

> *Oedipus*: Who then gave me my birth?
> *Tiresias*: This day brings you your birth and death.[7]

When the truth is revealed, Oedipus acknowledges that his physical eyes had not perceived it. Still identified with the person he believed himself to be, and too horrified to look upon it further, he stabs out his eyes and begs for death, but is sentenced instead to banishment. The suffering that he undergoes as, over many years, he integrates the truth of his earthly origin with all that he has been and known, leads him to fulfil the last part of the prophecy; that he would die a 'wonderful death' which would be a source of blessing to the world.[8]

This story contains a truth about the journey of our individual lives and of our western culture. Humanity is given hope that we can escape the 'shades of the prison house' to which exclusive reliance on physical perception has consigned us.[9] Sophocles shows us what we will achieve when we complete the journey and pass through the gate of higher consciousness, yet able to embrace the earth with our individual intelligence, born from the necessity to make sense of our material perceptions.

A material conception of the universe may dominate Western-global thought in our age, tempting us to think that earlier human experience is/was primitive, not as 'advanced' as we are now. But this attitude will last only for a short period of evolution as already many individuals, in sciences as well as arts, find their perception and understanding of the universe expanding to include again levels of reality beyond material existence.

Our cultural inheritance is littered with examples that reinforce such an observation because this journey deeply into matter and then out again was foreseen in many sacred stories.[10] In Indian mythology, the time of dense materialism was predicted and called, *Kali Yuga* (Age of Darkness). The texts also point to a stage when the 'terrible time will be over and creation will begin anew'. *Krita Yuga* will return.

Steiner, alive at the transition from the nineteenth to the twentieth century, confirmed this picture of our evolution. His investigations revealed our present age as the time predicted for the end of *Kali Yuga* and how human perception would expand to once again include the supersensible.[11]

In *Ode: Intimations of Immortality*, Wordsworth explores these stages of our consciousness. He experienced that they unfold as a matter of course within the journey of each human life. In the language of the Sphinx: between the time when human beings go on four legs and when in old age, with a staff to aid us, we go on three.*

> Our birth is but a sleep and a forgetting:
> The Soul that rises with us, our life's star,
> Hath had elsewhere its setting,
> And cometh from afar:
> Not in entire forgetfulness,
> And not in utter nakedness,
> But trailing clouds of glory do we come
> From God who is our home:
> Heaven lies about us in our infancy!
> Shades of the prison-house begin to close
> Upon the growing Boy,
> But he beholds the light and whence it flows,
> He sees it in his joy;
> The Youth, who daily farther from the east
> Must travel, still is Nature's Priest,
> And by the vision splendid
> Is on his way attended;
> At length the Man perceives it die away,
> And fade into the light of common day ...
>
> . . . . .
>
> What though the radiance which was once so bright
> Be now forever taken from my sight,
> Though nothing can bring back the hour
> Of splendour in the grass or glory in the flower;

---

* See *The Integrated Actor*, chapter The stages of life, for further discussion and a more extended quote from the poem.

> We will grieve not, rather find
> Strength in what remains behind;
> In the primal sympathy
> Which having been must ever be;
> In the soothing thoughts that spring
> Out of human suffering;
> In the faith that looks through death,
> In years that bring the philosophic mind …[12]

As children grow, they ever more deeply inhabit the physical and their reality increasingly consists of phenomena revealed through the five senses — the gateways of physical perception. Eventually, approximately in the middle of our life, the sense 'I am my body' culminates. Then, as the body starts to age and move towards its death, our connection to it loosens. With that, comes the possibility that awareness of reality can expand to once again include more than physical perception can reveal.

This journey is prophetically embodied in another story seminal to Western theatre history. The myth of *Persephone and Demeter* enacted in the temple mysteries of Eleusis, depicted the departure from Paradise and descent to Hades of Persephone, the human soul. She experienced this loss of paradise in order to return and unite with her beloved bridegroom, Dionysus, as an individuated being, conscious of herself. TS Eliot expresses this cyclic journey in the well-known passage from his *Little Gidding*:[13]

> We shall not cease from exploration
> And the end of all our exploring will be
> To arrive where we started
> And know the place for the first time …
> And all shall be well
> And all manner of thing shall be well
> When the tongues of flame are infolded
> Into the crowned knot of fire
> And the fire and the rose are one.

Steiner suggests that this cyclic process is also taking place within our culture, and that all human beings will eventually experience this 'loosening', and humanity evolve beyond materialism. It is this interpretation of the apocalyptic nature of our times that Christopher Fry intuits in his play, *A Sleep of Prisoners*:

> The human heart can go to the length of God.
> Dark and cold we may be, but this is no winter now.
> The frozen misery of centuries breaks, cracks, begins to move.
> The thunder is the thunder of the floes, the thaw, the flood, the upstart Spring.

Thank God our time is now
When wrong comes up to face us everywhere
Never to leave us till we take
The longest stride of soul man ever took.
Affairs are now soul size.
The enterprise is exploration into God.
Where are you making for?
It takes so many thousand years to wake
But will you wake for pity's sake?

From this perspective, all human beings are destined one day to develop *artistic sensibilities*.

Each mode of perception, physical or supersensible, must make its contribution and be integrated if the journey is to be complete. In the meantime, some individuals in each age choose to bear witness to the world behind appearances — serving as reminders to those who have chosen to develop consciousness through identifying with the world of matter.

The demand on the artist to stay conscious of non-material levels of reality and yet live in the 'normal world' can be so challenging it begs the question: have we reached a point in evolution and the evolution of our art when some aspect of artistic training could or should prepare us to deal with this condition? How can artists develop and maintain a healthy sense of self while they surrender to what is channelled through them?

Without such conscious preparation, they risk possession by what inspires them. The link between possession/obsession and the tyranny of artistic vision has often been expressed. Here is the famous description of the poet/artist from the poem, *Kubla Khan* by Samuel Taylor Coleridge:

And all who heard should see them there
And all should cry: Beware! Beware!
His flashing eyes, his floating hair!
Weave a circle round him thrice
And close your eyes with holy dread
For he on honey-dew hath fed
And drunk the milk of paradise.

One distinction between artistic sensibility and what is ordinarily perceived as madness, lies in the artist's gift and skill to communicate their extra-sensory perceptions. The greater the artist, the greater the capacity to render their medium transparent: some glimpse of extra-ordinary consciousness is revealed to the beholder. It may be that the very discipline required by art to render supersensible perceptions into form offers the artist an anchor to the 'real' world. Perhaps Blake understood this when he chose apprenticeship as an engraver, intuiting that only deep immersion in a process demanding utmost physical precision could balance his propensity to dwell in other levels of reality.

Because communicating extra-sensory experience in artistic form is therapeutic, the contribution that artistic practice makes to therapeutic process is well recognized. It has taken longer, however, to consider whether *conscious* therapeutic process would benefit the soul-health of an artist. This may be because of the fear that a healthy psyche might result in loss of the artistic gift, or because blurring the boundary between therapy and art may result in transgression of an individual's freedom to choose if, when and how, to undertake such therapeutic exploration. Our culture is only just beginning to consider such questions, which are increasingly relevant to many of us, and therefore, only just beginning to appreciate Chekhov's contribution to creating healthy processes for actors.

The 'disembodied self' and the inner critic

In his book, *The Divided Self*, RD Laing explores what he calls the 'disembodied' and 'embodied' self. Laing documents cases in which certain types of personality respond to childhood trauma by dissociating or withdrawing from their bodies. He observes how such individuals cannot sense the boundary, normally defined by the body, between their own experience and that of others. Someone affected in this way still enters into physical maturity and even functions as a 'normal' adult in some respects, but in others is 'stuck' or 'fixed' at the stage of development 'normal' in the tiny child or infant.

The consciousness of a brilliant artist such as Virginia Woolf may be seen as the consequence of this condition. Her novels and journals reveal her capacity to experience the thoughts, feelings and perceptions of those who peopled her environment, and the danger of being overwhelmed by their intensity. We may well imagine such a sensibility as hers remained as sensitive as in that earlier stage when, as an infant with 'no skin', all impressions passed through her as her own.

Her genius allowed her to expose those complex layers of perception to those who read her work. Yet for herself, the price she paid was that, at times, the lives of others seemed more real to her than did her own. Unable to inhabit her own body, she made way for the lives of her characters. Her self, absent from its body, left a vacuum into which another self or selves and their complex interweaving streams of consciousness, could enter. Or, with no defining boundary, her consciousness flowed out and merged with life around her.

Woolf reveals in a journal entry that she understood how someone's connection to their body related to their quality of consciousness, describing her impressions of Sir George Darwin:

> He is clearly affectionate, much interested in small events, and satisfied with his position. It is also clear that he has no feeling for beauty, no romance, or mystery in his mind; in short, he is a solid object, filling his place in the world, and all one may ever hope to find in him, is a sane judgment, a cheerful temper …[14]

A further consequence of Laing's picture of disembodiment is that the self experiences that it is not living but *observing its own life*. In extreme examples, the observing-self judges the observed-self relentlessly. The result is anguish. Like the proverbial centipede, the merciless examination that each action, observation, thought or feeling is subjected to makes it difficult, even impossible, to act. One difficult expression for an artist of this 'observing self' is the 'inner critic' who paralyses the creative mind. Yet, if its own life does not seem real, observation of itself is the only way the self can validate its own existence.

Who's Afraid of Virginia Woolf?

Virginia Woolf's journals, particularly those written at the end of her life, record her torment at the introspection she felt powerless to halt. Yet, what she experienced as a 'curse' was precisely what enabled her to observe and lay bare the web of subtext that underlies appearances. Many artists feel at the mercy of their gift, flung between the alternating states of paralysis and 'possession' when they are 'driven' into agonizing periods of manic action.

Is it because the state of disconnection or dissociation can lead to psychosis, that Edward Albee called his play, *Who's Afraid of Virginia Woolf?* For, unless we can direct our consciousness from a centre that is unassailable, we find ourselves the victim of sensibilities that leave us with no refuge or escape from continuous exposure to what is underneath our civilized, sophisticated surfaces. Rather than face another episode of madness, Virginia Woolf ended her own life. Who wouldn't be afraid?

Like Sophocles, Albee hints in the last words of the play that after the illusions, the false appearances are stripped away, a Self remains that cannot be destroyed. Vulnerable and fragile it seems to be, in contrast to the predatory power of the ego that we have witnessed rage its way through the first three acts and, like Dionysus in *The Bacchae*, strip away the false and civilized veneer.[15] Yet this 'still small voice' confessing powerlessness belongs to the same 'naked, new born babe', that calls to Macbeth from a part of himself he can still hear and offers him a different choice.[16] Reminding us as well of Oedipus, it indicates there is a Self which has been waiting to be born and which, outlasting pain, will live to 'stride the blast'.[17]

'Who's afraid of Virginia Woolf?' George asks his wife, Martha, recalling the joke they had heard that evening at the faculty party. The educated elite of our culture is now at the other end of the journey first made by heroes such as Oedipus. Despite its intellectual brilliance, it cannot escape the anguish to which it is subjected by such a level of self-conscious observation. With nowhere to hide, except within an alcoholic haze, it seeks to obliterate itself in a perpetual Dionysian ritual of drunkenness. Yet somewhere, from within that haze, a colleague has discerned the terrors of our time and cleverly woven that awareness into the traditional nursery rhyme. Now, like a mother, tenderly comforting her frightened child, George sings it to her; 'Who's afraid of Virginia Woolf?'

'I am, George. I am,' is Martha's response. It is a fragile beginning but it is the sacred name she utters that no one else can speak except the Self that knows itSelf to be the one, who, having passed through death, remains.

This day brings you your birth and death.

The Bhagavad-Gita and the way of the actor

In Hindu tradition, Krishna is the name given to the Sacred Self of whom we have been speaking. In this famous passage from the *Bhagavad-Gita*, he reveals his intimate name, again and again expressing the archetype and paradox in the core of the actor's being. For the knowledge that I AM all things and that all things exist in me, is both as innocent as the child at play and as awesome and terrifying as the power that creates the universe. Like Arjuna, we need to be instructed how to recognize and bear the 'Presence of the One who is the All', for unless we learn to mediate this power, it can destroy us.

Krishna counsels Arjuna: However men approach me, even so do I welcome them, for the path men take from every side is mine …

With the mind clinging to me, performing Yoga, refuged in me, how thou shalt, without doubt know me to the uttermost, that hear thou. I will declare to thee this knowledge and wisdom in its completeness, which, having known, there is nothing more here, needeth to be known. Among thousands of men scarce one knoweth me in essence.

Earth, water, fire, air, ether, mind and reason also, and egoism — these are the eightfold division of my nature.

This the inferior. Know my other nature, the higher, the life-element, by which the universe is upheld.

Know this to be the womb of all beings. I AM the source of the forthgoing of the whole universe and likewise the place of its dissolving. There is nought whatsoever higher than I, O Arjuna. All this is threaded on me as rows of pearls on a string.

I AM the sweet taste of waters, O son of Kunti, I the radiance in moon and sun; the word of power in all the Vedas, sound in ether, and virility in men; the pure fragrance of earth and the brilliance in fire AM I; the life in all beings AM I, and the austerity in ascetics. Know me, O Partha! As the eternal seed of all beings; I AM the reason of the reason-endowed, the splendour of splendid things AM I; and I the strength of the strong, devoid of desire and passion. In beings I AM desire not contrary to duty, O Lord of the Bharatas. The natures that are harmonious, active, slothful, these know as from me; not I in them, but they in me.

I the oblation; I the sacrifice; I also the butter; I the fire; the burnt offering I; the Father of this universe, the Mother, the Supporter, the Grandsire, the Holy One to be known, the Word of Power, and also ... the Path, Husband, Lord, Witness, Abode, Shelter, Lover, Origin, Dissolution, Foundation, Treasure house, Seed imperishable. I give heat; I hold back and send forth the rain; immortality and also death, being and non being AM I, Arjuna ...

We might add: I AM the choo-choo train, I AM the lion, I AM the spider, I AM the tree, I AM the suffering of Martha, I AM George. I AM Oedipus. I AM ...

Arjuna said: ... O Supreme Lord, even as thou describest thyself, O best of beings, I desire to see thy form omnipotent. If thou thinkest that by me it can be seen, O Lord of Yoga, then show me thine imperishable Self.

The Blessed Lord said: Behold, O Partha, a form of me, a hundred fold, a thousand fold, various in kind, divine, various in colours and shapes. Here today, behold the whole universe, movable and immovable, standing in One in my body, O Arjuna, with what else thou desirest to see. But verily, thou art not able to behold me with these thine eyes; the divine eye I give unto thee. Behold my sovereign Yoga ...

There Arjuna beheld a whole universe, divided into manifold parts, standing in one body of the Deity of Deities. Then he, overwhelmed with astonishment, his hair upstanding, bowed down his head to the shining one.[18]

Part of the joy actors have in their vocation comes from the awareness, at some level, of the privilege it grants them to sense, at times, that all humanity exists within them, that they can merge with it ... that the experience of every human being can be theirs.

But, how to manage having everyone inside you?

Krishna's affirmation of the Self reveals how the creator's consciousness is both inside its creation and, at the same time, outside, creating it. He refers twice to the yoga which prepares Arjuna to receive this revelation of the Self. Actors, too, need to be 'inside' their characters, yet at the same time, able to observe them as objects that they create outside themselves. Yet those who rely exclusively on instinct to allow other characters inside them or to slip inside another's body — the result, perhaps, of the unconscious state of not inhabiting their own — are in danger of confusing the boundaries in what is, in reality, a higher state of consciousness.

Actors too need a 'yoga' that prepares them to inhabit these extraordinary states; to remain *present* when, like Arjuna, their hair is 'upstanding', *to remember their name in the house of fire.*[*] Without such a 'yoga' they risk being lost in the same complicated landscape of sensibilities that tormented Virginia Woolf.

Trauma and the creative self

Perpetration of abuse — behaviour that violates another's 'beingness' — in all degrees and forms, blatant and subtle, violent, sexual, verbal and emotional, through neglect or superficiality was, for centuries, accepted as the 'norm'. It was justified as providing the necessary toughening, without which we would not survive. Perhaps, in the past, this was the way it worked for those who did survive. The trauma developed an initial sense of self and pressed it deep into the body, thus hardening the boundary between the self and the world and preparing it to battle for survival.

The childhood of Oedipus provides us with a metaphor for how trauma played its part in our descent into matter to become self-conscious. Rejection by his parents and exposure to die upon a hillside might well have served to anchor him more firmly to his body and the earth and is reflected in the detail, in some versions of the story, that a stake was driven through the baby's foot into the ground to ensure he could not escape — the name *Oedipus* means 'swollen foot'.

What Laing observed is that for many, trauma now has the opposite effect; separating self from body. This response is reflected in a change of attitude: much of what was once called 'toughening' is now acknowledged as 'abuse' that has been systemic at every level of our culture. This shift in perception is part of the larger shift in sensibilities that Fry suggests is taking place as the ice age of materialistic consciousness begins to melt. An aspect of confronting evil, which Fry connects to the awakening in 'our time', surely includes the recognition and exposure of abuse and its consequences.[19]

The gifted child

The insights of Alice Miller in her book, *The Drama of Being a Child,* have specific relevance to actors. At birth and for some time afterwards, the infant's consciousness is still undifferentiated from the primary object (usually the mother). As well, the baby is totally dependent on the 'other'. This creates a 'field' within which every child is

---

[*] See pages 11–14 for an excerpt of *The Egyptian Book of the Dead.*

highly sensitive; attuned to even tiny clues indicating the conditions necessary to ensure its survival.

Very few children receive an unconditionally loving response to every need expressed in the totally dependent early stage. No parent, however well-intentioned, can be available to meet every need, and many may not be aware of their unconscious need to repeat their own experience of deprivation or abuse. In the latter situation, without a healing intervention that can break the cycle, the pattern of wounding is perpetuated through the generations.

An environment of deprivation brings out the 'genius' in a child inasmuch as children, 'gifted' in this way, develop, to a high degree, capacities to sense into the unconscious dynamics or the subtext in a home. They absorb the implications and learn to be compliant to elicit from their parents what they need. Instinctively, they know to suppress responses they have learned will not achieve their goal, and exhibit those that will.

The fundamental need is for unconditional love, based on acceptance by the parents of the child as a separate being who is not an extension of the parents' needs. This condition being absent, the child learns to behave in a way that pleases, or at least avoids punishment. At best, the child learns to earn rewards such as approval, food or other substitutes for love.

The capacity to sense the subtlest nuance of what goes on inside the parent, Miller suggests, is a primal form of empathy. She observes that this capacity will be retained into adulthood by certain individuals and extend into all their interactions. We can imagine that an actor, who instinctively identifies with other characters, demonstrates this same gift of empathy.

This capacity for empathy can be a gift but it comes at a price. Miller observes how such gifted individuals often struggle to be certain of themselves or have a clear identity. Years of attunement to what 'the other' feels, thinks, or needs to ensure survival, may result in inability to even recognize, let alone allow oneself to have, one's own emotions. Those children, so gifted in feeling what other people feel, may find, that in this respect, they stay as children. They may be adults, contributing within an adult world, yet they are strangers to themselves, dependent on approval and recognition from that world to sense that they exist.

People gifted in this way may well be attracted to the therapeutic professions. Miller emphasizes the need for a conscious process of development if what begins as instinctive empathy is to be applied in healthy ways within a therapeutic context. For their gift to be of use, they need to exercise their empathy from a place of being whole and healed themselves, which means they need to understand, explore, and be released from the compulsive patterns of response which arise from their wounding.

Implications for the actor

The necessity for such a process in a healthy training to become an analyst or psychotherapist has been fully recognized over the last hundred years. The equivalent necessity for actors has either not been recognized at all, or left to chance. Actors exploit their extraordinary sensitivities, some producing work of genius, but for some it is at the expense of their often already fragile sense of self. The gifted child has learned that the price to be paid for feeling safe and approval in the family environment is that certain feelings and emotions are not to be expressed. The pain is resolved by pushing them below the threshold of consciousness where they cannot be felt at all.

Many actors are first drawn to acting when they discover that it offers them opportunities to safely feel and display a range of emotions which, till then, they may not have allowed themselves in actual life. Thus, someone who finds it difficult, even impossible, to admit to or express such things in life, can do so in the context of playing a specific character. It is as though, at last, they have permission to experience and release such culturally unacceptable emotions as rage or grief, jealousy or cruelty, to name a few. For some, the initial release connected to acting out unconscious painful wounds becomes an agony that begins to outweigh the ecstasy.[20] Those who reach this point and want to go on practising their art are then compelled to ask: is there a 'yoga' appropriate for actors?

The last hundred years have produced a large range of acting methodologies that have sprung from the necessity to make conscious what, in western practice, had become a set of wooden rules, or else was largely left to 'personality' and talent. There is nothing amiss if an actor's starting point is the unconscious need to experience catharsis of their own emotions, nor is a gift for playing certain roles always the consequence of being 'wounded' in some way as a child; but for those who do wish to understand and transform unconscious gifts into conscious faculties that support the path to be a balanced human being, Chekhov and those who build upon his work, offer a 'yoga' to the Self that is unassailable.[*]

Implications for the future

Approximately five thousand years ago we began the journey of transition from clairvoyant consciousness to physical sense perception that granted us our independent judgement and intelligence and produced a culture in which toughness qualified us for survival. Since the world wars, increasing numbers of vulnerable human beings survive. This heralds the return journey back to clairvoyant consciousness *with* that

---

[*] The word *yoga* implies the physical, mental, spiritual practice that leads to the spiritual goal of union with the divine.

hard-won intelligence and independent judgement; but how do we return without 'going mad'?

Laing observed that 'embodied' human beings are centred in themselves. Actors depend on the ability to 'slip into' someone else's skin or let someone else slip into theirs. Both tendencies can slide towards pathology. Is there any hope for actors who traverse this dangerous terrain unconsciously to emerge as healthy human beings?

In ancient times, selected pupils trained in initiation centres to retain perception of the disappearing non-material world. Strict rules and guidance ensured the safety of the neophyte. What aspects of a modern training would support actors to retain the intelligence and clarity of independent judgement developed through the course of evolution, enabling them to safely enter and inhabit the realms we access in our work?

The story of Oedipus is seminal for actors because it points to this possibility. He suffered when the self/persona he thought himself to be was stripped away. Yet, he came to recognize there was a second Self within him, not dependent on the circumstances of his physical birth or any outer facts of his biography. In fact it was this very Self that undertook dismantling of that false identity and layer by layer, stripped away the persona he had constructed to survive. Rejecting the temptation to conceal the truth that was emerging, this real or Higher Self, relentlessly pursued it instead. It is the path also of Lear, who 'hath ever but slenderly known himself'[21] and of all who answer the call to self-knowledge. They do not run from the catastrophe resulting from the hubris and actions of that false identity. Instead, they turn to face it and to say:

> Born thus, I ask to be no other man than that I am
> And I will know who I am.

> *Oedipus*, Sophocles

This quest to know the true Self is not to be confused with the bolstering of self-esteem; for this latter may imply merely a shift from dependence on others to confirm our worth, based on criteria like talent, wealth, achievement of success or fame, to dependence on ourselves. For if we judge our own worth by the same criteria as those we formerly required the world to judge us by, then the 'love' we are compelled to seek is still conditional. We live now in a time when actors who wish to avoid the pitfalls of losing themselves within the many selves they inhabit, or who inhabit them, may be confident that a technique is evolving; one that supports their quest to know themselves and provides a pathway to consciousness of the Self that knows it is itSelf in all its manifestations.

Steiner's mystery plays

In his first *Mystery Drama*, Rudolf Steiner explores the relationship between artistic sensibility and the conditions resulting from the disembodied state through the character of Johannes Thomasius. When we first meet Johannes, this young and gifted painter is plunged in deep despair at the drying up of his creative process. Yet, he describes with great precision that he feels the lives of those around him are more real to him than his own.

> *Johannes Thomasius*: I know what all these people lack;
> I also know
> they stand in life, and I in emptiness ...
> I had to sink myself in all the people
> who in their words revealed themselves just now: ...
> I was each; but for myself
> I died.
> I would need the faith
> that beings spring from nothing
> in order to have hope
> that from my nothingness
> a man could grow.

Though he cannot form a clear sense of himself, he is a 'permeable membrane' to the lives of those he meets. At the beginning of the play this sensibility torments Johannes. Over several scenes, we see him helped by his friend and mentor, Maria and their teacher, Benedictus.

Johannes learns to penetrate his consciousness through the discipline of meditation. In the eighth scene, we see the rebirth of his power to create. This same capacity that at times torments him, enables him to paint a portrait of his friend Capesius in which the scientist, Strader, perceives the very being of his friend. The painting stimulates the shift in consciousness made possible by art.

> *Strader*: I do admire Thomasius, and acknowledge
> that, in his picture, Capesius, whom I thought I knew,
> for the first time is really shown to me.

In subsequent chapters of his journey, we witness other problems that arise from Johannes' inability to find a firm sense of self within himself. For although his artistic sensibility grants easy access to supersensible experience, it makes it hard know whether that experience is his or belongs to others. This means he cannot function healthily in his relationships or in his work.

At first Johannes has no sense that the seeds of his unhealthy functioning may lie in former lives and how they may have impacted the early chapters of his present life. So far as he is conscious, he remembers that his childhood in this life was a happy one. He gives us clues, however, of another level, underneath; the kinds of clues an actor relishes in searching for a character's back-story.

Johannes tells of his parents' joy in his artistic gifts and their support for his unfolding talent. Yet, we might imagine the most loving and well-intentioned parents, unless they had attained enlightenment already, would find it hard to view their highly gifted child with equanimity. It is unlikely that they nurtured his capacities without some level of investment of their own egos in his progress. As we have explored, such all-too-understandable conditional acknowledgement can be what makes the crack through which the forming of the false identity, dependent on outside approval, first appears.

Throughout the plays, the trials specific to each individual pathway are explored in depth. These include the scientist, philosopher and scholar, wo/man of action, mystic and the artist. Within the scope of the four dramas Steiner was able to complete (he left notes for a fifth), we do not see the resolution of Johannes' struggles to transform his specific challenge and fulfil his potential. By the end of drama four, he seems, if anything, to be more deeply mired in the confusions of relationships and the illusions arising out of his complexities. It is not within our context to follow the journey of Johannes further, except to say that Steiner is precise in what he has identified to be the struggles of a soul gifted with artistic sensibility, yet also challenged by the difficulties that it brings.

Steiner on the 'dangers of the threshold'

In the ninth section of *The Threshold of the Spiritual World*, Steiner describes some of the dangers faced when we cross the threshold separating physical and supersensible realities unconsciously and, therefore, without the necessary preparation.

> For in order to live consciously in those [supersensible] worlds, an attitude of the soul is necessary that cannot be developed in the physical world with the same intensity with which it appears in supersensible worlds. This is the attitude of surrender to what is being experienced. We must steep ourselves in the experience and identify ourselves with it; and we must be able to do this to such a degree that we see ourselves outside our own being and feel ourselves within some other being. A transformation of our own being with which we are having the experience must take place. If we do not possess this faculty of transformation, we cannot experience anything genuine in supersensible worlds. For there all experience is due to our being able to realize this feeling: 'Now I am transformed in a certain, definite way; now I am vitally present in a being which through its nature transforms mine in this particular way.'

This transformation of self, this conscious projection of oneself into other beings, is life in supersensible worlds. By this process of conscious self-projection into others, we learn to know the beings and events of those worlds ...

When awakening to the supersensible world takes place in rightly developed human clairvoyance, the memory of the soul's experience in the physical world still remains. It must remain, otherwise other beings and events would be present in clairvoyant consciousness, but not the clairvoyant's own being. We should in that case have no knowledge of ourselves; we should not be living in the spirit ourselves, but other beings and events would be living in our soul. Taking this into consideration, it will be clear that rightly developed clairvoyance must lay great stress on the cultivation of a strong ego-feeling. This ego-feeling developed with clairvoyance is by no means something that enters the soul only through clairvoyance; it is merely that we get to know what always exists in the depths of the soul, but remains unknown to the soul's ordinary life as it runs its course in the physical world.

The strong ego-feeling is not there through the etheric body[*] as such, but through the soul which experiences itself in the physical body. If the soul does not bring that feeling with it into the clairvoyant state from its experience in the physical world, it will prove insufficiently equipped for experience in the elemental world.

On the other hand, it is essential for human consciousness within the physical world that the soul's feeling of self, its experience of the ego, although it must exist, should be modified. By this means it is possible for the soul to undergo within the physical world training for the noblest of moral forces, that of fellow-feeling, or feeling with another. If the strong ego-feeling were to project itself into the soul's conscious experiences within the physical world, moral impulses and ideas could not develop in the right way. They could not bring forth the fruit of love. But the faculty of self-surrender, a natural impulse in the elemental world, is not to be put on a par with what is called love in human experience. Elemental self-surrender means experiencing oneself in another being or event; love is the experiencing of another being in one's own soul. In order to develop the latter experience, the feeling of self, or ego experience, present in the depths of the soul, must have, as it were, a veil drawn over it; and in consequence of the soul's own forces being thus dulled, one is able to feel within oneself the sorrows and joys of the other being: love, which is the source of all genuine morality in human life, springs up ...

Therefore it is necessary for man's being that there should exist in his etheric body the two opposing forces, the capacity for transformation into other beings, and the strong ego-feeling, or feeling of self ... The relation of two such opposing forces can never be that of one effacing the other, but must be of such a kind that both are developed and act upon each other in the way of balance and compensation ...

---

[*] For an exploration of what Steiner means by 'etheric body' see *The Art of Speech*. For Steiner's own, detailed exploration, see *Theosophy*. For now, it is enough to indicate that the etheric body is the subtle body of life-forces which, for as long as we are alive within a physical material body, penetrate that body.

If the capacity for transformation which it is necessary for a person to possess in his etheric body were to extend in the same degree to physical existence, he would feel himself in his soul as something that, with regard to his physical body, he is not …

If, however, the human soul were to develop in the physical world the capacity for transformation necessary for the elemental world, its personal identity would be lost. Such a soul would be living in contradiction to itself. In the physical world, the capacity for transformation must be a power at rest in the depths of the soul; a power which gives the soul its fundamental tone or keynote, but which does not come to development in that world …

Clairvoyant consciousness must ever observe the boundary of the two worlds, and must not use in the physical world faculties adapted for a supersensible world. If the soul, knowing itself to be in the physical world, were to allow the capacity for transformation possessed by its etheric body to go on working, ordinary consciousness would become filled with conceptions which do not correspond to any being in the physical world. Confusion would reign in the life of the soul's thought. Observation of the boundary between the worlds is a necessary presupposition for the right working of clairvoyant consciousness …[22]

The threshold in relation to the actor

These observations were made with regard to developing clairvoyant consciousness, yet their relevance to the actor's work is clear. Actors may not have connected what they do with clairvoyance, yet in Steiner's terms, their gift is the unconscious capacity to cross the threshold that divides the worlds of physical and supersensible experience. The challenge is to manage those transitions *consciously*. Since actors possess the gift of transformation, they will benefit from knowing how, without the loss of personal identity, to manage both the 'projection of the self into others' that Steiner says 'is life in supersensible worlds' and the 'experiencing of another's being in one's own soul'.

In the *Mystery Plays*, we see how a range of characters deal with these transitions. Johannes, as we have discussed, is loosely connected with his body and dwells easily in the supersensible realms that inspire his art, but finds it difficult to maintain his sense of self. The character, Maria, achieves the capacity to cross the threshold by a conscious process of development and spiritual discipline. She is not gifted, like Johannes, in one of the acknowledged art forms, yet she is an artist in the way she approaches life and her relationships. Steiner makes it clear that her capacity to healthily traverse the back and forth between both worlds stems from a healthy development of self throughout her childhood and youth.

Benedictus: You did not climb too soon the steeps of spirit.
The longing for the spiritual world

did not arise in you before you had fully grasped
the senses' innocent joys …
You could laugh gaily, as a child can laugh
who has learned nothing yet
about the shadows of existence.
You understood the happiness of men,
and sorrowed for their pain, while still
no glimmer of a question stirred in you
about the origin of joy or grief …[23]

Felicia Balde is a gifted storyteller able to access the realms of inspiration while rooted firmly in the practical necessities demanded by a rustic life. She is able to maintain her sense of self, not thrown out of balance by the sensibilities in which Johannes tends to lose himself. Her gifts are called forth when a friend or visitor needs healing for their soul. Then, deep in the forest where she lives, Felicia weaves a world of fairytales that quench Capesius's thirst when his academic mind feels empty and dried out. He says that when she speaks like this, it is as though the ancient practice of the bards lives on in her.

Felicia has no personal attachment to her art. She is not compelled to struggle with the individual ego, and what she creates is given in response to need. The stories that she tells are not 'hers'. She is a glorious creation in her simple eccentricity.

Through Felicia, Steiner shows that artistic gifts do not need to come at the expense of healthy functioning in life. She performs her work soberly and with joy in the creative act. Its glory lies in the simple act of service, meeting human need without the glamorizing of its purpose, or the one whose gifts have made it possible.

If artistic training is to be artistic then like art itself, it must leave us free to engage with and receive the level of insight and nourishment we seek. As Chekhov said, 'First of all freedom'.* Although our methodology is grounded in initiation knowledge, it should serve the needs of three kinds of actors without imposing theories on anyone; those who come like Maria with a healthy sense of self and who are consciously in search of a path to be an actor that is also a path of initiation; those like Johannes whose artistic sensibilities are the result of an unconscious crossing of the threshold that leaves them vulnerable and who are conscious that they need a healing way to work that supports them to reclaim themselves and find balance; those who simply want to act and are looking for a healthy process that offers practical results.

The first century of Anthroposophy has yielded priceless treasures. For each art, Steiner showed how the laws specific to each medium connect to the greater universe.

---

* See page 9.

These treasures have been nurtured and devotedly imparted by and to the first generations who sought them. We cannot help but ask, as the trainings that once flourished die away, are these priceless treasures now redundant, have they yielded what they could for evolution? We sense that they have not and that we have just begun to understand.

Terms of reference

Steiner and Chekhov used these basic terms in ways that were precise to them.

Use of terms specific to Steiner

The threefold human being – body, soul and spirit
Amongst the attributes of the *physical body* are organs that enable physical perception of the world. In addition, our anatomy is structured so we can experience and then express feelings, thoughts and actions. Broadly speaking, these functions have their centres in our chest, our head, and metabolic system connected to our limbs. This body is a corpse, unless it is alive; what fills the physical with life is what Steiner calls the 'etheric'.

- The sensations, feelings and emotions, thoughts and impulses for action that compose our consciousness or inner life is what Steiner calls *soul*.
- *Spirit* is the self that is conscious of its own experience within the soul and which refers to itself as *I*.
- *Body* is the instrument through which spirit becomes aware of the world and expresses the thoughts, feelings and intentions made conscious in the soul.
- *Soul* is the arena within which spirit becomes conscious or aware of its experience while it dwells within a body.
- *Spirit* is the I who directs our process.[*]

We shall use Shakespeare's *Macbeth*, to illustrate.

Macbeth and his wife are confronted with the prophecy that Macbeth is destined to be King of Scotland. This stirs in them the longing for the power they have dreamed of and they resolve to murder Duncan, the present king, to gain the crown. In the course of the action, their *bodies* walk, talk, sit, stand, eat, drink, fight, defend, kill, ride, read, wash their hands, die, etc.

Within their *souls* there flows a constant stream of sensations. Those connected to the body, enter their souls through the five physical senses: they smell the air around the castle, the blood so freshly gushing from the body, now smeared on their hands; they see the blood, the forest moving, read each other's faces, letters. They hear the knocking at the gate, the owl's screech, the prayers of guards still half-asleep; they taste the wine, touch the crowns upon their heads, the daggers in their hands, etc. Emotions and impulses to action also fill their souls; we identify ambition, terror, fear, pity,

---

[*] For Steiner's detailed exploration of these terms see *Theosophy*.

cruelty, compassion, mockery, cynicism, disgust, defiance, horror, shame, guilt, courage, cowardice, regret, longing, gentleness, tenderness, bewilderment, ruthlessness, despair, emptiness, et cetera.

Shakespeare's language also reveals the activity of *spirit* which is conscious of itself through thinking that enables it to understand and order the flow of sensation and emotion it encounters in the soul. From time to time, as well, each character expresses thoughts and feelings that could only be expressed by a being that is *conscious of itself being conscious*. There are choices that only one who can weigh up and assess, and then reflect upon itself, could recognize and make. Lady Macbeth, for example, steels herself to murder by a conscious choice to obliterate the spirit from her consciousness.

> Come, thick night,
> And pall thee in the dunnest smoke of hell,
> That my keen knife see not the wound it makes,
> Nor heaven peep through the blanket of the dark,
> To cry 'Hold, Hold!'

Later, she can only will her *body* to perform the necessary actions by using alcohol to mask the consciousness of *spirit* in her *soul*. But *spirit* cannot be obliterated and returns ever and again, reminding her:

> Nought's had, all's spent.
> Where our desire is got without content.
> 'Tis safer to be that which we destroy,
> Than, by destruction, dwell in doubtful joy.

Macbeth, too, hears the voice of *spirit*. It wrestles with ambition in his *soul* as he contemplates the deed of murdering his king:

> Besides, this Duncan
> Hath borne his faculties so meek, hath been
> So clear in his great office, that his virtues
> Will plead like angels, trumpet tongued, against
> The deep damnation of his taking off;
> And pity, like a naked new born babe,
> Striding the blast, or heaven's cherubin, horsed
> Upon the sightless couriers of the air,
> Shall blow the horrid deed in every eye,
> That tears shall drown the wind. I have no spur
> To prick the sides of my intent, but only
> Vaulting ambition, which o'erleaps itself
> And falls on the other.

In successive stages, he overrides this voice until his soul is overwhelmed by the emptiness of life, lived in conscious violation of that spirit.

> It is a tale
> Told by an idiot, full of sound and fury,
> Signifying nothing.

The stages/levels of spiritual cognition

The map that Rudolf Steiner has bequeathed to guide us safely through supersensible experience requires that we examine that experience with scientific rigour. He called this work a science of the spirit, and identified four stages of cognition on the healthy path of supersensible perception. Chekhov's methodology provides us with a way to do this through the practice of our art.

Clear perception and thinking

First we develop the capacity to perceive and think clearly in the world of physical material reality. We learn to observe a phenomenon accurately and form a concept of it.

Imagination

We do not abandon clear perception and thinking, but use it to penetrate beyond perception of the outer form, to the energies, forces and dynamics that lie 'behind' material appearances. We use imagination to arrive at living pictures of the formative activities out of which those forms arose.

Inspiration

Instead of dismissing feelings as subjective and not able to reliably inform us of phenomena, Steiner suggests we cultivate them consciously and refine them to become an organ of perception for a further level of reality. This refined feeling sensibility, permeated with the clear, awakened thinking we developed earlier, allows us to sense that the forces and dynamics revealed by *imagination* are not only abstract energies but the expression of consciousness or *being*. Steiner calls this level of cognition *inspiration*.

Intuition

We gain further knowledge of that being's consciousness by sensing what activity is needed on our part to be a channel for that being to express itself through us. This involves commitment of our will to serve the being's will. Steiner called this level of cognition *intuition*, which is not to be confused with possession or being taken over by the other's will because at every point clear thinking permeates our sense of what that being asks of us. This makes us free to choose how we respond. In doing so, we achieve the highest level of cognition; a knowledge of this level of reality is only possible because we have consciously allowed it to express itself through us, we have participated in its being.[*]

These stages are described in linear progression for purposes of clarity. In life and practice they are more likely to appear something like this: *glimmers of imagination or inspiration encourage us to use our will, get up and try some of the explorations offered in this book, for example; action leads to experiences which we try to understand and which, in turn, lead to further inspiration and/or action.* What matters is to learn how to consciously move back and forth through all the levels so that they can fructify each other.

We shall use the four *qualities-of-movement*, which are the focus of chapter 1, as an example. Chekhov used precise observation and thinking to clarify his concepts of the four elements: earth, water, air and fire. Through intuition he allowed these four elements to express themselves through his body and clarified the four qualities-of-movement that allow us to imagine the supersensible activity out of which the elements arise. Exploring the movement leads to further sensations which intimate not just different forces and energies but qualities or states of being that exist and interact in the universe. The more I mould or float or fly or radiate, the more I experience that fire, air, water, earth are qualities of consciousness. They exist in me and I can make use of them, because I sense them also in the characters I play. I sense their being in the macrocosm. When I radiate, my body/soul knows the consciousness of fire. I have a glimpse of the creator's heart. When I mould, my body/soul knows, for example, something of the consciousness of Shelley's Earth and Demogorgon from *Prometheus Unbound* — is granted some dim sense of love that burns enough to densify, condense itself into a ground of being firm enough to stand on, a resistance I can press against and tells me, I exist. Floating, flying, radiating, my body/soul knows the path to Shakespeare's Ariel from *The Tempest*.

---

[*] Owen Barfield, a lawyer and the eminent philosopher and author of many books (*Saving the Appearances, Poetic Diction, History in English Words, What Coleridge Thought*, to name a few) was a student of Steiner's work. He explored the evolution of consciousness and its relationship to language and epistemology. He formulated the idea of original and final participation. Original participation refers to the ancient consciousness in which there was no distinction between inner and outer, or consciousness and the world. According to this view, humanity gradually lost this consciousness until we are confronted now by a universe that we perceive to be entirely empty of consciousness and from which we feel detached. Through this we find our freedom and can make our way back (through the stages of cognition earlier described) to a 'final participation'; one which we have consciously achieved in freedom.

For Chekhov's specific exercises for the training of the actor's imagination, see the various editions of *To the Actor*.

The 12 senses

Our understanding of the intimate connection between 'outer' and 'inner' deepens when we consider how our senses mediate between these worlds. For the last few hundred years there has been a cultural consensus in the West that the five senses, touch, smell, taste, sight and hearing, alone can validate that our experience is *real*. Steiner invites us to expand our definition of reality and differentiates twelve gateways through which experience declares itself to us:

sense of touch	sense of smell	sense of hearing
sense of life	sense of taste	sense of word
sense of movement	sense of sight	sense of thought
sense of balance	sense of warmth	sense of 'I'

The first group of senses (touch, life, movement and balance) allow us to perceive our own body. For everyday experience, their functioning is raised to consciousness only when we are 'not well'. The psycho-physical approach to training the body leads to a conscious awakening and strengthening of these four senses.

The second group (smell, taste, sight and warmth) are the gateways of perception that allow the world that we experience outside of us, to enter our soul and be known to us.

The last group (hearing, word, thought and I) allow us to perceive the inward aspects of phenomena, or what we might call 'being'. They are the gateways whereby supersensible impressions (those from the realm of soul and spirit), have access to our consciousness. I do not only hear a sound, for instance; I can learn to listen so that the sound reveals the inner being of the one who makes the sound. A recognition of the consciousness or being of another or the sudden realization that I sense what someone else is thinking, are possible because the sense of *I* or sense of *thought* are active.

Information provided by our senses causes a reaction in our soul, of antipathy or sympathy. Since the range of emotions we normally experience are largely a consequence of these two tendencies, the cultivation of sensory recall, along with personal emotional recall, has been, since the pioneering work of Stanislavski, a staple of an actor's training in the western world. Chekhov also recognised the powerful connection of sensations mediated to the soul through the body with our feelings and emotions and evolved his own process for releasing its potential.[*]

---

[*] See chapter 3, Qualities and sensations.

Although an experience may first enter our soul more through one sense than another, it is the way our senses interweave and work together that provides us with the continuity of consciousness we think of as our *self*. The senses are not isolated from each other and cannot be dogmatically divided into groups. Yet for purposes of training, the familiar senses may be refined and cultivated further; the less familiar can be awakened and developed. Great actors have always revealed a larger spectrum of experience than 'everyday'. Chekhov shows us we can all expand our senses and develop the capacities through which such 'large' experience becomes accessible and harnessed in the service of our art.

Use of terms specific to Chekhov

The actor's instrument

Musicians express music by developing skills that allow them to project their will into an instrument. Think of a violin sonata played by Isaac Stern; over many years his violin becomes as intimate to him as his own body, yet the instrument he plays remains physically external to him. Like dancers and singers, actors learn to play upon themselves. They train to *be* the instrument through which they can express their art.

If musicians are to play or sing not only notes, but move us with their *music*, if actors, singers and dancers are to get beyond technical proficiency and move us to the heights and depths of our humanity, they must express soul and spirit through their instrument. Ideally then, the training of the actor's instrument includes the training of the soul and spirit and the intricate relationship they have to body and to nuances of voice and tone. For actors, the voice and body are the instruments through which the inner life is expressed.

The psycho-physical principle

Chekhov named the fundamental nature of his technique *psycho-physical*. He recommends we cultivate together the body/soul capacities an actor needs. This goes against the trend in our culture to keep them separate from each other (or dismiss the soul altogether).

Dancers or elite athletes, for example, train their bodies to do what is required by obliterating from their souls a range of emotions and sensations. The adrenalin high that fuels the drive to perform, or win, overrides sensations and emotions such as fear, pain and exhaustion, or feelings such as empathy and compassion.

Chekhov suggests that actors undergo the opposite of such a toughening, unlearn the soul/body split at the core of so much cultural conditioning and learn, instead, with every movement that our bodies make, to be conscious of a corresponding movement or sensation in our soul. Such a training develops awareness of how body, soul and spirit are connected. If a sensation exists in my awareness (soul) then I (my spirit) can express it, in and through my body. Conversely, I become aware that every action of my body awakens a corresponding journey of sensations in my soul.

We could express it thus: no outer expression that is not inwardly experienced: no inwardness not outwardly expressed.

In such a way, actors train their instrument to be that 'sensitive membrane' we have spoken of; able to receive and transmit the range of impulses within the human soul; those arising from the world of matter (the visible/tangible) and from the realm of spirit (the invisible/intangible).

In such a way, spirit, soul and body weave together. In fact, it lies within the very nature of what Chekhov and Steiner have suggested, that the healthy development of one cannot take place without the others. I am convinced that if Chekhov were to formulate his understanding of the actor's process today, he would not hesitate to add *spirit* to the name: calling it a *spiritual-psycho-physical* process for the actor.

Incorporation
The expression of an impulse through the body.

Archetypal and particular
Chekhov uses the term *archetype* or *archetypal* in several different contexts in his work. In general, archetype refers to an underlying principle that appears in various specific forms. There are many bullies in the world, and many friends, but the ability to recognize the essence we identify as bully or as friend is the ability to recognize the archetype.[*] This is connected to our ability to form a concept.

We can also identify the archetypal quality in gestures and movements that we make in daily life. For instance, we can observe and imitate many different ways we use our body to express acceptance (sympathy) or rejection (antipathy) of an object or another person. What do those different gestures have in common? Can we express that in a movement?

Chekhov calls an *archetypal gesture* one that expresses the archetype or essence that is shared by the particular examples. He suggests that we come closest to an archetypal-gesture or movement by working in a *full-bodied* way.

Full-bodied and naturalistic: our working principle — the actors' secret
A full-bodied movement engages our whole instrument; each toe and finger, limb as well as trunk, neck and head are equally committed. Complete engagement of our

---

[*] See chapter 4, section on Archetypes.

body stimulates the most intense sensations in our soul. When we have aroused these sensations through archetypal full-bodied movement, then we learn how to sustain this movement inwardly and imbue our everyday, more naturalistic movements with the original commitment and intensity. This imparts to them a fullness of substance and intention and leads to an ability to radiate that substance into the surrounding space. Our goal is to be at ease within the whole spectrum of expression, from full-bodied to naturalistic, which we designate as a scale from 10 to 1. A full-bodied movement is at level 10. We want to sustain and radiate the strength of sensation aroused at level 10 through all degrees of outer movement down to level 1.

Soul and body are intimately interwoven. The stages (10–1), which span particular and archetype, can always be a model. To activate the body until it is completely penetrated with whatever action we are focused on means we cannot help becoming conscious of the strong sensations that arise within our souls, and which constitute the inner counterpart of any outer movement. We learn to sustain and radiate those strong sensations, applying them in whatever style or manner is artistically appropriate. This process grants reliable access to artistic impulses. It is not dependent on the personal emotions of the actor at the time and leaves the actor free and in objective relationship to his/her creation.

We call our ability to let our full-bodied outer preparation disappear into the specific intensities required to shape the space with inner substance, our *actor's secret*.

Warm-up

Those who worked with Chekhov speak of his intention that his methods would provide a barre class for actors. No dancer, however famous or accomplished, would dance without a layered warm-up which carefully prepares the joints and muscles for what will be demanded of them in a way that maintains their health and function.

The vast array of explorations in this book, expands the actor's barre, enabling us to warm up body, soul and spirit. There should be no extremity of soul or body demanded by our art which cannot be prepared for or brought to its conclusion, healthily. As we surrender to this interlocking web of processes, the psycho-physical sensations they arouse will teach us how to make from them specific pathways that will lead us healthily through whatever process we require. It is assumed that early stages of a process are always used to warm-up for advanced levels and their applications.

Imaginary stage

The device of imaginary wings, imaginary stage and imaginary audience means that at any point in our process we can 'perform' our work. We designate a part of our working space to be the wings where we prepare or warm up the aspect of technique we wish to focus on, and a part to be our imaginary stage where we perform to an imaginary audience. Such 'performances' help us develop the split-level consciousness Chekhov refers to, in which we are within our creation and simultaneously able to behold it as objective creation outside of us.

Improvisation

Improvising takes many forms. Generally it refers to the state of surrender to the unknown, when we leave the safety of what has been planned in advance and explore what arises spontaneously. Most successful improvising depends on clear rules and guidelines to establish the conditions in which the unpredictable can then arise. Much improvising has as its goal the generation of ideas and situations and the willingness to follow where they lead. Its goal in the context of this book is to support the development of a psycho-physical technique. Unless stated otherwise it refers to a stage of exploration where having practised or developed a specific skill we improvise a dialogue or situation which provides the opportunity to apply and sustain that skill. The following are guidelines for this approach:

General indications for working

The steps of each exploration need not be accomplished in a single session. Each step can take as long as it requires to be fruitful. As skill is gained, it becomes a warm-up for the next stage of the process. We learn to pay attention and observe the soul component in our action, whether we work with full-body or anywhere within our scale of 10–1. We may be amazed at the sensations, feelings and emotions that 'surface' to become artistic impulses. These principles apply throughout our explorations.

Let the scenario unfold organically

It is important not to plan a situation, decide on character, or, as in the case of the letter scenario which is used many times, to think out what the letter might contain and its effect on you. Focus on the skill you are practising, sustaining the sensations that arise and letting them 'suggest' the content of the letter or what happens.

Thorough preparation

Use full-bodied gesture or movement until you are ready to let go of it. Being 'ready' means you can sustain and radiate the intensity of the impulses aroused by full-bodied/ outer action without the need to continue using it. Play with varying degrees of outer gesture (10–1) as you work. Remember that, in this context, the goal of improvising is not plot or character development as such, but to gain proficiency in generating and sustaining strong sensations or emotions from a full-bodied gesture and letting these determine what happens. We let go of outer gesture when we can sustain its inner counterpart. We return to outer gesture to revitalize the inner when we sense it weaken.

Creative individuality

If scenes or characters emerge from individual or interactive work (as, at some point, they most powerfully will) let them unfold, *so long as they continue to be anchored in the gestures and sensations that produced them.* You will learn to trust your own artistic intuition, letting what it reveals from other levels of your psycho-physical awareness surprise you. This work has power to elicit from artistic depths within you a wealth of knowledge of both character and situation of which you had been previously unaware. You could not have thought it out beforehand; the ideas possibly, but not the rich texture of sensations accessed by each simple exploration and that spring from the deeper wisdom that your body holds and which the psycho-physical technique releases in your soul. These artistic depths within you Chekhov called your *creative individuality.*

Space and the dynamic 'field' of interaction

Full-bodied work generates intensity of inner life. When we learn to radiate that inner life we transform the space into a 'magnetic field', charged with that intensity. This creates a dynamic meeting place for interaction with another character or partner.

Letting go of the intensity — de-roling

Despite a widespread acknowledgement that actors need to de-role after rehearsing or performing, how to do this is often left to chance. A psycho-physical training teaches us to rely on an objective starting point for what we do. Returning to an equally objective form at the completion of our work reminds us not to identify ourselves with the intensities we generate. Developing the habit to complete an exploration or performance by returning to the full-bodied preparation that we started with, then consciously releasing it, contributes to a healthy working culture which acknowledges that we are conscious creators who exist in a free relationship to what we make.[*]

Use of terms specific to *A Spiritual Path for the Actor*

Our working culture

To take what Chekhov called the first baby steps to consciously achieve the multi-levelled consciousness necessary for a *Theatre of the Future,* we need to cultivate a working culture of permission, patience and respect.

---

[*] See the use of heart exploration as way to de-role, chapter 6, Performance and the Threshold, page 265.

Artistry

The artist's goal is transparency. Nothing that they do or don't do obscures what they intend to express. Achievement of this stage is what is meant, within the context of this book, by *artistry*. When it is achieved, the audience experience reality that is not to be confused with naturalistic efforts to accurately represent appearances. On the contrary, great artists make levels of experience that lie beyond appearances, real for the beholder.

Chekhov's psycho-physical technique guides us to this goal. Paradoxically, although each specific exploration can generate profound, immediate experience, the process as a whole does not lead to quick results. Only the accumulation of capacities achieved with long-term, patient exploration can amount to mature artistry. Only practice can transform talent or those first brilliant flashes of imagination, inspiration or intuition into faculties, consistent and reliable, that can be consciously invoked and depended on. We need to give our colleagues and ourselves permission to explore and find out what it means to move beyond the naturalistic reproduction of behaviour. To explore the deeper truths full-bodily requires time and courage to move beyond the shortcut of immediate effects that correspond to everyday appearances.

A note on criticism — a culture of compassion

Even when we have assembled the elements of sensibility, technique and gift, these still do not, in themselves, make art. Artists must invest their passion; be willing to surrender, jump off the edge, be vulnerable, pour their 'lifeblood' into their creation. This makes them sensitive to judgement or criticism. For the artist's very self has been offered and awaits the verdict. Only when we cultivate awareness of the Self that cannot be annihilated can we hope to reach the objectivity enabling us to separate creation from creator; able to fruitfully receive and offer the critical appraisal without which our artistry cannot mature.

For those already driven by perfectionism, this additional demand seems stern: *that, as well!* Yet we cannot learn from our 'mistakes' without a healthy process, and will continue to be offended by constructive criticism until we develop consciousness of that Self that is unassailable; and have compassion for the self whose worth depends on recognition or approval.

To build a culture of compassion and respect within a working group, ensemble or a class — where our evolution as an artist and human being is held and honoured — is central to a new holistic way.[24] We need to give realistic encouragement that does not flatter or deceive, to distinguish between kindness and dishonesty, to guard against exploiting talent by tearing its attractive fruits from the context of that human being's need to grow in harmony with their humanity.

Building a bridge to speaking

In order to prepare the ground for an organic, natural relationship between the Chekhov work and Speech it is important, from the very early stages of our process, to dissolve the artificial barrier that has separated body from experience and Speech from movement in our increasingly intellectual culture. The organic flow from movement into speech is encouraged from the start by recognising that the movement in the muscles that enable us to speak cannot be separated from our whole moving instrument. It is, in fact, warmed-up or brought into a state of appropriate tonicity by such full-bodied preparation.[*] Such appropriate tonicity is, in fact, the condition necessary for speech to be vital and alive. Therefore, most of the explorations in *The Art of Acting* include steps that provide such an organic transition into speaking. This in turn creates a bridge to the more detailed exploration of the art of Speech Formation in *The Art of Speech*.

---

[*] Tonicity refers to the degree of tonus or muscular response that an experience engenders in the body. The expression can be used instead of 'tension' which can have unhealthy connotations. To avoid this, Chekhov used the term 'appropriate or necessary tension'. I have used the term 'tonicity' in order to connect with Musgrave Horner's book: *Movement Voice and Speech* which explores this concept thoroughly; the book which sent me on my search for Speech Formation. See Appendix C, An autobiographical note, and *The Integrated Actor*, My teacher at the crossroads.

THE PRACTICE

When God at first made man,
Having a glass of blessings standing by;
Let us (said he) poure on him all we can;
Let the world's riches which disperséd lie,
Contract into a span.

The Pulley, George Herbert

Chapter 1

The Psycho-Physical Principle

[Those who were given responsibility by the Creator,
to create the human being …] borrowed portions of
fire and earth and water and air from the world …
then they took and welded them together …
making up out of all the four elements each separate body
and fastening the courses of the immortal soul in a body
which was in a state of perpetual influx and efflux
as in a vast river … in all the six directions of motion, backwards and forwards, right and
    left and up and down …
the affections produced by external contact caused still greater tumult … when the body
    of anyone met and came into collision with some external fire,
or with the solid earth or the gliding waters,
or was caught in the tempest borne in the air,
and the motions produced by any of these impulses
were carried through the body to the soul.
All such motions have consequently
received the general name of 'sensations'…

The Timaeus of Plato[25]

Awakening our body as a sensing organ

The tools of the psycho-physical approach inspire us with creative impulses that intellectual analysis by itself cannot supply.[*] Yet our intelligence is thoroughly engaged when we dive into and ride the wave of such an impulse which is not less intelligent because it is fused with the intense sensations that energize our work; the passionate intelligence of the creator.

As mastery develops, a rich range of soul experience becomes available to us, almost effortlessly. We learn to radiate these inner states into the acting space, to change them with clarity and certainty, and transform the soul-substance of the space we inhabit in increasingly complex situations, in solo, partner work and in ensemble.

The following preliminary explorations prepare us to become aware of our body as a mediator of sensation.

---

[*] See the Terms of reference for a description of the psycho-physical principle.

The body as sensing organ exploration 1 (partner work)
A is blindfolded and guided by B in silence but with a firm and gentle touch that A can trust.

1. Begin indoors with B introducing A to a range of sense experience. Take time to stop and listen, touch, smell, taste, walk on different levels, surfaces, etc.
2. Go outside and expand the range of sensory experience.
3. At the conclusion of a designated time, say 20 minutes, bring A to rest and remove the blindfold.
4. Change roles.

The body as sensing organ exploration 2

1. Find a space where you can move without touching anyone and shut your eyes.
2. Using your imagination and your body, recreate some of the moments of your journey in *exploration 1*. Recall the sensations as strongly as you can and let them permeate your body and the way you move.
3. Come to rest, open your eyes, move around the room and observe the shift from your previously heightened sensory awareness to the familiar sight-dominated way of functioning.

The body as sensing organ exploration 3

1. Shut your eyes and move around the room. Observe your awareness sharpen as you use your whole body and your other senses to inform you. If you touch a person or an object in the space, use your other senses to explore and get to know them.
2. Choose one person and get to know their hands.
3. Move away from each other. Open your eyes. As you move around the space, can you sustain the heightened sensitivity throughout your instrument that was awakened when you could not see? As you meet each person, close your eyes and explore each other's hands until you recognize the ones that you explored earlier.

The explorations that follow and any variations you devise increase the range of psycho-physical awareness and can be used throughout the training to warm-up to any other explorations.

The four qualities-of-movement

Earth water fire air . . .
these are (a part of) the . . . division of my nature[*]

We will use the set of tools Chekhov called *qualities-of-movement*: *moulding, floating, flying* and *radiating* to explore and understand the psycho-physical basis of this work.[26] No sooner do we start to play with them, than we encounter what the first ancient Greek philosophers identified as the four elements or the four fundamental states of being of which our physical universe consists. In the *Timaeus*, for example, Plato describes how the gods created not only the greater universe or macrocosm out of them, but also the microcosm of ourselves.

Even present consciousness recognizes how the solid/earth, liquid/water, gaseous/air and warmth/fire states compose and permeate our physical existence. So, when we work with the four elements or states of being and their corresponding qualities-of-movement, we work with universal principles.

The psycho-physical nature of experience manifests when we connect the dynamic interactions of the elements in the weather patterns we witness as outside ourselves, and the storms or calm we experience within our souls. Is the storm Lear feels within his soul, the storm that blows around him and vice versa — or is Shakespeare's portrayal merely a literary device? Is metaphor possible because all outer life has its corresponding inwardness? Are they in reality not two worlds, but one? These are the deeper implications of a psycho-physical approach.

Whatever the ultimate answer, working with the four qualities-of-movement takes us deep into the nature of the four elements and confirms their intimate connection to our souls.

MOULDING

I am . . . of that which is immoveable
. . . I AM the mountains

To *mould*, I need resistance; the same resistance that the earth outside me offers to the earth of which my body is composed; its bone and flesh. Yet no element exists in isolation from the rest and I cannot mould without the watery element to soften earth, the air I am compelled to breathe more deeply to exert myself and the fire of will that warms me through. Nevertheless to *mould*, I engage with a level of resistance, a density

---

[*] Unless acknowledged otherwise, the quotations that preface each section are from the passage quoted earlier from the *Bhagavad-Gita*.

specific to the element of earth. To awaken the sensation of resistance, it is helpful to begin with a partner.

Qualities-of-movement exploration 1 – moulding (partner work)

1. A runs across the room with a strong intention to get to the other side. B tries to prevent A from arriving.
2. Gradually, allow the struggle to transform into 'wrestling'.*
3. Sense how you support each other through the resistance that you offer. Wrestle with as large a surface of your bodies as you can; hips, backs, shoulders, arms and hands. You are *moulding* with each other's bodies. Check that you engage your body's lower half to support the upper and thus experience *full-bodied* movement.
4. Gradually separate while sustaining the moulding quality-of-movement. Imagine that *space* now gives you the resistance that was formerly provided by your partner. Now you are moulding space.
5. Extend and enlarge your movement until it becomes archetypal; far away from everyday, naturalistic movements. Become aware of the intense sensations that accompany such full-bodied movement.
6. When these sensations seem inwardly sustainable, lessen the degree of outer movement in stages until it becomes minimal or even imperceptible, (10–1) Can you sustain the sensation of shaping or moulding a resistance through your inner activity?

Qualities-of-movement exploration 2 – moulding

Psychotherapeutic principles acknowledge that emotions are locked within our muscles and the structure of our cells. By moving with the quality of moulding, a rich store of sensation, emotional and feeling life can be released as inspiration for the actor.

1. Warm-up with full-bodied archetypal moulding.
2. Reduce outer movement, inwardly sustaining the sensations that arose while you were moulding, and practise standing, walking, sitting, picking up an object, saying a simple word like 'yes' or 'no', or any other everyday activity. If the sensation of moulding fades or weakens, strengthen it by engaging once again in full-bodied or 'archetypal' moulding.
3. Move between 'inner' and 'outer' (or full-bodied) moulding, exploring the soul experiences that arise. If a situation or scenario suggests itself, not as an intellectual idea but in the flow of sensation, follow and explore it.

---

*See pages 126–128.

Qualities-of-movement exploration 3 — moulding — the letter

The purpose of this exploration is to develop the capacity to mould and inwardly sustain this quality-of-movement within a simple everyday scenario. Return to full-bodied moulding as often as you need, to remind you of the strength of the original sensation.

1. You enter the room, find a letter on the table, open it and read it, then leave. Warm up with full-bodied moulding and when you are ready, perform the sequence in a quality of moulding. Pay attention to the sensations and emotions that suggest themselves and how they transform the simple action into an event which seems part of a greater story.
2. Invite a partner to observe your action and to share with you their feedback. Did you succeed in sustaining the quality of moulding? What did they receive from watching you?

The goal is to be attentive to the intense sensations which arise from moulding and to let these provide the impulse for artistic inspiration. Ideas for plot development may well suggest themselves and can be welcomed and included, so long as they do not become an end in themselves and usurp the purpose of the exercise, which could be stated thus: can you allow the action of the scene to unfold entirely within the quality-of-movement we call, *moulding*?

If you succeed in this, your partner will perceive your state of soul as something tangible which permeates the space. Our capacity to mould inwardly, creates an atmosphere. When we mould, we sense the activity in the universe that densifies and creates solid substance.

Qualities-of-movement exploration 4 — moulding — relationship to speaking

While engaged in full-bodied moulding as though space has the consistency of malleable clay, we shift our hands to mould where breath emerges. Experiment with moulding sounds of language and words. Are there consonants or vowels which more obviously tend towards the density and solid form that moulding generates? These can be enjoyed and tasted on their own, as well as formed in words and phrases. Experiment and find your own.

Qualities-of-movement exploration 5 — moulding — Speech-exploration

1. Return to full-bodied moulding.
2. Imagine the many different ways in which the earthly element can manifest: hard impenetrable rock, smooth or rough, sharp and jagged, dense but penetrable earth,

thick clods, viscous mud or clay, tiny pebbles, large surfaces of rock. Adapt the moulding in response to walking or climbing through or over them, digging into them, sculpting, moulding or creating them, compressing them, etc.

3. While moving, explore your quality of speaking. Search for consonants or vowels that emerge from and integrate with your actions. Experiment, creating words and phrases to be spoken while you move.

Qualities-of-movement exploration 6 — moulding — Speech-exploration[*]

The following examples may inspire you to play with speech and to create your own. First let their sounds and rhythms organically emerge out of full-bodied movement. Then reduce the degree of outer movement (10-1) and sustain the quality of moulding in your speech.[†]

digging deeper	bigger boulders
gripping granite	tying knots
moulding mountains	tearing tree trunks
carving crags	

FLOATING

> *I AM the sweet taste of waters . . .*
> *of bodies of water I AM the ocean . . .*

If we make a transition from moulding into floating, the shift from one sensation to another will make this second quality-of-movement easy to identify.

Qualities-of-movement exploration 7 — floating

1. Warm-up with full-bodied moulding.
2. Imagine, now, that the resistance we are moulding full-bodily in the space becomes less dense. It changes into the consistency of liquid or the watery element. If we allow this imagined change of density to affect the way we move, the quality with which we move through this 'watery' space will metamorphose from moulding into *floating*.
3. Extend and enlarge your floating until it becomes quite archetypal. Moving with the quality of floating may remind us of the different ways that water can behave. As we let our bodies play with some of these, our souls will register a shifting spectrum of

---

[*] All speech explorations in *The Art of Acting* by Dawn Langman unless otherwise indicated.
[†] See *The Art of Speech*, chapter 1.

sensations; from water that is dense and powerful like great waves of the ocean, through to the lightest bubbling of a stream where water drops already mingle with the air and almost take us into the next element. Somewhere in-between we find that we are purely floating, carried effortlessly by eddies and currents, balanced between light and weight.

4. When you are able to sustain these strong sensations by activating your inner 'muscles', lessen the outer movement by degrees from level 10 to level 1. Inwardly floating, practise standing, walking, sitting, picking up an object, saying a simple word like 'yes' or 'no', or any other everyday activity.

5. Move for a while between full-bodied and 'inner' floating in all its different qualities. Observe the states of soul aroused. Do they remind you of specific moments of experience, moods, someone that you know or have observed? If a situation or scenario arises in the flow of sensation, follow and explore it.

Qualities-of-movement exploration 8 – floating – the letter

1. After warming up with full-bodied floating, repeat the simple action of entering the room, finding a letter on the table, opening and reading it, then exiting. Your goal is to sustain the quality of floating through the sequence, and to allow any sensations or emotions that suggest themselves to permeate the action.

2. Again you can invite a partner to observe and give you feedback.

If you succeed, your partner will perceive your state of soul as something tangible that permeates the space, making it appear more fluid. Our capacity to float inwardly creates an atmosphere. When we float we sense the activity in the universe which creates the liquid quality.

Qualities-of-movement exploration 9 – floating – Speech-exploration[*]

We can explore our quality of speaking while we float. Once again, we search for sounds or words which organically emerge from our full-bodied quality-of-movement and which display a liquid quality.

1. Return to full-bodied floating.
2. Play with the ways that water manifests.
3. Experiment, finding words and phrases to speak while you move, letting the sounds and rhythms emerge organically.
4. When you stop speaking, focus once again on moving and prepare for a transition into the next quality-of-movement.

---

[*] See *The Art of Speech*, chapter 1.

Qualities-of-movement exploration 10 — floating — Speech-exploration

Search for any sounds or words which emerge from full-bodied floating. Then try the following examples.

ocean waves: hurling and burling the sloggering brine

— Hopkins

floating in calm water: limpid liquid lazily

bubbling brook: babblingly bubblingly happily lappingly

Floating in practice

Sometimes an image in a text will guide us to explore the use of a specific tool. Or while working with a tool and with the language from a text resounding through one's soul, the link will suddenly appear that gives rise to further fruitful exploration and connections. I was warming-up one day with the four qualities-of-movement in preparation for working on the character of Hecuba from *The Trojan Women* by Euripides. Suddenly, while surrendering in full-bodied movement to that aspect of the watery element connected with the ocean's weight and density, words from the particular adaptation we were using came flooding into me:

I am remembering pictures I have seen of men at sea.
How, when the storm hits,
If the winds are not too high,
Each man fights to live.
But when the sea rolls higher than the ship
And smashes them,
They lose the will to fight.
God's savage waves have swamped me.
I cannot think.
I cannot speak to question or to curse.[27]

Such an image could not but inspire a full-bodied exploration which led, in turn, to further moments from the text, illuminating them within the stages of the metaphor — how she clings to bits of wreckage but finally, battered by successive blows, is beaten by the waves on to the rocks, yet still the last glimmer of her life force holds on to existence.

A technique that grants permission to explore such images full-bodily led me to a clear journey of sensation and levels of intensity related to this character's specific circumstance. I found that this clear journey of sensation contained within the action of this metaphor that could be unlocked by floating, provided a foundation for the journey of the character throughout the play.

FLYING

... of purifiers ... I AM the wind

Because air is all around us all the time, it is likely we have taken it for granted. Creating the shift from floating into flying through the air highlights the sensation.

Qualities-of-movement exploration 11 – flying

1. Return to full-bodied floating, but as you continue, imagine that the watery substance you are moving in, with its specific weight and density, transforms into air. Now, relatively, you sense that you have no resistance. Allow this imagined change of density to affect the way you move. It is as though your bones are hollow, your body has no weight, the air can pass through you and you can *fly* through space. Play with the range of airy qualities, flying through a light-filled sunny sky, heading through dark and stormy clouds and out into the light again.
2. Extend and enlarge your movement until it becomes archetypal/full-bodied.
3. Become aware of the sensations.
4. When you can sustain these strong sensations, lessen the degree of outer movement by stages from level 10 to 1 checking as you do that you activate your inner 'muscles'.
5. Inwardly flying, practise standing, walking, sitting, picking up an object, saying a simple word like 'yes' or 'no', or any other everyday activity.
6. Move between full-bodied and inner flying. It is particularly striking to stand or sit or walk while you are inwardly flying. Play with the scenarios and characters that suggest themselves.

Qualities-of-movement exploration 12 – flying – the letter

1. Now try the action with the letter while sustaining the quality of flying.
2. Invite a partner to observe and give feedback.

Your audience may not be conscious they are watching *flying* but will perceive your state of soul as something tangible that permeates the space making it appear dynamic and light or thunder-filled. Our capacity to 'inwardly fly' creates an *atmosphere*. When we fly, we sense the activity in the universe which creates the airy quality.

Qualities-of-movement exploration 13 — flying — Speech-exploration

1. Return to full-bodied flying.
2. Follow the different manifestations of the airy element; a gentle breeze, a gusty wind, a hurricane, etc.
3. While you fly, explore your quality of speaking. Look for sounds which emerge out of your movement and integrate with flying. Let the sounds, rhythms and phrases emerge organically. Experiment with degrees of movement 10–1.
4. Standing in a circle, let the sounds and words fly around between you, the rolled 'r', the gentleness of *breeze*, the fierceness of *hurricane*, the increasing intensity of *wind, west wind, O wild west wind.*[*]

Qualities-of-movement exploration 14 — flying — Speech-exploration

To play with speaking while flying:

> radiant rollick
> rolling airily
> restlessly rippling

RADIATING

> *I AM the brilliance in fire . . .*
> *the radiance in sun and moon*

Pay attention and observe the soul component in your action as you make the following transition into radiating.

Qualities-of-movement exploration 15 — radiating

1. Return to full-bodied flying.
2. Imagine flying right into the centre of the sun; burning up into pure energy, as though you have merged with and become the sun. Sometimes you will be like quick tongues of flame and sometimes slow, deep penetrating warmth. Whichever form it takes, Chekhov calls this quality-of-movement, *radiating*. Once again, be attentive to what happens in your soul and follow through these next steps of transition.
3. Become aware of how intense are the sensations which accompany full-bodied radiating/fiery movement.
4. Lessen the degree of outer movement from level 10 to level 1, sustaining the sensation of radiating.

---

[*] See *The Art of Speech*, chapter 1.

5. Inwardly radiating, practise standing, walking, sitting, picking up an object, saying a simple word like 'yes' or 'no', or any other everyday activity.
6. Move back and forth through levels 10–1 and improvise as the impulses direct you.

Qualities-of-movement exploration 16 – radiating – the letter

1. Apply radiating to the letter scene.
2. Invite an audience.

Our audience may not be conscious we are radiating but will experience our state of soul as something tangible which permeates the space with fiery intensity, incandescence, or can make it smoulder. Our capacity to radiate inwardly creates an atmosphere. When we radiate, we sense the activity in the universe which manifests as fire.

Qualities-of-movement exploration 17 – radiating – Speech-exploration

While we radiate, we can explore our quality of speaking. Once again, we look for any sounds which have a fiery quality and integrate with radiating.[*]

1. Return to full-bodied radiating.
2. Play with the ways that fire manifests; those described above; quick tongues of flame, a steady candle flame, a furnace, slow and penetrating warmth, etc.
3. Create words and phrases while you move. Let the sounds and rhythms emerge organically.

Qualities-of-movement exploration 18 – radiating – Speech-exploration

Try the following examples to play with radiating:

> furious fire
> flickering flame
> sizzle and frizzle
> steam and fry
> shower of sparks
> slowly smoulder
> warmth infuse/imbue
> emanating warmth
> immanence

Now that we have practised radiating, we can begin to sense how it is fundamental to the whole creative act. There is a sense in which we cannot create unless we access

---

[*] See *The Art of Speech*, chapter 1.

the fire which is the primal source. Experiencing this will help us understand the way that Chekhov uses the term *radiating* in a different context later. It will also help us deal with a tendency to get bogged down when we first begin to work with moulding.

Qualities-of-movement exploration 19 — radiating in relation to moulding

1. Warm up with full-bodied radiating
2. While in the centre of that fiery activity, transform the radiating into moulding, without losing its intensity or energy.

If you can achieve this in one step, you will discover that the fire is not lost within the density but condensed into the solid form. The radiating is not lost, but totally transformed into the moulding and the moulding is still full of fire.

Sometimes you will achieve this transformation by working through the stages; feeling how the fire gradually densifies as the radiating makes its way through flying, floating and at last is totally absorbed into the density of moulding. Through this, you may experience how energy condenses into matter, and arrive full circle at the quality of moulding.

To mould directly out of radiating and let the radiating be released directly out of moulding will help you overcome the tendency for moulding to become bogged down and stuck. Likewise, the experience that fire is the creative source from which the other elements condense, can help us learn not to confuse an image or the state a character displays with the creative energy required by an actor to create that state or image.

So, in the example I described of Hecuba, the character is numbed by trauma and weak to the level of exhaustion. To create this state in such a way that it can radiate to the audience and to the other characters and drive the action of a scene requires the utmost fire.

In another example, the characters of *Waiting for Godot* are suffering from existential boredom. Yet an actor who naïvely shows that he is bored will only bore the audience. An artist will create the state of boredom out of inner fire. The practice of transforming radiating into flying, floating and moulding will develop this capacity to distinguish the energy required for the process of creation from the work that is created.

Transitions

Once confidence and skill are gained, it's important to develop flexibility in moving from one quality-of-movement to another in any order. This cannot be achieved by sacrificing thoroughness of penetration of our instrument. It is always a temptation to believe that the *idea* of doing something means that we are *doing* it. This is where we face the choice to really train our psycho-physical capacities or to fall into the trap of believing that having an idea is the same as creating an experience.

So, at the beginning of our training we choose to lay a firm foundation rather than resort to shortcuts. Remember our dancer who thinks they do not need a barre class for today. We want to know that we can demonstrate a clear transition from one quality-of-movement to another. We warm up with full-bodied movement first, reducing the degree of outer movement (10–1) when we are confident we can inwardly sustain the intense sensations. Observation by a partner confirms whether our transitions arise from an abstract idea or the heightened moment of intense sensation signalling a shift.

Warm up full-bodily to each transition. The simple actions will reveal dramatic possibilities as you experiment with different orders of transition.

Qualities-of-movement exploration 20 – transitions – the letter

At any point you want to try you can adapt the tiny action with the letter to accommodate transitions into different qualities-of-movement.

1. Warm up floating
2. Enter the room, see the letter and begin to mould.
3. Pick it up and open it, begin to read it in the quality of moulding.
4. As you read, pay attention to the moment where the moulding sensation changes and becomes an impulse to fly. Similarly the flying sensation will transform into the impulse to radiate, and leave the room.
5. Invite feedback from a partner or an audience of classmates.

When these transitions are the result of intense sensations which provide the impulses for change, even such a simple action is transformed into engaging drama.

Qualities-of-movement exploration 21 – Speech-exploration

The following texts easily relate to one of the four elements or states of being. Warm up, then experiment with speaking through the range of movement, 10–1. Our aim is to discover how a quality-of-movement which permeates our whole instrument supports that part of our instrument which speaks, to manifest that quality in words.

Earth

> Then lips cracked open in the stone hard peaks
> And rocks begin to suffer and to pray.
>
> *The Harp and the King*, Judith Wright

He clasps the crag with crooked hands.

The Eagle, Lord Tennyson.

Water

The sea is calm tonight
The tide is full.

Dover Beach, Matthew Arnold

Summer's bubble sound of sweet creek water.

The Bull, Judith Wright

Roll on thou deep and dark blue ocean, roll!

The Ocean, Byron

Air

Wild air, world mothering air
Nestling me everywhere.

The Blessed Virgin Mary compared to the Air We Breathe, Hopkins

O wild west wind, thou breath of Autumn's being ...

Ode to the West Wind, Shelley

Fire

Look! Look! See all the little fire-folk sitting in the air.

The Starry Night, Hopkins

The sun sprang forth.

The Triumph of Life, Shelley

The wind had become furious again and more furiously helped to spread the fire ... Sparks caught the manes of many horses and there were infernal creatures racing across the grass, flaming steeds that trampled everything in their path ...

The Name of the Rose, Umberto Eco

And then with a rush and rumble of stone (the dome of the house) fell in a flurry of fire; but still unabated the flames danced and flickered among the ruins ...

The Return of the King, JRR Tolkien

The Celtic verse, *St Patrick's Breastplate*, contains the opportunity to practise speaking as we make the transition from one element to another while working with its quality-of-movement.

At Tara today in this fateful hour
I place all heaven and its power:
And the sun with its brightness
And the snow with its whiteness
And fire with all the strength it hath
And lightning with its rapid wrath
And the winds with their swiftness along their path
And the sea with its deepness
And the rocks with their steepness
And the earth with its starkness.
All these I place with God's almighty help and grace
Between myself and the Powers of darkness.

Hamlet's speech to Rosencrantz and Guildenstern also contains opportunities to create images related to at least three of the four elements. Experimenting with the qualities-of-movement will open up possibilities inherent in the language. Although it contains no direct reference to water, I have found that *floating* provides an excellent entry point into what can seem a daunting 'slab' of language to beginners. Full-bodied floating enables us to launch into a stream or river of words and carries us along in its waves and currents until we are at ease in its changing dynamics.[*]

> *Hamlet* [to Rosencrantz and Guildenstern]:
> I have of late, but wherefore I know not, lost all my mirth, forgone all custom of exercises; and indeed, it goes so heavily with my disposition that this goodly frame, the earth, seems to me a sterile promontory; this most excellent canopy the air, look you, this brave o'erhanging firmament, this majestical roof, fretted with golden fire: why it appeareth nothing to me than a foul and pestilent congregation of vapours. What a piece of work is a man, how noble in reason, how infinite in faculties, in form and moving, how express and admirable, in action how like an angel, in apprehension, how like a god: the beauty of the world, the paragon of animals; and yet to me, what is this quintessence of dust?[28]

Shelley's *Ode to the West Wind* contains numerous opportunities to make transitions between the different elements.

Qualities-of-movement exploration 22 — transitions — Speech-exploration
The opening lines from the great invocation spoken by Prometheus provide the opportunity to move through all four elements and qualities-of-movement.

---

[*] Please note: this matching of the qualities-of-movement with appropriate images is not to be confused with the creation of the character. It constitutes a stage of working on the speaking of the language which is valid in itself and needs to be mastered if the character is to finally embrace and inhabit the dimensions inherent in the words of Shakespeare.

O divine ether
And swift winged winds and river fountains
And of ocean waves, the multitudinous laughter,
And Thou Earth, boon mother of us all
And Thou, bright round of the all seeing sun
You I invoke.

Prometheus Bound, Aeschylus.[29]

Qualities-of-movement exploration 23 — moods and emotions — Speech-exploration

We have discovered the power each quality-of-movement has to elicit in us certain moods, feelings or sensations. The following phrases make a bridge between a quality-of-movement, such inner states and our capacity to express those states in speaking. Practise in a full-bodied way. According to our process, when sufficient skill has been achieved, the outer movement can be diminished.

Moulding

deep despair
truly trying
keeping courage
neurotically niggling
gravely grieving
mourning moaning
grasping greedily
deep in debt
gaining knowledge
getting closer to my goal
quiet courage/quietly courageous
begging boldly
quiet beauty

Floating

lovely lady
lightly laughing
lurching lumpily
listlessly lazy
lovingly lilting
full of love
all over the place

Flying

restlessly rippling
rather ridiculous
rapidly reasoning
really royally

really radiant
rushing around

Radiating

fuming furiously
savagely seething
finding focus
seriously focussing
sustaining focus
fragile and sensitive

<table>
<tr><td>recklessly racing</td><td>fighters yes!</td></tr>
<tr><td>raging recklessly</td><td>choose showers of flame</td></tr>
<tr><td>rowdy rumbustious</td><td>these souls on fire</td></tr>
<tr><td></td><td>soon sleepers wake</td></tr>
<tr><td></td><td>see spirits higher</td></tr>
</table>

modelled on Rudolf Steiner

The four temperaments

This principle, of the intimate relationship between our soul and body, forms the basis of Chekhov's psycho-physical approach. This relationship between the four elements and our soul/body fusion is demonstrated in the old idea of the temperaments. Certainly, up to and including Shakespeare's time, to understand the four temperaments, how they arise out of the play within us of these four elements, and how they are expressed in our behaviour, was the basis of psychology.

Someone, in whom the earthy element was dominant, was a *melancholic*. Melancholics tend to be weighed down by the sorrows and pain of our existence.

If the watery element was dominant, it would manifest in the *phlegmatic* temperament; characterized by love of ease, reluctance to be stirred yet also a capacity to absorb the shocks of life without becoming overly excited.

When the airy element was dominant, a tendency for moving rapidly from one thing to another, the capacity to be occupied with many things at once, would be observed. Such a person was identified as *sanguine*.

Lastly, when the fire element predominated, it was better not to cross such a person who was known as a *choleric*. Yet their fiery will forges the determination that does not give up at the first obstacle to an initiative.

Most of us can recognize that we might respond with any one of these four tendencies depending on the situation. Our initial explorations made it clear that all the qualities-of-movement and their related states of soul belong to each of us. These tendencies, which belong to everyone, would only have been recognized as *temperament* in someone in whom one of the above behaviours was predominant. Anyone stuck in one of these four tendencies, who seemed incapable of flexibility in their response to the range of life experience, was regarded as in bondage to their temperament.

It is possible for human beings to transform the raw material of their given nature. Such conscious work with any of our one-sided tendencies makes it possible to harmonize the possibilities that lie within us. This means we can enjoy the gifts each temperament provides but are not compelled to act out of its destructive tendencies.

Here are some characteristics of a person who is controlled by their temperament. In contrast are the gifts each temperament bestows when it is ennobled through the conscious work of transformation.

Temperament	Ennobled	Untransformed
Melancholic	Compassionate Capable of depth	Depressed Pessimistic
Phlegmatic	Harmonizing Creating balance Methodical Patient	Indolent Interested only in own comfort
Sanguine	Enthusiastic Interested in everything	Shallow Uncommitted
Choleric	Positive energy to change things	Destructive to resistance

When you are confident working with the qualities-of-movement, improvisation work can be extended into playing with the temperaments. They will form a rich layer in the composition of complex characters. In the case of a simpler character, if we can identify the temperament, the qualities-of-movement will grant immediate, yet profound, access to its delineating features. The result will be a colourful and powerful portrayal. We can use the template of the four temperaments as an opportunity to practise differentiation in a set of characters.

Four temperaments exploration 1 (for a group of four)
Return to full-bodied movement if you lose touch with the strength of the original sensation.
1. Each choose a temperament so the four are represented in each group.
2. Warm up the quality-of-movement related to your temperament.
3. Play instinctively with the behavioural tendencies related to your temperament and let them permeate your quality-of-movement.
4. Move into each other's space. Allow your four qualities-of-movement to create a dance together.
5. Let your full-bodied movement lessen by degrees from 10–1 until your four 'characters' relate in a naturalistic way, standing, sitting, walking, and speaking simple words.

6. Return to full-bodied movement and when you are thoroughly warmed up, improvise a situation such as this: the four of you are sitting in a car, on your way to an important meeting. You become aware that you are lost and need to find out where you are and how to get to your appointment.
7. When the improvisation is complete, swap your qualities-of-movement and try again. Do this until you each have played each role.
8. Play with other situations.

Four temperaments exploration 2

Use the four temperaments as a way of achieving a broad sketch of these characters from Shakespeare's *Romeo and Juliet*. If you work in groups of four, each one can have a turn at each. When each interaction is complete, share your observations and move on to a different warm-up and a different character.

Melancholic — Romeo
Sanguine   — Mercutio
Phlegmatic   — Benvolio
Choleric   — Tybalt

Mercutio: Romeo, I would have you dance!
Romeo: I have a soul of lead
             So stakes me to the ground I cannot move.
Mercutio: If love be rough with you, be rough with love.

                    . . .

Tybalt: What! Art thou drawn among these heartless hinds?
             Turn thee Benvolio, look upon thy death.
Benvolio: I do but keep the peace: put up thy sword,
             Or manage it to part these men with me.
Tybalt: What! Drawn, and talk of peace? I hate the word
             As I hate hell, all Montagues and thee.
             Have, at thee coward!

1. Decide on your first set of choices.
2. Learn your lines.
3. Move apart and warm up with full-bodied quality-of-movement. Allow the aspects of your temperament that are appropriate to permeate your quality-of-movement. Let your words unfold within the movement. Experiment with speaking them until they are familiar and integrated.
4. Move towards each other and let your full-bodied qualities-of-movement interact. Let the words unfold within the movement.

Stay engaged and reduce the outer movement by degrees from 10–1, checking that you can sustain the inner quality.[*]

Layering

In a creative process, it is important not to be dogmatic with our choices. Here we use the qualities-of-movement to master our capacity to play with temperaments which, in turn, contribute a rich layer of substance to a full character development. It would be naïve to reduce a complex character like Hamlet, for example, to a simple temperament. Yet rich layers are revealed when we explore those tendencies in him.

To do this, we invent an advanced-level exploration with the qualities-of-movement which requires the capacity to consciously layer more than one skill. When this is achieved, the exploration will yield profound sensations which attract and integrate with further revelations of the character. Layering is explored in detail in the next chapter.

---

[*] Other possible characters to explore and play with:

Melancholic: Jacques, *As You Like It*; Antonio, *The Merchant of Venice*.

Phlegmatic: The Earl of Gloucester, *King Lear*; Sloth: Marlowe's *Dr Faustus*; Falstaff, *Henry 4th* parts 1 and 2; *The Merry Wives of Windsor*.

Sanguine: Ariel, *The Tempest*.

Choleric: The Duke of Cornwall (the hot duke), *King Lear*; Henry V, *Henry V*; Paulina, *A Winter's Tale*; Hotspur, *Henry IV*, Part 1; Katherine, *The Taming of the Shrew*.

The connection of this work with Steiner's indications about the temperaments in the *Speech and Drama* lectures will be explored in *The Integrated Actor*.

Chapter 2

Body

Hamlet, Shakespeare

Inhabiting the body

An art of acting that aspires to be a spiritual path recognizes that it cannot train the body as though it were a machine. *The Egyptian Book of the Dead* suggests that the wellbeing of the soul as she continues on her journey into realms beyond the physical depends on knowing the true names of things; this includes the body through which she would express herself. For to name the body truly would mean to understand it is not a machine to be driven to achieve its maximum level of mechanical performance.

Nor is it a corpse but a living form. We have a habit of confusing the body with the mineral substance of which it is composed. This habit can begin to shift if we consider how the mineral substances, at death, decompose, returning to the elements. During life, something held those substances together in the distinctive form we recognize as human and, as well, imbued that form with life. At death that 'something' withdraws from those substances, which of themselves do not provide us with our human form or life.

Let us consider, then, that this 'something' consists, in part, of that distinctive form we normally refer to as our body. For working purposes, we cannot think of this apart from what imbues that form with life. This, to borrow Steiner's terminology, we will refer to as the *life* or *etheric* body. It is a paradox to be explored that we cannot truly understand the 'physical' without considering the 'non-physical' or supersensible. And it is just this exploration that we undertake when we embark upon the training for the actor which Chekhov called psycho-physical.

Such training includes cultivation of the faculties with which to sense these subtle realms of form and life. Working with psycho-physical techniques will assist us to become aware of streams of life and movement that are always flowing through our bodies. These levels of activity, in turn, are interwoven with our life of feelings and emotions. This is why the psycho-physical techniques prove such a potent tool for the actor, as we shall see.

When embarking on this work to finely tune our body/soul to be that subtle membrane Chekhov has described, many of us discover that relating to our 'bodies' can be difficult. Even something as simple as to throw and catch a ball or beanbag with a partner will expose a fundamental problem. Initially our movements may be uncommitted, uncoordinated; we lack balance and our throws and catches may well be either over- or under-extended. It is as though we are not able, at the simplest level, to inhabit the body with which we try to carry out these actions.

What is the matter with us?

Counter tensions

If we consider some of the well-known Ancient Greek sculptures, such as the Nike of Samothrace, we get a sense that the human being of that earlier time seemed 'held together' in a way that many of us, now, do not experience. It is as though some power that is invisible, that once integrated human beings to move as a wholeness has withdrawn. In our present time many of us experience that we are 'not together', awkward, self-conscious, 'all over the place'. Those of us who 'suffer' in addition, from artistic sensibility as was described early on, will especially be aware of disconnection from our bodies.

We shall consider the implications of this phenomenon to our evolution and to artistic style in *The Integrated Actor*. For now, we are concerned with whether we can find again what we have lost and what the ancients seemed to know instinctively. And if we can make use of it to benefit the early stages of the training of our 'body'.

What sensations are aroused in us when we incorporate the figures of the sculptures and try to live in to the way they inhabit their bodies? Can we glimpse, through them, how, in ancient cultures human beings were held within some greater pattern, an order which they felt to be divine? To have this sense today, we must achieve it *consciously*.

My own experience of disembodiment manifested in extreme awkwardness unless I was playing 'someone else'. I was intrigued with my physical abilities when I *was* someone else. On one occasion, when I was rehearsing the central character of Marlowe's *Dr Faustus*, I was astonished to find that I had leapt several yards across the space. I had no idea that I could do such a thing — me, Dawn, who in my daily life was incapable of even modest jumps. As myself, I could not be present in the simplest movements and would perform them clumsily.

Unless I was someone else, any movement, whether it be dancing, even walking, was painfully awkward and self-conscious. Observation of my students over many years suggests that many of us suffered from the same condition. It revealed itself in the simple act of throwing balls or beanbags with a partner or in Chekhov's staccato and legato explorations.[*]

The following process was developed, as much for myself as for my students, as a preparation for these 'advanced' requirements. It enabled me to sense for the first time, something I imagined 'normal' people took for granted: what it was like to be at home in their own bodies. What a relief! Through practice, the sensation becomes familiar and something we can call on anywhere, in any situation, any time. I called this process *working with the counter tensions*.

---

[*] See section on Dynamics, page 106.

Counter tensions exploration 1

1. Examine some of the well-known classical Greek sculptures. The discus thrower, spear thrower or the Winged Victory (the *Nike of Samothrace*) will serve.[*]
2. Incorporate each image, using your own body to 'become' each statue. Pay attention to any changes in sensation that occur.
3. Now bring it to life. Try moving as that statue would, if it were alive, with the qualities embodied in its image.
4. Discuss your observations with a partner.

Counter tensions exploration 2

Consider the *Nike of Samothrace*. We see a figure who is fully grounded, thoroughly inhabiting her body and at the same time, able to soar freely on her wings. She is not, like Hamlet, 'crawling between heaven and earth', but striding out and at the same time flying. Can she teach us her secret? How to have such presence, such perfect harmony and balance between the visible and what cannot be seen?

If we look closely, we perceive that her body is held within a network, a frame of counter tensions. Do we see a downward thrust? Then there is an equally visible upward thrust supporting her. Do we see an impulse upward? Then, equally, we sense the downward thrust, holding and supporting her. So, in myriad angles and tensions, forwards and backwards, right and left, and possible diagonals; each specific thrust or effort is supported by a counter thrust, pulling in the opposite direction. The result is a body which is perfectly at ease, supported as it is, at every point.

1. Experience this principle at work by playing with a partner, leaning into and stretching away from the support and weight of each other. I can trust myself to stretch out totally in one direction if I am firmly held and supported in the opposite. And so we play, shifting balance endlessly, stretching ourselves fully; each limb risking to extend itself further as I trust my partner to support me with an opposite and equal tension.

Counter tensions exploration 3 (partner work)

Now we are ready to formalize this exploration into six directions. Initially, I suggest working with a twisted sheet or some strong tie which you can loop around your partner's chest enabling you to hold and support your partner firmly as they move in each direction. A to lunge forward first.

---

[*] See illustrations, pages 79, 129 and 131.

Figure 5 – NIKE of SAMOTHRACE

1. B stands behind A and firmly loops the tie around A's chest, holding both ends firmly. Although it is important that support be firm, it should not be over-tense or tight. It should be sensitive as well, allowing sensations of a subtle interchange of energies and tensions to pass between you.

2. B, loose your hold for a moment; just enough that A can step back slightly, in preparation for a forward lunge.

3. As A lunges forward, with arms and hands extended forward at shoulder level, B, tighten your grip; enough that you give A confidence to extend fully because of the firm support.

   The degree and quality of firmness should not be a restriction, but strongly (and safely) supportive. It will facilitate transmission of the subtle energies between you, resulting in a perfect balance of the tensions which will not be stuck or hardened but dynamically alive. If A is not to be pulled back by B, or to be catapulted forward when B releases A, you need to activate the muscles in the lower half of your body, especially hips, thighs and calves and grip the earth with your feet.

4. When you sense this balance, and when A is ready, B begin, gently, to release your hold and therefore your support for A. As you do so, A replace that support by sustaining the activity in the muscles of your hips, legs and feet. A, reach down into

Figure 6 – Counter tension 1

the earth itself for forces to support you and grasp those forces with your feet, legs and hips; as though you grow roots into the earth. This brings about a depth of penetration of your body's lower half. This sensation of inhabiting the lower half of your body can bring relief to those for whom it is not familiar.

5. Both should be satisfied that A can now provide, by their own activity, the support initially supplied by B. A can then recover from the lunge to a standing position.

6. Walk a few steps *while sustaining the sensation of support* you worked so hard to find. Move around the space.

Figure 7 – Counter tension 2

Figure 8 – Counter tension 3

7. Try this same exploration backwards, right and left.

8. Up and down are possible if you have facilities for working on two levels. B supporting A, first from above while A is lunging downwards, and then from below, while A lunges upwards.

9. Swap roles.

Counter tensions exploration 4

Your goal was to sense the support that comes from fully inhabiting your body's lower half. Now you can practise accessing this sensation by yourself and apply it to every movement.

1. Perform a lunge in each direction, without a partner, and creating, through your own activity, the support you need. Each time, balance the power of the outer thrust with an inner thrust of equal power, in the opposite direction.

    You are learning consciously to do what *Nike* does instinctively.

Counter tensions exploration 5 (partner work)

This exploration should bring about an increased ease and confidence in working with our bodies, which will serve as a basis for our work.

1. Throw and catch a ball. Permeate your actions with all you have achieved in your exploration of counter tensions.

Impulse and sustaining

Many training processes emphasize working out of impulse. Yet, our present culture and stage of evolution may require that we learn to distinguish between an impulse and an idea generated by our intellect.[*] An impulse will always be experienced kinaesthetically; a sensation of energy and life that grips and has the power to organize an actor's instrument.

How do we become receptive, our instrument attuned so that body and voice are channels to receive and transmit an impulse? How do we become transparent to its quality and texture and duration so that it can manifest itself through us? So that we

> … blur no whisper, spoil no expression.
>
> *Song of a man who has come through*, DH Lawrence

To be a conscious channel we learn not to impose our will on what wants to express itself through us but to unite our will with its impulse. Chekhov has suggested a large range of explorations to develop psycho-physical awareness. Each one can be regarded as an opportunity to extend the range of impulses we are receptive to as we become that 'subtle membrane'.

An actor cannot be passive and without initiative. Practising makes it clear that responding to an impulse involves an active choice at every moment and the utmost degree of awake intelligence and sensibilities. Thus, we prepare to be an instrument through which the complex web of impulses of which each story, poem, character or drama is woven, can reveal itself.

Impulse

The relationship of any action to its impulse is clear when that impulse is received through one of the traditional five gateways to our physical perceptions. We move in response to a sudden noise, a smell, a taste, the sight or touch of something: such actions, vitally embedded in the web of interactions of this world, are satisfying to perform and witness.

If we expand the range of our senses and become responsive to subtle realms as well, we can experience that everything we do is embedded in a finer weaving, supported in a web of interaction with a greater life than what these 'normal' senses see or hear. For, movement that is not the automatic action of machines, comes from 'somewhere'. Our goal is to grow attentive to that 'somewhere' and responsive to the impulses originating there. Any movement that is not such a response cannot be alive

---

[*] See page 20, and chapter The Evolution of consciousness in *The Integrated Actor*.

and will be less satisfying to perform or witness. We learn how to listen, to sense before we act, receive before we give and, as our work progresses, become responsive to complex impulses.

We prepare to attune to subtle realms by learning first to respond to an impulse channelled through the sense of touch. Observe your experience. Can you recognize when you respond to a genuine impulse or to something constructed by your intellect? Of course, an idea can become an impulse, but we are tempted sometimes to avoid the fear of emptiness by snatching *an idea of something,* anything! You will learn to recognize the difference between an idea that is abstract and an impulse.

Impulse exploration 1 (partner work)
A to initiate the impulses. B is neutral and available; attentive and able to respond.

1. A touches B on the arm or leg or back. The touch or impulse should have a clear dynamic, direction and intensity.
2. B be attentive to how A's touch affects your body and respond in movement.
3. Pay attention to the life of the impulse and do not keep on moving once the impulse has run its course.
4. Keep doing this with a variety of impulses from a variety of directions onto different parts of the body, for example: firm, soft, sustained, sharp, smooth, quick, curved, direct, blunt, longer or shorter duration, light, penetrating.[*]
5. Swap.

Impulse exploration 2

1. Recall some of the impulses received from your partner.
2. Remember them as sensations in your body and as each one comes to you, respond. Move only for as long and in just the same direction and with the same intensity and quality that you imagined.

Impulse exploration 3
Sometimes an impulse might be provided by something that you see or hear around you. Sometimes you might experiment with one arising purely from imagination. Do not move unless you have received an impulse.

1. Create your own impulses and respond to them in movement.

---

[*] See later explorations of this chapter for changes in tempo and dynamic. For those familiar with Laban's work, the effort actions also provide a wide range of possibilities.

Impulse exploration 4

1. Use different sounds as your impulse; a bird call, the sound of scratching, footsteps or the banging of a door, etc.

Impulse exploration 5 (partner work)
Use the sounds of language, consonants and vowels, as your impulse.

1. A speaks a consonant into B's back space.
2. B allow the quality and dynamic of the sound to move you and become the impulse for your own speaking of the sound. Only speak a sound you have first received as an impulse.
3. When you have immersed yourself in the experience, swap roles.

Sustaining
The sensitivity to impulse is concerned with the start of a creative act. It asks that I be attentive to what it is that wills to come, *before* the action that reveals it in space and time. The cultivation of this organ to perceive what wants to come and where it comes from cannot help but make us equally attentive to the *end* of the creative act. With this, develops the ability to *sustain*, to stay present after the conclusion of the act. Only then can I accompany the impulse as it disappears from the world of space and time and journeys back into the realm whence it came, but now enriched by my participation. There it may be gathered into what becomes potential for a new impulse, a new creative act.

Many of us will recognize the following experience. We throw a stone into a lake or a tranquil sea and observe how the ripples that are set in motion spread until they disappear. Perhaps we have strained to follow what happens to the energy and movement after it ceases to be visible, even further than our eyes can see. Does it cease to exist because it no longer has a physical medium in which to travel? Can we perform an action so that it honours the life of the impulse in the realm beyond?

When we rock a baby, do we mechanically shove the cradle back and forth, concluding with a final jerk, or do we sense that what wants to be expressed through rocking continues afterwards and delivers the baby finally to outer stillness — without severing participation in that other world in which the baby is still woven and embedded?

Sustaining exploration 1
Using your imagination, throw a stone, and rock a baby, so that you awaken your ability to sense such delicate perceptions.

Sustaining exploration 2 (partner work)

To throw and catch a beanbag or ball with a focus on impulse and sustaining leads to an experience that *end and beginning exist in a continuum*. The visible action is but a tiny part of a greater wholeness, most of which remains imperceptible, unless we train our subtle organs of perception.[*]

1. Face your partner, one of you holding a ball. Make eye contact, and when you sense the impulse to throw to your partner, respond.
2. When you have thrown the ball, sustain your attention and follow its progress as it moves beyond your action until the moment when your partner throws it back to you and in doing so, returns it to you as a further impulse.

Sustaining exploration 3

1. When you sit or stand or perform any simple action, remain attentive beyond the duration of the act. Continue, inwardly, to be aware of what happens to the impulse once you complete the action; how it either vanishes or comes to rest within the realm of things unseen, or metamorphoses into a completely new or different impulse.

Sustaining exploration 4

1. Repeat *sustaining exploration 3*, but with a word or sound.

Sustaining and commitment

The cultivation of sensitivity to the 'beyond' results in a transformation of our speech or movement. We are committed. No longer do we pull back from an action as though we don't believe that what we did or said is real. To withdraw our interest and attention has the effect of cancelling or 'rubbing out' what we did, erasing its reality. It is as though we want to think it never happened and we never said or did it.

Through remaining active by sustaining, the space becomes alive with substance. We create a 'field' in which the actors and the audience perceive that the space between the things and actions of the finite realm is charged.

Equally, actors who have learned to focus their attention and become receptive to the impulse prior to the act, have the power to charge the space and render it 'magnetic' to an audience.

Impulse and sustaining belong together and require each other. Both have their life in realms beyond the manifest. To respond to any impulse by revealing it, letting it

---

[*] Discussed further in the exploration of Chekhov's *Sense of the Whole* in chapter 5.

manifest without attending to its future progress by sustaining it, is to cut it off, losing faith in what it brought. On the other hand, you may discover that an action that is not the response to an impulse will have no life within it to sustain.

To try to hold on to an impulse, not be able to let go of it; to try to keep the action going when the life has gone from it, is to stifle and imprison it in a dead form. This is not sustaining. We may discover that the mastery of working with an impulse involves the mastery of working with sustaining. Blake understood this when he wrote:

> He who binds to himself a joy
> Doth the winged life destroy;
> He who kisses the joy as it flies
> Lives in eternity's sunrise.

Eternity from *Several Questions Answered*

Space

Having learned to be attentive to the realm beyond the visible and audible, we now turn our attention to the realm in which the impulse manifests. If an impulse is to be expressed it must appear in space and time.

Let us first consider space.

We initially become aware of space by being conscious of the forms that occupy it: whether they take up a larger or a smaller space and how much space there is between them. The nature of that 'space between' — whether it exists, consists of 'anything' or is a nothingness in-between what *does* exist — is to be explored. This question has vital implications for actors, who are constantly placed (by themselves or others) as forms within a space.

We have observed already that the most powerful, compelling actors do not only occupy the space but have the power to affect it, to change its quality and shape its substance. To such actors, space itself is as much the medium in which they work as are their bodies and their voices.

Working with impulse and sustaining has taught us that to enter and exit the world of form, we become aware of what lies beyond the form.

Expansion and contraction

When we look into the universe, we see that everything alive, all living forms exist in a continuous cycle of expanding and contracting. On a minute scale, a tiny flower opens and closes in response to sunlight. On a larger scale, a human being is born into a tiny body that grows and expands into maturity and gradually shrinks into old age. On a massive scale, scientists explain that our universe, which has come about as the consequence of cooling and contracting, is now expanding at an exponential rate. The point will come when it will disappear and bring about an end of earthly time and space.

Centuries of poetry bear witness to the fact that our souls also experience expansion and contraction.

> My heart leaps up when I behold
> A rainbow in the sky.
>
> Wordsworth

> .... Here! creep,
> Wretch, under a comfort serves in a whirlwind: all
> Life death does end and each day dies with sleep.
>
> *sonnet*, Hopkins

Within the cycle of the seasons we sense our souls contract in winter and expand fully in midsummer. On the journey of our lives from birth to death, they contract in fear or grief, or expand into trust, relief or exultation. These to name but a few.

For Chekhov's own descriptions of expanding and contracting, see pages 6–7 of *To the Actor*. The following explorations are developments of his exercises and, like them, designed to sensitize us to the psycho-physical continuum of *expansion* and *contraction*.

Your goal is to achieve the capacity to radiate each gesture, and transitions from one into the other. On this basis you can develop endless variations of such simple situations as are here described, making them complex, adding other characters. You will also find that this objective starting point for action will not result in lack of inner life. Instead, you may be surprised at the depth of emotion that is accessed effortlessly when your soul's sensations are embedded in objective ground. No longer is the means to generate intensity left to the vagaries of personal emotional availability.

Expansion & contraction exploration 1

1. Stand, alert and available, and slowly contract your hand. Follow the contraction inwardly until your hand is totally contracted. Follow the sensation of contraction

further than your hand is able to reveal. Observe how deep within the core of that contraction at some point will be born the impulse to expand. Follow that impulse as it engages with and slowly penetrates your hand.

2. Follow the expansion until your hand is fully extended. Stay attentive as you follow the sensation of expansion further than your hand is able to reveal. Observe the moment when it seems that from the furthest reaches of expansion is born the impulse to contract. Sense the moment it engages with your hand, penetrating it, contracting it until your hand becomes a fist.

3. Allow the cycle to continue. As you engage deeply in this continuum, pay attention to the subtle changes of sensation that accompany your actions.

4. Let your hand gradually draw your body into its activity until your whole instrument is involved, expanding and contracting. It is this full-bodied state that Chekhov has described and illustrated in his book.

5. Explore these states *and what exists between them* in a full-bodied way, paying close attention to the journey of sensation that unfolds. Observe your sensitivity increase to the most subtle changes in sensation which arise in response to every tiny movement one way or another. It is these sensations which grant access to another whole arena in our souls' gamut of experience.

Expansion & contraction exploration 2

1. Use exploration 1 to warm up. Stay attentive to the spectrum of sensations your preparation has aroused. These will act as a barometer or lens through which to sense the movement in your soul that follows.

2. Move around the space, continuing to expand and contract bodily, observing changes in your soul as they remind you of everyday experience.

3. Express with your body every shift in your sensations. If your soul expands, then stop a moment and expand your body to what feels like an accurate reflection of that degree of movement in your soul. Likewise with contraction.

4. Pay attention to the interplay between expanding and contracting which is always taking place within our souls, not forgetting to translate it into gesture. For example:
I see my friend. I feel my soul expand.
I see him/her smile. I feel my soul expanding further.
I see her looking worried. I feel my soul contract.
I remember that person or that thought or something that I did . . . my soul starts to contract/expand . . .
I see that painting on the wall . . . my soul expands/contracts further. I hear that door slam . . . my soul contracts.

I see my dirty windows … my soul …
I see the tree outside … hear birds … my soul (etc.)

Expansion & contraction exploration 3 – the letter – expansion to contraction

Once facility is gained, improvise the following:

1. Designate a space for preparation, adjoining your imaginary stage. In your 'wings' prepare your instrument with a full-bodied gesture of expansion.
2. Then, of contraction.
3. Then, expansion once again.
4. When you are ready, release the outer gesture, sustaining the inner gesture/sensation of expansion.
5. Sustaining the inner gesture/sensation of expansion, enter your imaginary stage. You see a letter. Pick it up, open it and read it.
6. As you read it, let yourself contract. Continuing to do so, exit your imaginary stage into the 'wings'.
7. Before releasing your intention, once again pour your inner life into a full-bodied gesture, this time of contraction and then let it go.
8. Repeat this with a partner watching. Invite your partner's feedback as to how you demonstrated the transition from one state to another. Share your experience of working with expansion and contraction in this situation with the letter. What sensations or emotions were aroused in you?
9. Swap roles.

Expansion & contraction exploration 4 – the letter – contraction to expansion

1. Improvise the letter scenario beginning with contraction. As you read the letter, let yourself expand.
2. Share feedback.
3. Swap roles.

Expansion & contraction exploration 5 (partner work)

In this exploration the focus is on sustaining the initial choice of gesture for the whole encounter.

1. Standing at a distance from each other, A prepares a full-bodied gesture of contraction; B, a full-bodied gesture of expansion.

2. When you are ready, release your outer gestures and, sustaining your inner gestures and their accompanying sensations, approach each other. Allow your expanded or contracted states of soul to be the lens through which you each experience your meeting. Let them determine what takes place between you and how you depart.
3. Make your way back to your starting point.
4. Once again, slip into the full-bodied gesture with which you began.
5. Release it.
6. Share your experience with your partner briefly.
7. Swap roles and repeat.

Expansion & contraction exploration 6 (partner work)

A further step would be to start your interaction within the field that you have generated by your initial choices. Now let your partner's gesture affect and change your own. This meeting could evolve into a complex interaction of varying degrees of both conditions.

1. Prepare with the full-bodied gesture of your choice.
2. Within the 'sensation body' this creates in you, approach your partner. Stay attentive to the way your partner's 'body of sensation' affects your own. You may experience a continuing interplay of extreme or subtle impulses back and forth between expanding and contracting. Express this interplay in gesture. Allow it to determine the story of your meeting, how it unfolds and concludes.
3. Sustain the degree of the gesture you are in when you withdraw from each other, and then pour your soul once again into the full-bodied gesture.
4. Release it and walk away from that commitment. Meet your partner and share your observations.

Expansion & contraction exploration 7 – working with text

Improvising with expansion and contraction, approach each other with this practice dialogue, letting the words arise within the field your combined gestures have created, swapping roles, etc.

A. I didn't expect to see you here today.
B. I didn't expect to see you either.
A. How've you been?
B. Fine.
A. I've missed you.
B. I've missed you too.

Expansion & contraction exploration 8

Give yourself permission to work with the range of outer gesture, (10–1). This does not need to look like a performance.

1. Apply expansion and contraction to any character that interests you. Resist the urge to predetermine what gesture might apply or what transition, choose one or the other and begin. After full-bodied preparation, let the sensations guide you into moments of your character's experience. If words of text arise organically explore them.

Expansion & contraction exploration 9 — (partner work)

Don't restrict yourself to what you think you already know about your character. Each gesture has something to reveal to you and will grant access to creative sources that may be blocked by a predetermined choice.

1. Apply the expansion and contraction technique to any scene you're interested in that involves a partner.

Working with Hamlet (expansion and contraction)

A complex web of interactions can be woven entirely out of these simple tools. This web provides a vital context for experimenting with Hamlet's speech quoted in Appendix A, to which we will also apply the other tools explored throughout the book.[*]

By act 2, scene 2, Hamlet has feigned madness to gain time while he decides how to deal with the appearance of his father's ghost. Claudius and Gertrude have requested that his friends from university, Rosencrantz and Guildenstern, spend time with him and find out, if they can, what troubles him. They meet. Hamlet is overjoyed to see his friends but cannot trust that they have not been summoned to the court to spy on him. They also are conflicted, put into a situation that is impossible; under orders from the king, unable to be honest, and yet, from the way that Hamlet greets them, we sense their friendship for the prince and concern for his welfare.

Such a complicated subtext offers an ideal opportunity for expanding and contracting to provide a simple and objective means for entering its territory. The exploration can be undertaken first in pairs, with one as Hamlet and the other as his friend. When you are ready to include another character, then work in groups of three. It is an interaction that can be undertaken in any gender combination. At this first stage of the work, no words need be spoken. It is enough to explore their meeting silently.

---

[*] See Appendix A.

Expansion & contraction exploration 10 – Hamlet – commitment to the single gesture – pre-text (partner work)

Work silently. Do not predetermine what will happen or how each character might react.

1. Decide who will be who.
2. Decide who will begin in a contracted and who in an expanded state.
3. Stand at opposite ends of the space.
4. While allowing your understanding of the character and situation to permeate your imagination, prepare with the full-bodied gesture of your choice.
5. When you sense you are ready, make contact across the space.
6, Release the outer gesture, sustaining the inner gesture and sensation, and approach each other. Allow the contraction or expansion to determine the quality and length of meeting that takes place between you, the dynamics of your inter-action and how you separate.
7. Return to your starting point and slip into your full-bodied gesture.
8. Let it go, relax and share with your partner any observations and discoveries.
9. Swap gestures.
10. Swap roles.
11. Swap gestures in new role.

Expansion & contraction exploration 11 – Hamlet – pre-text (partner work)

Work silently with full-bodied gesture, resisting the temptation to take short cuts.

1. Build on *expansion & contraction exploration 10* but allow your gestures to influence and change each other.

Expansion & contraction exploration 12 – Hamlet – pre-text (partner work)

1. Build on *expansion & contraction exploration 11*, but introduce working with the range of outer gesture (10–1), always sustaining the intense sensations generated by your full-bodied preparation.

Expansion & contraction exploration 13 – Hamlet solo work and text

Don't plan before you speak. Surrender to the power of the gestures to reveal unexpected insights, emotions and surprise turnings in the paths of Hamlet's soul. If you do not know Hamlet's speech already, have a copy of it somewhere easily accessible.[*]

---

[*] See Appendix A.

1. Warm up expansion and contraction.
2. Experiment with the text. Allow the words to come to you, to reveal themselves to you through the lens of your psycho-physical gesture/s.
3. Let the words affect your gesture. Sense how the words and gestures interact, affecting subtle changes in each other.

These allow you to explore Hamlet's soul, helping him express what had been unexpressed, maybe even to himself.

Expansion & contraction exploration 14 – Hamlet (for groups of 2 or 3)

1. Warm up expansion and contraction with the text.
2. Experiment with the dynamics that arise and how, within their web, Hamlet tries to speak to his friend/s and they to listen.

Part of the mystery of space is that it requires us to explore what lies beyond the range of normal sense perception. We look into the tiniest flower where the structure is so small that we can hardly see it with the naked eye, or into a drop of water. Just at that point where everyday perception ends, if we view it through a magnifying glass or microscope, we see that tiny point of matter open out into another world. An infinite space expands within the smallness when we are able to expand our consciousness.

Expansion & contraction exploration 15

1. Contract with the full-bodied gesture, as described by Chekhov. When you cannot, physically, contract any further, continue to contract in your imagination. Sustain your attention and follow the sensation of contracting beyond what you can physically manifest until you sense the moment when it turns around. In this inner space, invisible to physical perception, the sensation of contraction metamorphoses into an impulse to expand.
2. Allow that impulse to organize your instrument, expanding it into the full-bodied gesture that Chekhov has depicted.[*] When you reach the limit of your physical boundary, continue to expand in your imagination into that infinity beyond the physical. At some point you will sense the expansion transform into an impulse to contract.
3. Train yourself to experience both poles as part of a continuum that has its origins outside of normal sense perception.

---

[*] See Chekhov's *To the Actor*.

Expansion & contraction exploration 16

1. Returning to the so-called outside world, observe a flower when its petals fall away. Or see the leaves begin to die on trees when they have reached their maximum physical expansion in the summer. Sustain, in your imagination, the movement of expansion beyond those material forms. And as those structures crumble and contract, sense what is released into infinity.
2. Incorporate this journey in full-bodied gesture.

Portraying death

Expansion and contraction suggest how we might portray death differently. We can show the mineral form contract and crumble at the same time as the spirit leaves that form behind, expanding to the infinite beyond. After a performance of *King Lear*, a member of the audience approached me: 'How did you do that?' he asked. 'I saw Lear's spirit leave his body while his body was collapsing.'

Through practice, we become familiar with these movements in our souls. We discover that our souls move constantly between expanding and contracting, in relation to the outer world and to their own inner landscape. In this or that degree, in relationship to this or that experience, we learn to recognize these movements; first how they happen to us, and then how to create them consciously.

Expansion & contraction exploration 17 – relation to speaking

Using the natural tendencies of the consonants 'b' and 'p' to make the bridge from movement into speech, we can sense how 'b' tends to fold or contract around an object or itself, while 'p' tends to expand.[*]

1. Play with 'b' and 'p', first letting each single consonant, on its own, unfold organically within the full-bodied gestures, neither swallowing nor forcing it.

Expansion & contraction exploration 18 – Speech-exploration: expanding and consonants

The following words and phrases provide the opportunity to consciously connect this work with speaking language.

1. Begin in a gesture of contraction and jump[†] into three successive levels of expansion, accompanying each new level with the next line. Make use of the energy of 'p'

---

[*] See *The Art of Speech*, chapter 1.

[†] Later in the chapter we shall see that jumping into a gesture of expansion could be experienced as layering expanding with a *staccato* dynamic.

to carry the phrase out into the space. By the time you reach the third level, you should be in a full-bodied gesture of expansion.

First level:	peapods popping
Second level:	peacocks prancing
Third level:	power proudly

Expansion & contraction exploration 19 – Speech-exploration: expanding and vowels

1. Observe the natural tendency of long vowels and diphthongs to expand. With each successive stage of expansion, try the following:
   a. Do not *hold on* to the vowel to expand it further. Breathe in as much as you need to let the vowel expand but then release the vowel on your breath as you speak.[*]
   b. Impulse and sustaining teach us to expand a word, not by holding on to the vowel for longer, but by following its impulse beyond its physical sound in the space.
2. Speak 'far' three times so that each word communicates a further distance by disappearing further into the inaudible. In other words, we hear the expansion of the distance, not in the word, but in the space beyond the words.

Expansion & contraction exploration 20 – Speech-exploration: expanding and vowels

The following words may be played with in any order, on your own or with a partner.

1. Imagine that each arrow represents a further level of expansion:

> Far → far → → far → → → far away → → →
> Far, far away → → →
> How far can you fly? → →
> All around the earth → all around the sky →
>
> See → see → → see → → →
> Free → free → → free → → →
> Go → go → → go → → → go away → → →
>
> Look → look → → look → → → look there → → →
> Where? → where? → → where? → → →
> There → where? → →
> There → where? → → there → → →

---

[*] Later in the chapter we shall recognise that gestures of expansion connected to long vowels have a *legato* dynamic.

2. Now we are ready to apply these principles to express the following image from a sonnet by John Donne:

> At the round earth's imagined corners, blow
> Your trumpets, Angels, and arise, arise
> From death, you numberless infinities
> Of souls and to your scattered bodies go ...

And from Wordsworth's *Daffodils*:

> Continuous as the stars that shine
> And twinkle on the Milky Way
> They stretched in never-ending line
> Along the margin of a bay.

3. In the following example, the outer and the inner aspects of expansion come together in Romeo's soul as he beholds Juliet on the balcony. Love has expanded his soul and, as well, he must reach out physically to Juliet across the space. The text contains a mixture of short and long vowels. Play with expanding the short vowels by breathing through them in such a way that you extend them into longer ones, as though you are caressing them.

> See how she leans her cheek upon her hand.
> O that I were a glove upon that hand
> That I might touch that cheek ...

> O! speak again, bright angel; for thou art
> As glorious to this night, being o'er my head,
> As is a winged messenger of heaven
> Unto the white upturned wondering eyes
> Of mortals that turn back to gaze on him
> When he bestrides the lazy pacing clouds,
> And sails upon the bosom of the air.

Expansion & contraction exploration 21 – Speech-exploration – contracting and consonants

1. Contract, in three successive stages so that each stage of gesture supports you as you speak. Form each /b/ so that that it enfolds first its own word and then the entire phrase in a gesture of contraction. By the third level, you should be completely contracted in a full-bodied gesture.

First level: building bowers
Second level: beauty blushing
Third level: bud beholding

Expansion & contraction exploration 22 – Speech-exploration – contracting and vowels

1. Observe how short vowels can support the expression of a contracted gesture when we speak:

    Stop that at once!
    Get a grip on yourself!
    A little bit of grit
    Lock it up!

2. Now try:

    Lock it up and throw away the key!

In 2, the transition from short vowels into long assists us to express the shift from contraction to expansion.

Expansion & contraction exploration 23 – Speech-exploration – transitions

1. Blake's words provide another opportunity to experiment with making the transition from one state to another.

    To see a world in a grain of sand
    And a heaven in a wild flower
    Hold infinity in the palm of your hand
    And eternity in an hour.

And from Judith Wright's poem *The Wattle Tree*:

    Now from the world's four elements I make
    my immortality; it shapes within the bud.
    Yes, now I bud, and now at last I break
    into the truth I had no voice to speak:
    into a million images of the Sun, my God.

This early venture into language invites us to consider the following suggestions:

- consonants can provide the impulse which can drive the expanding or contracting gesture of a word or phrase;

- the length of vowels can help reveal the expanded or contracted gesture of a word or phrase.

Expansion & contraction exploration 24 – working with text

Explore expansion and contraction in these two moments from Shakespeare's *Cymbeline.*[*]

1. Warm up with full-bodied gesture.
2. Let the words unfold out of the movement.

   Expansion – First, Imogen receives the news from her husband's servant Pisanio, that if she journeys to Milford Haven she can meet her banished husband, Posthumus:

   > O for a horse with wings! Hear'st thou Pisanio?
   > He is at Milford Haven; read and tell me
   > How far 'tis thither. If one of mean affairs
   > May plod it in a week, why might not I
   > Glide thither in a day?

   Contraction – But later when she wakes beside the decapitated body of the queen's son, Cloten, who wears her husband's clothes, and believing him to be Posthumus:

   > Good faith,
   > I tremble still with fear: but if there be
   > Yet left in heaven, as small a drop of pity
   > As a wren's eye, fear'd gods, a part of it.

Expansion & contraction exploration 25 – Hamlet

We have explored how these gestures provide access to the subtext in the meeting of the characters. Now the gestures support us to explore and reveal the structure of the language and the images that it contains. It's important that we recognize this difference and not confuse these two contrasting purposes which may only coincide at a later stage. For present purposes, we make simple choices in pairing images and gestures.[†]

---

[*] Again, I stress that these experiments are not in any way to be a substitute for character development, nor to suggest a definitive interpretation. Our goal is simply to apply the tool we have been working with to the speaking of a text.

[†] These choices are not intended to suggest any final way of approaching the text or character, although they will no doubt lead to insights into character and suggest an approach to the structure of the language. Other necessary aspects related to speaking such as rhythm, breath, projection and articulation are explored in *The Art of Speech*.

1. Warm up expansion and contraction.
2. Apply to Hamlet's speech, allowing each phrase and image to unfold within a full-bodied gesture or sequence of gestures. Renew the gesture with each line, as follows.

Expanding	this goodly frame, the earth
Contracting	seems to me a sterile promontory
Expanding	this most excellent canopy, the air, look you
	this brave o'erhanging firmament,
	this majestical roof fretted with golden fire
Contracting	why, it appeareth nothing to me
	but a foul and pestilent
	congregation of vapours
Expanding	what a piece of work is a man
	how noble in reason
	how infinite in faculty
	in action how like an angel
	in apprehension how like a god
	the beauty of the world
	the paragon of animals
Contracting	and yet, to me,
	what is this quintessence of dust?

Expansion & contraction exploration 26 – Hamlet

Enjoying the interplay of gesture and speaking, explore this complex relationship between contraction and expansion in these further words of Hamlet:

O God! I could be bounded in a nutshell and count myself the king of infinite space were it not that I have bad dreams.

Expansion & contraction – further investigations

When you are confident in your ability to use expanding and contracting, investigate the following:

(a) Can we use contraction to exclude or cut us off from the invisible dimensions of the spirit?
(b) Can we use it to enfold the spirit, by wrapping the physical around it, so to speak?
(c) Can we expand in order to merge with spirit?
(d) Can we expand so far that we 'go out of ourselves'.
(e) How can we play such an expanded character and remain centred?

Expansion & contraction exploration 27

We learn how to 'be in the centre' of our space; not to expand beyond what we can consciously inhabit because only then can we be grounded healthily in our soul/body constitution. Some actors describe a sensation of 'leaving their body' during a performance. In the light of this, I suggest the following:

1. Practise expanding by degrees and checking that with each level of expansion you can centre yourself.

You may need to discover how to do this. The explorations about balancing of gravity and levity, to be found later in this chapter may assist. In chapter 3 we investigate what Chekhov refers to as the 'actor's centre in the chest'. These are just two possibilities. As we proceed further in the work you will learn to recognize the sensation of centredness and the many ways this method offers to achieve it.

We are ready to consider time.

Time

We considered in the section on impulse and sustaining, that without connection to the invisible and inner life of things, our art will appear mechanical and empty, even if we move with technical proficiency.

Our psycho-physical investigations have begun to cultivate ability to pay attention to these subtle realms. We want now to develop this attention in relation to the theme of *time*. When we move at different tempos, precise sensations manifest within our souls which can become as flexible and mobile as our bodies.

Tempo — fast and slow

Within our solar system the planet Mercury moves comparatively quickly, circling the sun three times each year. Saturn's cycle round the sun, on the other hand, takes approximately twenty-nine years to complete. We speak of certain souls as 'Mercurial', others as 'Saturnine'. This points to the psycho-physical phenomenon that we cannot separate the tempo of a movement from the soul qualities which it attracts.

Nature demonstrates all possible varieties of tempo, from the slow progression of a snail along its path to the sprint of predator and quarry. Observe a cat. At one moment it bounds at top speed with an energy that seems inexhaustible. Then, attention caught, it moves with focused slowness so intense that at times it seems almost not to move. Finally, its movement held back and gathered into outer stillness, it explodes in a lightning-quick pounce.

To move in that continuum of wakeful energy, from stillness or in tempo quick or slow, develops mobility and flexibility; a sense of readiness, availability. Yet mobility and flexibility are not merely physical or outer attributes; a knee-jerk reactivity. Animals in their natural condition tend not to tear muscles or ligaments or traumatize their joints. This is because when they move, they express something not visible to everyday perception; the life force with which they are at one.

Because we have the task of making conscious what was once our instinctive connection to the macrocosm, we had to first lose connection with it.[*] The painful consequences of this loss become our motivation to connect again. In the process we may often find that we resemble the legendary centipede who, when questioned about the order of his stepping with his many legs, became incapable of moving.

---

[*] See chapter 5, The Evolution of Consciousness, in *The Integrated Actor*.

Tempo exploration 1

1. Listen and then move to a recording of the well-known theme by Mikis Theodor-akis from the film *Zorba the Greek*. This provides a clear experience of gradually increasing tempo.
2. Observe your sensations as the tempo changes. What feelings and emotions are aroused? Share your observations with a partner or the class.

Tempo exploration 2

1. Observe different animals and the growth of plants.
2. Incorporate, in turn, as many of them as you can, finding movements that demonstrate the different tempos with which they move. Tune in to the energy that moves through the plant or animal. This will mean your movements are not just quick or slow but that you are able to respond to impulses that arise from the invisible and which move through you quickly or slowly. Perhaps they flash through you with the speed of lightning, or pour themselves through you with the infinite slowness of a growing seed that transforms so slowly its movement is invisible to normal sight. Such an example may lead you to experience the movement contained in stillness.
3. Extract the range of tempos from your examples and express them in an archetypal movement sequence.

The degrees from fast to slow to stillness move in a continuum. Within this, each contains the others, and together they express the unbroken stream of energy of life. This energy exists beyond the way it manifests in time as fast or slow, just as we observed how contraction and expansion exist beyond the way they manifest in space. This energy constantly transforms and moves through the continuum of time, its tempo always in a state of flux. I may choose to join it consciously and let it through me or to ignore or block it. But it is never *not*.

Tempo exploration 3

1. Incorporate the range of movement of a cat. Become aware of that stream of energy, the life that pours through you.[*]

Stillness need be no less active and alive than very fast movement. We can stand completely still and sense the 'streams of movement in the stillness' permeate our instrument, into the very centre of our bones. As we do so, we sense the stillness is

---

[*]See also page 109 and chapter 5 in *The Art of Speech*.

alive with the possibilities of tempo which at any moment may express themselves. We may also sense the interplay of qualities that weave through the continuum of tempo and which musicians call *staccato* and *legato*.

The dynamics of staccato and legato

A movement may be sharp, sudden and explosive, capturing one pin-prick in the tapestry of time. Or it may be smooth, sustained, joining the single points in a seamless flow. We see a frog's or lizard's tongue whip forward, almost faster than the eye can see, to stun and catch its prey. In the ocean we see tiny fish dart like lightning, back and forth. A great whale, on the other hand, leaps in massive curves out of the water and plunges to the depths, seeming to pour itself into the liquid mass of its environment.

Chekhov investigated how the interplay of these dynamics, could translate into expressive faculties an actor needs. He showed how we can use tempo and dynamic as a tool for opening another avenue of psycho-physical awareness. In doing so, he gave it an important place in the toolbox of the actor. Chekhov formalized the work with these two dynamics into a movement exploration that allows the actor to experience their archetypal qualities.

Staccato & legato exploration 1

Now we integrate our work with the movements we observed in nature with the work on counter tensions and on impulse and sustaining.[*]

1. Choose a legato movement you observed in nature and incorporate it.
2. Practise until you can detach the 'legato-ness' from the naturalistic details and express this archetypal quality full-bodily.
3. Move freely in this legato dynamic until you sense that it is all around you.
4. Stand and imagine the legato-ness surrounding you. Attune yourself to this, and receive it as an impulse, allowing it to slowly turn you to the right and lunge. Allow the impulse to pour through your instrument, along the full length of your arms and way beyond your fingertips.
5. When the impulse has run its course, return to your centre and repeat the process, except that now the impulse takes you to the left.
6. Repeat this process in the other four directions: above and below, front and back. Pay attention to the inner aspect of the movement; the sensation it arouses in your soul.

---

[*] See pages 80–83 and 84–88.

7. Repeat these stages 1–6, choosing a staccato impulse. Attune yourself to let it through; a lightning flash passing through your body as you lunge.

Staccato & legato exploration 2

1. Choose staccato or legato to begin. Prepare your instrument by warming up your choice.
2. Practise sustaining the sensation. Let it inspire you to explore, moving freely round the space. Remember to return to archetypal/full-bodied movement when necessary.
3. Allow the sensation to remind you of specific moments of experience and action. Perhaps a character suggests itself. Whatever impulse it inspires, follow where it beckons, saying yes to the offer that staccato or legato has released from your creative depths. Always stay within the landscape that your psycho-physical awareness has created in your soul. If sounds or words suggest themselves, express them too.
4. Repeat the process with the opposite dynamic.

Interplay of tempo and dynamic

Although tempo and dynamic are related, they are not the same. A single staccato movement may be fast in tempo but a series of staccato movements may occur in an overall tempo that is fast or slow. A movement with legato dynamic may be slow or fast in tempo. Speed can manifest in a momentary flash, sharply defined, an instant that seems separate from before and after. On the other hand, we can observe a series of such instants, fast movements which seem bound by an inner power of sustaining. This enables each such separate moment to flow seamlessly into the next. This sustaining can weave also through a slower tempo, giving it a powerful dynamic.

Tempo & dynamic exploration 1

1. Find and listen to music that demonstrates different combinations of tempo and dynamic.
2. Move freely to the second and third movements of Beethoven's *Waldstein Sonata*, focusing on tempo changes and the interplay within them of staccato and legato. Allow the music's different tempos and dynamics to move through you, exploring the full range of bodily expression (10–1) once you are familiar with the music.
3. Alternate between full-bodied archetypal movement and imagining yourself as the conductor of the piece, or the pianist, a member of the audience, or even the composer in a combination of hearing and notating. How would you sustain the

tempo 'inwardly' when the outer action might be playing, conducting, sitting, listening or writing?

Tempo & dynamic exploration 2

Your aim is to become skilled in recognizing and responding to the different combinations: fast tempo with staccato dynamic; fast tempo with legato dynamic; slow tempo punctuated with staccato dynamic; slow tempo with legato dynamic.

1. Choose a simple action from daily life. It should lend itself to being built into a sequence. Then add another. Then another, etc. For example: walk a few steps, pick up a book, open it, read a page and sit down.
2. After full-bodied preparation in each combination of tempo and dynamic, sustain the sensations thus aroused.
3. Perform the activity or sequence within the combination of tempo and dynamic you have prepared. Pay attention to the inner life that each combination inspires in your artist's soul. If a specific character or situation presents itself, follow its impulse. Allow it to emerge and follow where it beckons, always staying in the inner landscape generated by your psycho-physical awareness.

Tempo & dynamic exploration 3 – the letter

Choose each specific combination of tempo and dynamic in turn: (fast tempo with staccato dynamic; fast tempo with legato dynamic; slow tempo with staccato dynamic; slow tempo with legato dynamic).

1. After full-bodied preparation, perform the letter sequence, using it to experiment with changes of tempo and dynamic.

Tempo & dynamic exploration 4 (partner and group work)

1. Explore ways in which, when a group of people move together, these different tempos and dynamics can interweave, providing impulses to which you can respond; in turn, providing them to others.[*]
2. Experiment with a partner first, then in a group of three, until all members of the group form one ensemble.

The improvisation can be archetypal, expressed in full-bodied movement or connected to an everyday scenario; a busy street, for instance, in which everyone moves with a staccato dynamic at a faster tempo. Someone enters moving with legato

---

[*] See the explorations for the building of ensemble in chapter 6.

dynamic in a slow tempo and gradually permeates and transforms the original atmosphere. Or vice versa. Experiment with other possibilities.

From movement into speech and language
Steiner suggests tempo and dynamics apply to the art of speaking consonants and vowels. Instinctively we sense a legato tendency in /v/ or /l/, for instance, and a staccato tendency in /t/. As we develop confidence in working with our psycho-physical awareness, such observations will increase the range of what we can express in speech.

Tempo & dynamic exploration 5 — Speech exploration: cat sequence

1. Warm up *tempo exploration 3*.
2. As you move through the continuum of stillness, slow, fast, stillness, stalking, charging, strike, sometimes you are the prey, being followed, sometimes the predator, following.
3. At some point when it is organic, begin sounding 's', letting it arise out of the movement and exploring its natural tendencies to express the different stages.
4. When it is organic let 's' slide into words letting them arise as a natural expression of the movement, so that movement, sound and word are integrated.
5. Now into your continuum of movement, insert a continuum of words, playing until the integration of movement voice and speech is a seamless expression, for example: *still-stillness-silence-sensing-secret-slowly-stalking-stealthy-swift-sudden-strike-pounce*.

Tempo & dynamic exploration 6 — Speech exploration: consonants and vowels

Tempo and dynamic can be matched to any sound, but which specific sounds lean more in one direction than another?

1. Allow a *sense of ease*[*] to accompany the movement work for tempo and dynamic and at some point when you're warmed-up, your mouth embedded as it is in your whole body-instrument, play with consonants. Let them be born out of the movement. Which ones seem inherently to lend themselves to expressing a staccato or legato dynamic — or both?
2. Repeat, using vowels.
3. Let words or phrases be born out of the movement — for example: 'quick', 'slow', 'sharp' or 'smooth'.

---

[*] See chapter 5, page 234.

Tempo & dynamic exploration 7 – Speech exploration: staccato and legato

The following suggestions have been developed to accompany the exercises Chekhov gave for practising staccato and legato in the six directions, and then for bringing them into relationship.

1. Practise these full-bodily, letting the words be born out of your movement, then when you're ready, incorporate using (10–1).

Staccato	Legato
flick a stick	limpid liquid lazily
trick it quick	moving muesli smoothly
lizards lick	lovers leaving lingeringly
crickets click	melting moments mazily
lightning quick	leaves falling driftingly
in the nick	musing music dreamily

2, Create your own

Tempo & dynamic exploration 8 – Speech-exploration: transitions

Here, the transitions and the combinations of specific consonants encourage your organs of articulation to be agile and flexible. If you prepare full-bodily, your whole instrument will be attuned and your mouth will be warmed-up and available to express staccato and legato dynamics in speech and language.

1. Initially, work at each part separately.

staccato:	Jets spit
	through cracks in rocks
legato:	curl in liquid pools of light
transition:	then
staccato:	cataract

2. Weave the changes in dynamic into a single sentence.

Working with Hamlet

Now we can use these principles to play with our Hamlet speech. Do not focus on the character but let the tempo and dynamic of the text itself become the starting point. We want to intimately penetrate the text – the shifts in thought and image. We want to learn how to use the sounds Shakespeare gave to communicate *different possible intentions*. So, for the moment, we develop mastery of tempo and dynamic to extend our repertoire of vocal skills.

Hamlet's words and sounds suggest dynamic interplay between staccato and legato, demanding vocal flexibility. Facility in speaking language at this level will, in turn, support the complex layering required to build a character like Hamlet.

Do not be concerned at this stage with the complexities of Hamlet's character but allow the changes in dynamic to inspire you with possibilities. Work full-bodily, playing with the sounds and words as they arise within each possible dynamic, as we have been doing.[*]

Tempo & dynamic exploration 9 — working with text — Hamlet

1. Test out the words, the sounds; tasting and chewing them, getting to know the language, digesting it. Let staccato and legato reveal their wisdom to you; aspects of the character and what he feels or thinks that you could not have arrived at by analysis. When the language comes from deep within your instrument, then you will be able to integrate it with your work on Hamlet's character. Here are some suggestions, which can equally be played with in reverse.

Legato	This goodly frame the earth
Transition (either)	seems to me
Staccato	a sterile promontory . . .
Legato	. . . the beauty of the world,
	the paragon of animals
Transition (either)	and yet to me
Staccato	what is this quintessence of dust?

Tempo & dynamic exploration 10 — working with text

1. Try out these transitions:

Martha in *Who's Afraid of Virginia Woolf*:

Legato	George, who can hold me at night so that it's warm
Staccato	and whom I will bite till there's blood.

Lady Macbeth:

Legato	Look you like the innocent flower
Staccato	But be the serpent under't.

2. Experiment with changing tempo in the moments of transition.

---

[*] Again, I am not implying that this is how the lines should be delivered or interpreted. It is simply another way to enter Shakespeare's language and explore how he communicates, in turn teaching us expand the expressive range of our instrument.

Tempo & dynamic exploration 11 −Speech-exploration

1. Here is another sentence for playing with tempo and dynamic, this time reversing the transitions in exploration 8 :

> Slowly, slowly, the snake unfurled its coils. Then, in a flash,
> a shiver of lightning, it vanished. The rocks were silent.

Tempo & dynamic exploration 12 − working with text − Hopkins

The poetry of Gerard Manley Hopkins provides many opportunities to play with and enjoy the interplay of changing tempo and dynamics.

1. Once again, work full-bodily, letting sounds, words, phrases, sentences be born out of movement before attempting to reduce it 10−1.

> . . . and thrush
> Through the echoing timber does so rinse and ring
> The ear, it strikes like lightnings to hear him sing;
> The glassy pear tree leaves and blooms, they brush
> The descending blue; that blue is all in a rush
> With richness; the racing lambs too have fair their fling . . .
>
> *— Spring*

> This darksome burn, horseback brown,
> His rollrock highroad roaring down,
> In coop and in comb the fleece of his foam
> Flutes and low to the lake falls home . . .
>
> *— Inversnaid*

> Some candle clear burns somewhere I come by . . .
>
> *— The Candle Indoors*

> I caught this morning morning's minion, king-
> dom of daylight's dauphin, dapple-dawn-drawn Falcon, in his riding
>
> Of the rolling level underneath him steady air, and striding
> High there, how he rung upon the rein of a wimpling wing
> In his ecstasy! Then off, off forth on swing,
> As a skate's heel sweeps smooth on a bow-bend: the hurl and gliding
>
> Rebuffed the big wind. My heart in hiding
> Stirred for a bird, − the achieve of, the mastery of the thing!
> Brute beauty and valour and act, oh, air, pride, plume, here
> Buckle! . . .
>
> *— The Windhover* (abridged)

... And I have asked to be
Where no storms come,
Where the green swell is in the havens dumb,
And out of the swell of the sea.

— Heaven Haven (a nun takes the veil).

As kingfishers catch fire, dragonflies draw flame;
As tumbled over rim in roundy wells
Stones ring; like each tucked string tells, each hung bells
Bow swung finds tongue to fling out broad its name ...

Sonnet

Examples from dramatic texts at such an early stage present a danger. Speech that does not arise out of deeply textured character development, may well appear facile or simplistic. Nevertheless, it is exciting to experiment with some obvious examples of specific tempos and dynamics, provided we do not confuse this work with character development or use it as a substitute. They can then be explored and enjoyed, showing how tempo and dynamic are clear components of specific moods, moments and events. As well, changes in the tempo and dynamic may suggest to us an aspect of the character's experience we would not have thought of otherwise.

Tempo & dynamic exploration 13 — working with text — Shakespeare

1. Remember to allow the language to emerge (to begin with) out of full-bodied movement. When a sense of ease[*] has been achieved, experiment with reducing the degree of outer movement (10–1). If you can do this without losing the tempo and dynamic when you speak, your goal in this respect has been achieved.

   Juliet anxiously awaits news of her beloved:
   Gather apace ye fiery footed steeds,
   Towards Phoebus' lodging; such a wagoner
   As Phaeton would whip you to the west
   And bring in cloudy night immediately.
   Spread thy close curtain, love performing night!
   That runaways eyes may wink and Romeo
   Leap to these arms, untalked of and unseen!

   In King Lear, *Cordelia, reunited at last with her father, first watches him asleep:*
   O my dear father! Restoration hang
   Thy medicine upon my lips, and let this kiss

---

[*] See chapter 5, page 234.

Repair those violent harms that my two sisters
Have in thy reverence made.

Then lets him know he is forgiven:
No cause. No cause.

Lady Macbeth tries to override Macbeth's conscience:
I have given suck
And know how tender 'tis to love the babe that milks me.
I would, while it was smiling in my face,
Have plucked my nipple from his boneless gums
And dashed his brains out, had I so sworn as you
Have done to this.

Time seems to stand still for a moment as Othello, intending to kill Desdemona as she sleeps, contemplates her lying in their bed:
It is the cause. It is the cause my soul.
Let me not name it to you, you chaste stars!
It is the cause. Yet I'll not shed her blood,
Nor scar that whiter snow of hers than snow
And smooth as monumental alabaster.

Romeo is in the orchard and sees Juliet on the balcony:
What light through yonder window breaks?
It is the East, and Juliet is the sun!
Arise fair sun, and kill the envious moon,
Who is already sick and pale with grief,
That thou, her maid, art far more fair than she:
Be not her maid, since she is envious;
Her vestal livery is but sick and green
And none but fools do wear it; cast it off.
It is my lady; O! It is my love:
O! that she knew she were.
She speaks, yet she says nothing: what of that?
Her eye discourses. I will answer it.
I am too bold, 'tis not to me she speaks …[*]

In King Lear, *Edgar, hunted for his life, disguises himself as Poor Tom the madman*: Who gives anything to poor Tom? whom the foul fiend hath led through fire and through flame, through ford and whirlpool, o'er bog and quagmire; that hath laid knives under his pillow, and halters in his pew; set rats bane by his porridge; made him proud of

---

[*] This speech, in its entirety, gives many other opportunities for changes in tempo and dynamic.

heart to ride on a bay trotting horse over four inch bridges, to curse his own shadow for a traitor. Bless thy five wits! Tom's a-cold. O! Do de, do de, do de. Bless thee from whirl winds, star blasting and taking! Do poor Tom some charity, whom the foul fiend vexes. There could I have him now, and there, and there again, and there …

Layering

The rich possibilities that emerge when we play with combinations of the tools is one of the many gifts of Chekhov's psycho-physical technique. However, layering one skill with another will only yield fruit when we bring each separate skill to the exploration. We cannot do this if we mistake the *idea* of a skill with the actual capacity to demonstrate its substance and potency. Therefore, we cannot take short-cuts, thinking to avoid the necessity to work with full-bodied exploration. At this point in our journey, we have available the four qualities-of-movement, expansion and contraction, tempo and dynamic. Let's play first with layering moulding and expansion.

Layering exploration 1

1. Warm up each separate tool of expansion, contraction and moulding.
2. Mould into a full-bodied gesture of expansion and explore with archetypal movement.
3. Sustaining the sensation of their fused activity, relinquish the full-bodied gesture. Perform a few simple, everyday, naturalistic actions.
4. Build the movement until it once again becomes full-bodied and archetypal.
5. Continue to mould but transform your gesture of expansion into full-bodied contraction. Mould contractedly.
6. Sustain the sensation that arises from the fused activity of moulding and contraction.
7. Relinquish the full-bodied gesture and perform a few simple, everyday actions.
8. Remain contracted but let the moulding change to floating, and so on, through all the combinations.
9. Begin again either with a quality-of-movement or expanding or contracting and layer it with a fast or slower tempo and staccato or legato, until you have worked through these possibilities as well.

Layering exploration 2

Returning to the connection between the qualities-of-movement and the temperaments, explore the possibilities for Hamlet's character, of layering together a basic temperament of sanguine, which through extreme circumstance has been overlaid with melancholy. Or experiment with layering a phlegmatic lethargy punctuated on occasions by choleric bursts of fire. All possibilities and combinations can be supported by the text and can provide rich material for exploration.

Character development is the theme of chapter 4, but I want to indicate where such simple processes may lead once we master the basic skills such tools provide.[*]

Layering exploration 3

When you have mastered layering two different tools, layer in a third. Eg: *fly* with a *staccato* dynamic, *contractedly*. Depths of sensation and emotion and rich possibilities of character suggest themselves from the combinations possible so far:

> *Qualities-of-movement*:
> radiating, flying, floating and moulding
> *with*
> Contraction and expansion
> *with*
> *Tempo and dynamic*
> stillness/slow/fast — staccato/ legato

Layering in practice

Working with an image as a starting point.

In an early speech, Hecuba[†] describes herself as 'a winter-frozen bee'. What a rich vein to mine! I imagined I was flying freely with expanded wings, collecting nectar from each flower in the summer warmth. Then, as winter came upon me, felt my wings contract and gradually freeze until I could only manage a last faint flicker of movement. I was making a transition from a quality-of-movement — flying — which began expandedly and then contracted.

As I refined this further, I felt how these sensations attracted the qualities of *freely* and *contentedly*.[‡] I then felt a transition into qualities of moving into *numbly*, *weakly* and *exhaustedly*. Such full-bodied exploration taps into a seemingly limitless source of inspiration that in turn is anchored in reliable, objective processes for accessing aspects of the inner life of any character. This set of choices could be summarized as follows:

- Hecuba as she experienced her life before the war: flying and expansion with the qualities of freely and contentedly.
- Hecuba as she experiences life within the play: flying ever more contractedly with the qualities of numbly, weakly and exhaustedly.

---

[*] See *The Integrated Actor*.

[†] From Euripides' *The Trojan Women*.

[‡] See chapter 3, Qualities and sensations.

Gravity and levity

To physical sense perception, reality consists of the world of finished objects defined by their edges. Space is the emptiness surrounding them. The uses we make of matter are based on this perception and would seem to prove its validity. We stand at a point in history where the consequences of accepting such perceptions to be exclusively what constitute reality, threaten the existence of our planet, suggesting that we need to question such a premise.

As Martin Buber has observed, it is entirely possible to reduce a living being to a 'thing' or, to use his terminology, a 'thou' to an 'it'.[30] *Oedipus* leads us to consider Steiner's proposal that human beings can develop freedom, only if they first detach from that universal consciousness of which they formerly experienced themselves to be a part. This detachment both enables, and is in turn enabled by, development of the abstract intellect.

The *Egyptian Book of the Dead* demonstrates this ancient consciousness.[*] It reveals the sacred names of things that constitute our earthly existence (foot, floor, lintel, etc.). These names attest to the *livingness* and *beingness* of reality. The loss of such perception can be seen as an advance or a decline in consciousness, depending on our point of view. Obviously, each 'reality' presents both gifts and challenges.

The Art of Acting invites us to undertake the conscious work to reacquire those once instinctive sensibilities. It requires that we integrate our intellectual, intuitive and feeling consciousness. Certainly, a mastery of style appropriate to texts from different times and cultures, as explored in *The Integrated Actor*, will not be possible without such understanding. For now, let us see how the training of our psycho-physical awareness might lead us to a deeper understanding of what we normally refer to as *gravity* and *levity*.

Gravity & levity exploration 1

1. Surrender to the weight of your body. Let gravity take hold of you until, finally, you fall to the earth. Sink further until you rest within it.
2. This is your home, your mother. Here you belong and sense you are supported and secure. Would it be possible to sustain this sensation of support as you journey on your earthly path?
3. Stand slowly and consciously, permeating every stage with this sensation.
4. Sustain it as you take a single step forward into space, then a second, third, etc.

---

[*] See pages 11–14 for an excerpt.

5. Extend your movement into simple actions, checking that you have not disconnected from the earth, your home, your mother, your support.
6. Return to full-bodied union with the earth.
7. Explore the words:

> Thou Earth, boon mother of us all, You I invoke.
>
> *Prometheus Bound*, Aeschylus

8. Imagine strings of light attached to every part of you. Let them draw you upwards. You stand up by allowing light to draw you upwards, *lifting* you to the periphery. You stand, not by your own will but because the light's will draws you up. Repeat steps 3–5 as you sustain this new sensation.
9. Return to full-bodied movement and explore these further words from Aeschylus's, *Prometheus Bound*:

> O divine aether! You I invoke.

10. Move between weight and light, letting the earth draw you down, the light draw you up. Attend to the sensations that arise in each condition. Become familiar with them, able to sustain them.
11. Alternating them, explore the soul states that arise as you sit, stand, walk, etc.
12. Move full-bodily back and forth between the poles of light and weight until you find a balance. Locate where this activity of balancing takes place in you? This can provide us with another entry point to what Chekhov called our *actors' centre.*[*]
13. Stand and sustain the activity of balancing. Recognize it is a choice to consciously balance these two poles of physical existence, and that some part of you must *will* to engage in such activity. Then, acknowledge who makes this choice silently or, if you wish, speak: 'I' or 'I AM'.
14. Explore how to sustain the balancing sensation as you move freely in the space and play with the words:

> O divine aether, And thou earth, boon mother of us all, You I invoke.

I prefer to use the active form 'balancing' because the noun suggests a passive and finished state. Balancing must be maintained by active choice and is not a static condition which, once achieved, perpetuates itself. Our goal is confidence in our ability to access consciously the centre of activity which balances levity and gravity and to investigate the contribution their polarity can make to the actor's repertoire of inner life. The sensation of connectedness resulting from this process is a healthy departure point for other work.

---

[*] Explored in chapter 3.

Gravity & levity exploration 2

1. Warm up gravity and levity.
2. Sustaining the sensation of that centre in you that can balance light and weight, consciously enter and remain within the realm of gravity. Stay connected with your centre as you descend deeply into heaviness. This enables you to observe yourself while you surrender to the journey.
3. Observe what feelings or emotions are drawn into the field of gravity. Explore them and any situations they suggest.
4. Repeat steps 2 and 3 but focusing on levity.

Gravity & levity exploration 3 — the letter — gravity

Don't try to make the action look real or naturalistic. Your purpose is only to let gravity inspire your life of feeling and sensation.

1. Warm up to gravity, levity and balancing. Stay connected with your centre and prepare to stay working with the pole of gravity.
2. Begin full bodily, weave between degrees from 10–1 allowing the sensations that arise to inspire your exploration of the letter scenario.
3. Finish with a full-bodied gesture balancing light and weight.
4. Consciously release your focus and relax.

Gravity & levity exploration 4 — the letter — levity

Repeat steps 1–4, focusing on levity.

Gravity & levity exploration 5 — the letter — from gravity to levity

1. Warm up as above.
2. Begin the letter scenario in full-bodied gravity. Weaving between degrees from 10–1, transform to levity as you read the letter.
3. Finish with a full-bodied gesture balancing light and weight.
4. Release.

Gravity & levity exploration 6 — the letter — from levity to gravity

1. Warm up, as above.
2. Begin the letter scenario in full-bodied levity. Weaving between degrees from 10–1, transform to gravity as you read the letter.
3. Finish with a full-bodied gesture balancing light and weight.
4. Release.

Gravity & levity exploration 7 — Speech-exploration

1. While moving full-bodily, explore which consonants, words and phrases express the quality of gravity and how to imbue them with its weight. For example:

   death drags me down

2. Do the same with levity. For example:

   fluffy feathers softly drifting
   floating ever higher upward

3. Observe how the consonant /l/ moves easily in both directions.

   Leaden lump … fall … lift … leap … life and light

4. Use Romeo's lines already quoted in the moulding/melancholic exploration, to play with /l/'s cyclic tendency to move from light to weight:

   I have a soul of lead
   So stakes me to the ground I cannot move.

   Or in these two lines from *Hamlet* play with the cyclic tendency of /l/ to move from weight to light.

   O that this too too solid flesh would melt
   Thaw and resolve itself into a dew.

5. Further lines to play with while exploring full-bodily the transition between levity:

   I saw eternity the other night
   Like a great ring of pure and endless light,
   All calm as it was bright …

   and gravity:

   The darksome statesman hung with weights and woe
   Like a thick midnight fog moved there so slow
   He did not stay nor go

   The World by Henry Vaughan

If we approach gravity with imagination, we sense forces which bestow the gift of substance and dependability. But yet, if we identify with these exclusively, lose ourselves in matter, forget the light, they can drag us down into the dark, imprisoning the self within the body, convincing us it *is* the body.

If we approach levity with imagination, we sense forces which lift us far beyond concerns of earth and which inspire us to soar in bliss. But yet, if we identify with them exclusively, lose ourselves in light, forget the earth, they can dissolve the consciousness we are a self, obliterate it in the blinding radiance.

And we have sensed, as well, forces which balance both of these and consciously mediate between them. In *The Integrated Actor* we consider what other levels of spiritual cognition contribute to a further understanding of these forces.

The 'Three Sisters' — falling, lifting and balancing

Actors who studied with Chekhov relate how, in his later years, he experimented with *falling, lifting, balancing.* He jokingly referred to these as The Three Sisters, no doubt to redress the gender imbalance in naming The Four Brothers.* He observed that our movement *flows* when we *balance* the *falling* and *lifting* tendencies.

The *Three Sisters* reveal an archetype that provides an objective starting point for portraying some of the draining or disturbing aspects of life. This means we need not be exposed to the psychic risks to which personal emotion-memory expose us if we depend on it exclusively.

Gravity & levity exploration 8 — the three sisters

1. Explore full-bodily, the cycle of falling, balancing and lifting. As you flow, let weight pull you down and light pull you upwards in differing degrees and with different tempos and dynamics. Something now reveals itself within the journey of sensations that arise. We find within the cycles of sensation mysteries of living and dying, youth and age, sickness and health, levels of energy increasing then diminishing to weariness, exhaustion. Attracted to these cycles of sensation may be feelings and emotions, such as despair and hope, courage and surrender.
2. Within the cycle experiment with balancing for shorter or longer periods, or not at all.
3. Play with the degrees of outer movement (10–1) while sustaining the sensations thus aroused.

This teaches us to distinguish between a character's condition, which might be anywhere on the scale from weak and exhausted through to dying, and the energy required to portray it artistically.

Gravity & levity exploration 9 — Speech-exploration: the three sisters

The full-bodied exploration of these cycles and rhythms releases the forces and energies we need to speak while 'dying' or in a state of weakness; without such

---

* See chapter 5.

energies, we will have no forces to create such moments or to project them powerfully. Weave the following words into your full-bodied exploration of the cycles and progressions that arise from *falling, lifting* and *balancing.*

1. Play with this generic monologue, backwards and forwards, in any order over varying lengths of time, in various scenarios that end in 'death':

> What use wail or weep or wonder why …?
>
> Weaker and weaker … I must go on … no strength left …
>
> I can't go on … dying … dying … remember … dead.

Through these archetypal processes we find ourselves flowing in the stream of life, aware of how its once strong engagement with the body diminishes and finally relinquishes its hold. Feelings and emotions are attracted into this sensation stream contributing a deeper layer of impulses to inspire us.

Layering the *Three Sisters* with a set of choices Chekhov called *qualities-and-sensations*[*], enables us to play with such well-known 'deaths' as those of Romeo and Juliet; Edmund or Lear himself from *King Lear*; Desdemona from *Othello*; Pyramus and Thisbe from *A Midsummer Night's Dream*, etc., and after working with the indications for tragic and comic styles in *The Integrated Actor*, to layer these tools as well into the scenes.

---

[*] See chapter 3.

Ancient Greek gymnastics

Classical Greek sculpture reminds us of a stage in evolution when human beings felt they were at home in their bodies. The images demonstrate a balance of polarities; gravity and levity, centre and periphery, contraction and expansion, stillness and movement. We can sense that the human form was god-like to the Greeks.

Their gymnastics also gave expression to this body/spirit harmony. In his *Speech and Drama* lectures, Rudolf Steiner suggested the importance for the actor of working with the five Ancient Greek gymnastics exercises: running, leaping, wrestling, discus and javelin. Our context for doing so is not the achievement of athletic prowess, per se. We will use them to develop and expand our range of psycho-physical awareness.[31]

RUNNING

Modern western culture is obsessed with running. In every park, on every road, people can be seen; jogging their way to what they believe is health and fitness. I, too, once engaged in such a punishing regime. The agony I went through, pushing myself in the attempt to keep fit, is a clear example of abuse arising from the loss of psycho-physical awareness. The desperate faces of my fellow joggers, passing me, bore witness to the fact that I was not alone. Most of us were cut off from our source, pounding the pavements, often long after exhaustion had set in. We believed that activity arising from the imposition of our will upon the body made us healthy.

Occasionally, someone ran for the pure joy of it. Life streamed through them, picking up their feet; the universe around them. Could we learn their secret? What do we do when we run? What could we be doing differently?

Greek gymnastics exploration 1 – running

If we slow our running down to observe it, we discover two stages. First, we are about to:

(a) fall, but then, with each step, we . . .
(b) catch ourselves from falling by an upward thrust which, at the same time, drives us forward.

We are working with our old friends, gravity and levity. If we speed the process up again, we can consciously, run so that, in every moment, we balance weight and light. The light is lifting us so we do not fall. The weight is grounding us, establishing the firm connection of our feet with the earth. Someone, so deep inside us that we do not notice them or what they do, balances these forces and wills to move us forward, effortlessly held and carried and exhilarating in their certainties.

Greek gymnastics exploration 2 – running

Running teaches us to be present in our feet and legs in the way we need to stand and walk upon the stage. The 'presence' actors strive for comes by being 'present' in our bodies; able to inhabit them with no less intense activity when we stand or walk, than when we run.

1. Stand, walk, run, building momentum, until you reach top speed. Then reduce your speed as you move through the stages in reverse until you come to stillness once again.
2. Do this several times. Observe the sensation in your legs and feet when you are running at top speed and sustain this through the grades of tempo down to and including stillness. Can you be equally present in whatever state of outer rest or movement you may be?
3. Again build momentum and when you reach top speed, stop. Gather the movement and contain it in the stillness, sustaining the sensation of movement in your legs and feet. Sense the energy and movement, now outwardly stilled, continue inwardly. 'Continuing to run' while you stand sustains the powerful sensation of activity within your limbs and leads to the sense of being present in your body when you stand. Don't allow the sensation to dissipate.

Greek gymnastics exploration 3 – running

1. Alternate running and sustaining its sensation in stillness.
2. Sustain the 'body of sensation' you achieved by running, walk on to your imaginary stage and stand before your imaginary audience.
3. Try it out in front of fellow students/colleagues. Invite their feedback.

LEAPING

While I am running, my relationship to gravity and levity remains unconscious, largely automatic. But, if I jump or leap, I make a choice to do something new. I estimate changes in height and distance and consciously prepare what I need to execute these changes of intention.

Greek gymnastics exploration 4 – leaping

The sequence of sensations arising from the execution of a leap transform into flexibility of response to changes of tempo and intention in the rhythm with which I move on stage or speak a text, an ability to sense how many inner leaps are needed if my performance is to grip the audience's interest; engaging them from start to finish in the story, poem or character's evolving path.

1. Set up a course of different obstacles at varying heights and distances. Run through the course, leaping over them.
2. Make conscious the play of levity and gravity within you and within which you operate each time you leap; the moment when you recognize a leap is imminent; the inner preparation that enables you to leap when the moment comes; the choices this involves.
3. Pay attention to the psycho-physical sensations associated with the journey from the moment when a leap declares its imminence through to its completion.
4. Experiment with recreating these sensations within a sequence of everyday activity: walking, standing, sitting, changing your position, picking up a book, the letter scenario, etc.

Greek gymnastics exploration 5 – leaping – Hamlet

Warm up leaping. Recreate this sequence of sensations as you play with Hamlet's *I have of late* speech on page 283.

1. Move around, stepping, leaping, dancing, exploring and enjoying the constantly evolving changes in the rhythms of this language. As you become familiar with the text, you will sense the 'leaps' as they approach. You will sense the necessary preparation, and how much energy you need to execute them in the overall progression.
2. Identify the many 'leaps' Hamlet makes within his soul as he journeys through the text.
3. Compare this with speaking words 'on automatic' without the inner shifts required.
4. Repeat this process with any texts you may be working on.

WRESTLING

When we run and leap, we penetrate our feet and legs with our will as we engage with the earth's resistance. When we wrestle, we also penetrate our arms with our will as we engage with the resistance of another human being. The sensation that our arms are imbued with conscious will is the basis of a conscious work with gesture.[*]

Of course, our arms and hands do not move in isolation. When wrestling, commitment to intention will only flow out through our arms and hands, if it also permeates our torso, legs and feet. The lower half of our body thus supports and mediates the energy that streams up through the earth through our partner's body and our own. Wrestling prepares our body to be an integrated instrument for gesture, for full-bodied work of any kind and, in particular, the full-bodied gesture we shall work

---

[*] See *The Integrated Actor*, chapter Building the bridge between gesture, voice and speech.

with in chapter 4. It's important to discover how our own will is awakened when we pit ourselves against our partner's will.[*] Our goal in this context however, is not domination or imposition of our will but sensitive engagement with each other's will.[32]

Greek gymnastics exploration 6 — wrestling

1. Stand opposite your partner with arms outstretched and palms facing. Fall toward each other, arresting each other's fall as your hands meet. As you engage with each other's weight and resistance, sense your will awaken, first penetrating hands, and arms, then torso, legs and feet.
2. As you sense your way into your partner's resistance, strength and weight, can you also sense how they support you? How, in order to engage with their resistance, you inhabit your entire instrument.
3. When you sense your strength and energies are equally engaged, wrestle with each other through the space.
4. At some point, wrestle your partner to the ground.

Greek gymnastics exploration 7 — wrestling

1. Warm up wrestling with a partner.
2. Pay attention to the sensation aroused throughout your instrument by engagement with your equal wills.
3. Separate from your partner and sustaining your 'body of sensation' continue 'wrestling' with each other through the space, increasing the distance between you.
4. Sustain the sensation of wrestling and transform the action into gestures such as holding, embracing, caressing, reaching, attacking, etc., weaving a dialogue of gestures between you through the space.
5. Move towards each other and re-engage with your partner's body, allowing the other gestures to metamorphose once again into wrestling.

Greek gymnastics exploration 8 — wrestling, with qualities-of-movement

We have experienced how the qualities-of-movement extend our range of expressiveness beyond our habitual tendencies. Now we use them to extend our range of interaction with another human being; initially in the close proximity of physical engagement, and then as it transforms into gestures that weave across the space.

1. Wrestle with a partner in each quality-of-movement.
2. When your quality-of-movement is established, separate, but sustain the same sensation as you 'wrestle' with each other through the space.

---

[*] See chapter 3, *the will centre*.

3. Within that quality-of-movement, and sustaining the sensation of resistance you had wrestling with your partner, allow a series of full-bodied gestures to unfold between you.

4. In addition to the ones above, play with gestures that express greeting or farewell, rejection of each other, suspicion, questioning or desire to comfort or conciliate.[33]

Greek gymnastics exploration 9 – wrestling

A process, from wrestling into gesture – into speech, enables us to fully inhabit any text.

1. Warm up wrestling.
2. Wrestle with space while your partner reads from a text of your choice.
3. Metamorphose your wrestling into full-bodied gestures which express the words.
4. When your gesturing is confident, speak so the words arise out of your gestures, so that the quality of gesture penetrates your speech.[*]

The final Greek gymnastic exercises involve the projection of objects through space. Throwing a discus trains us to sense the relationship between periphery and centre as embodied in the spiral or the vortex. Through a series of expanding spirals, originating in the contracted centre of ourselves, we release the discus into the horizon. We learn to surrender to the power of the periphery to draw the discus out into itself. In contrast, when we throw a spear or javelin, our aim and focus is precise. Where the discus invites us to project out to the whole periphery, the javelin requires that we project to a *point*.

DISCUS

If our purpose is simply to throw a discus as far as possible, then we need no more than muscular strength. Of equal importance, however, to the Greeks who developed these gymnastics, was harmony and beauty. For this to be achieved action must be imbued with sensations arising from more subtle realms; in the case of the discus, the 'infinite' horizon. Ability to expand our consciousness to include the horizon is exactly what actors need when they project their consciousness – not only to the other characters on stage, but also to the audience.

Because we do not aim at a specific *target* when we throw, the discus draws our attention out to the whole periphery. Because it is released through a sequence of full-bodied movements, the tension necessary for the action is equally distributed throughout our instrument, the muscles of our face relax and our countenance becomes a 'neutral mask'.

---

[*] For an in-depth examination of speech and gesture, see *The Integrated Actor*.

Figure 9 – The discus thrower

This is important for an actor's face. We cannot be a 'sensitive membrane' that reflects the changing nuances within our souls if our face is fixed in tensions which result from inappropriate exertion. This makes the audience aware not of the soul life of the character, but of the actor's effort.

So, when we throw the discus, we learn to release the muscles of the face as we follow the discus's flight with our gaze. This release is only possible if the strength of our action is drawn not only from our muscles but from earth and sky and is equally distributed throughout our instrument.

Greek gymnastics exploration 10 – discus

1. Based on the illustration, devise a series of three or four contracting and expanding spiral movements which culminate in releasing an imaginary discus into space. Imagine the horizon draws you with each spiral further into its periphery. After each expansion, you are drawn further in and down – into the magnetic pull of a tightly coiled contraction.
2. When this sequence is perfected, introduce a real discus. Remember! Your goal is not distance, achieved in isolation from the aspects we're exploring.
3. When you can throw the discus with a sense of ease,[*] check the quality of tension in your face and consciously release any strain or effort from your facial muscles; letting the periphery draw your gaze out into it.

Greek gymnastics exploration 11 – discus (partner work)

Apply these principles as you throw imaginary objects to your partner. Let your face respond to each new 'object' as you pick it up, throw it and as it travels on its path to reach your partner. Do not fix or try to project the expressions on your face but let the subtle movements in your soul move across your countenance. We want transparency of countenance to be instinctive in all our work.

1. Throw and catch a beanbag with a partner, increasing and decreasing distances between you.
2. Let the beanbag go and work with gesture only.
3. 'Throw' and 'catch' specific objects; a rose, a stone, a raw egg in its shell, a dead rat, feather, snowball, a pebble into a pond, a fish back into water, etc.
4. Keep your face relaxed, as with the discus, allowing the expressions on your face as you respond to flow across your countenance.

---

[*] See chapter 5, page 234.

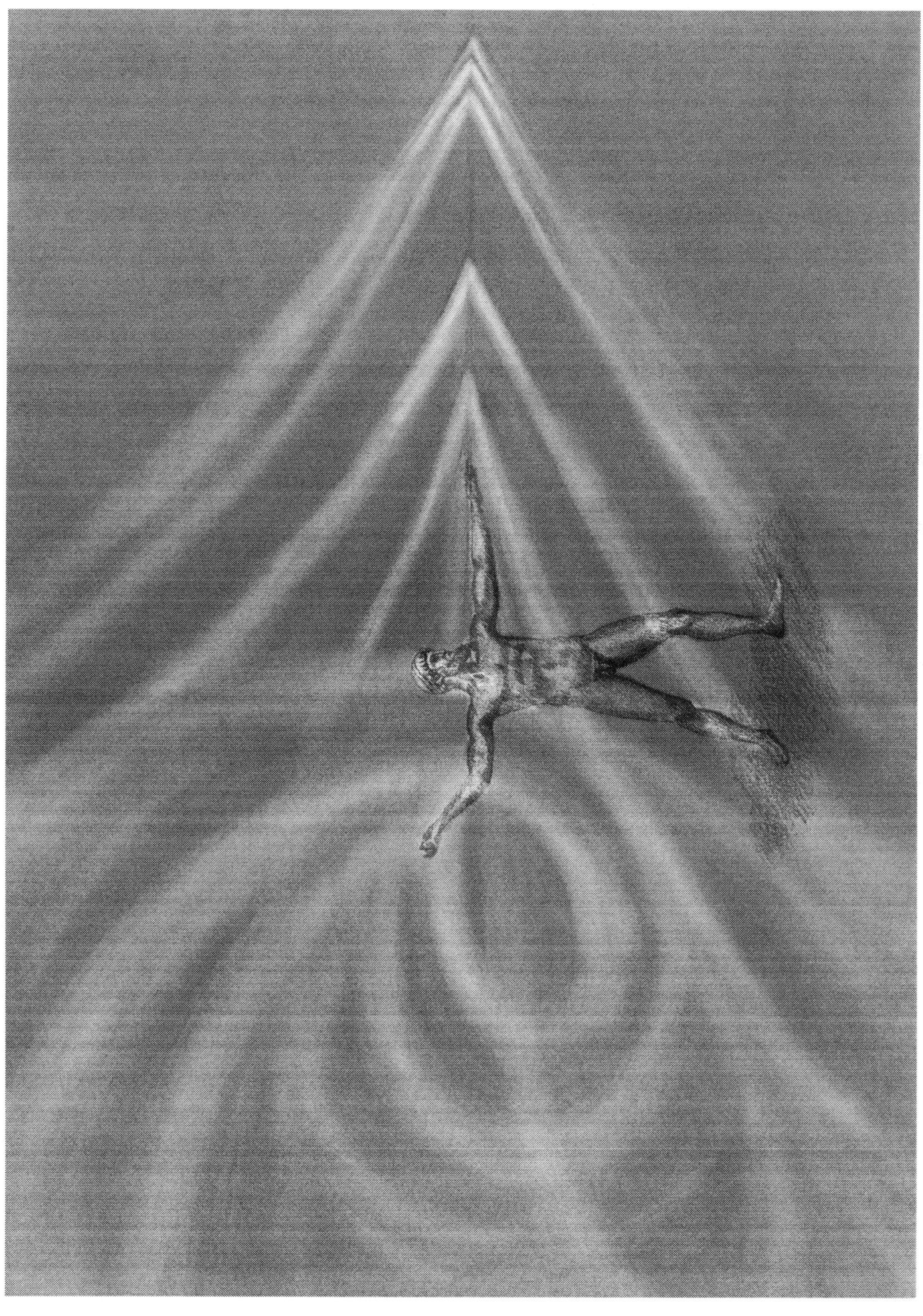

Figure 10 – The spear thrower

5. Play with distance. This will develop your capacity to extend the horizon to which you can project your responses.
6. Give each other feedback.

JAVELIN

As with the discus-throw, when we throw the javelin we strive for an action which is not cut off from the universe, but receives its impulse from that greater wholeness. If we shove the spear forward from our shoulder with sheer muscular exertion, our movement is *hard and less efficient*. To avoid this, we must gather from as far into the space behind as we intend to project into the space in front.

Greek gymnastics exploration 12 – javelin

1. Study the illustration. Notice that as the distance to the goal in front increases, so, equally, does that from which he gathers from behind. Note also that it is not abstract, empty distance indicated in the space behind but a fullness of impulse, a sense of life and energy, infinite vitality, connectedness.
2. Create a sequence of actions that culminate in throwing an imaginary javelin and allow you to experience this forwards and behind relationship.
3. Begin with less ambitious distances, increasing them one step at a time.
4. Check that the distance and the goal to which your action is directed are precise.
5. Each time you perform the sequence, embody the invisible activity revealed in the illustration.
6. When your action sequence is perfected, find a safe environment and throw a real javelin.

The spear will reach its target when we *unite our will* with the impulse to achieve that goal. Once again we learn that harmony is achieved when we balance the physical with the non-physical; the visible with the invisible.

Spear throwing is connected to another skill that actors need; projection. When we throw a javelin we learn that projection does not happen by itself. First we must *intend* to project an impulse and second, have the skill to allow it to stream through us without pushing and imposing our will upon the audience.

This is especially important when an actor speaks on stage. Actors that we strain to hear perhaps do not realize that they need to commit their will to reach the audience. Others may be so committed, but without the skill. It is this latter situation which often causes actors to resort to shouting.[*]

---

[*] The relationship between projection of the voice and of the javelin will be explored fully in *The Art of Speech*, chapter 3.

Since throwing a real javelin may not always be practical, Chekhov extracted from the act a sequence of archetypal gestures that embody its tensions and dynamics but which can be performed in any space. He used it as the basis for teaching actors to project their presence in the space.

Greek gymnastics exploration 13 – javelin

1. If you can, warm up with a real javelin. Otherwise, practise your archetypal action sequence until you recognise the activity and quality of consciousness involved in projecting or not projecting. You want to know how to turn it on and off at will. Notice the tendency to lose attention after the moment of release, and stay attentive.
2. Sustain your interest in what you have projected into space. Follow its path until the target has been reached. Genuine interest and attention are required, not 'acting' it.
3. Sustain the sensation of attention, intense involvement and interest in reaching your goal as you walk around.
4. Project this sensation out into the space, towards your fellow actors, other characters, towards an imaginary audience.
5. Stand still and sustain it.
6. Repeat this process several times, from outer gesture to sustaining and projecting the sensations aroused by it as you move around the space. From time to time, consciously let go of the sensation and then 'tune into' it again until you can call on it at will; the intense projection of your consciousness out into the space

A healthy training of the physical body is only possible when we proceed from the premise that the physical is never 'only physical'.[34] We train our instruments to be receptive to the streams of energy and forming processes that have their origin outside of time and space. The consciousness of these subtle realms and processes can be felt as sensations in our soul. The component of training that awakens these sensations in an actor is certainly a part of what Chekhov meant by 'psycho-physical'.

This range of sensations, while interwoven with the life of our emotions, is distinct from them and needs its own process to awaken them. As our training

Figure 11 – The spear thrower

deepens, the actor will begin to sense what Chekhov called the 'archetypal body' and Blake referred to as the 'human form divine'.[35]

This perception of an archetypal body forms a basis for creating character. If actors cannot sense their archetypal body, they remain fixed in their habitual tendencies. This means they cannot start from a neutral place and any characters they play will tend to resemble themselves. Although an industry-based perspective encourages acting based on type, this need not obscure what Chekhov called the actor's need and longing for a path of transformation.

Later, in chapter 4 we explore Chekhov's tools for creating characters that differ from ourselves; the art of 'changing shape' or 'morphing'. In chapter 3, we focus on the spectrum of sensations most commonly associated with our souls; feelings and emotions.

Chapter 3

Soul

the individual soul in this world
is an eternal fragment of myself ...

I am seated in everyone's hearts
I am the self
abiding in the hearts of all beings ...

mind and reason also ...
these are the division of my nature

... and I the strength of the strong.

The threefold nature of our soul-life

The soul is the vessel for our consciousness. The content of our consciousness is generated when we perceive and, as a consequence, think, feel and act. The processes that make these functions possible are spread throughout our body, yet our everyday awareness cannot help identifying each with a specific centre — perception with our sensory organs, thinking with our head, feeling with the heart and our capacity to act with our limbs and metabolic system.

Steiner refers to the last of these functions as *willing*. The term *will* is used here to differentiate between the action carried out by the body (the doing) and the *force* that drives the action (will). This activity of will exists on many levels. Some lie below the threshold of our consciousness and are not yet conscious impulses within our souls; our evolution as a human being partly consists of making conscious ever deeper levels of our will.[36]

Thinking, feeling and willing weave together. By consciously attending, we can observe how one or other may dominate our consciousness, according to the situation. Although the momentary dominance may shift, nevertheless, some of us seem predominantly 'thinking types' or 'feeling types' or 'action types'. Character development can be deeply informed by exploring these 'types', and to make this range of possibilities available as choices for the actor, Chekhov invites us to focus first on each one separately.

THE THREE CENTRES: THINKING, FEELING AND WILLING

Chekhov's concept of a *centre* was a location in the body which channels an impulse from the world into our soul and also from our soul into the world. First, we explore the centres through which our thinking, feeling and will impulses are channelled in their archetypal aspect, granting access to what is universal in the human soul. On this foundation, we can then approach what Chekhov called 'imaginary centres'; an objective tool for accessing the soul-life of a vast range of diverse individuals. We begin with those instinctive connections that we make between our thinking and our head, our feeling and our heart, our will and what we commonly refer to as our 'guts'.

THE FEELING CENTRE IN THE HEART (HEART-CENTRE)

I am the Self abiding in the heart of all beings

Within the range of characters an actor is called upon to play, unhealthy or destructive emotions may be repeatedly invoked. Chekhov struggled with the question: is there a way for actors to penetrate the 'darker' aspects of human nature that supports their emotional stability and health? One key that he discovered was to work with what he called the 'imaginary centre in the chest'.

On pages 7–8 of *To the Actor*, Chekhov tells us how to do this. He does not refer directly to this centre as 'the heart', perhaps because within his lifetime the heart was commonly conceived to be a muscle whose function is to pump our blood. In the half-century since then, it is more acceptable to think in terms of physical phenomena as spiritual activity condensed and to imagine our heart as that subtle field of energy centred in our chest that spiritual tradition refers to as the chakra of the heart.

Two stories from the heart

When my teachers in New York first introduced me to the centre-in-the-chest exercise described by Chekhov, the only sensation that arose in me was emptiness. I tried to bring the images alive within myself, but they remained an intellectual abstraction. For almost two years this continued and the exercise became a source of great frustration and a growing sorrow that my heart was dead.

I discovered that explorations relating to other aspects of the work aroused sensations in that region which seemed to be like what I imagined Chekhov had intended. And they arose because they were approached indirectly. As a result, I offer these as preparations for working with the centre in the chest, as Chekhov has described it. These draw together threads from gesture work, qualities and sensations, and other explorations still to come such as radiating and giving-and-receiving.

My experience relates to an anecdote about the evolution of his methodology from the years when Chekhov taught at Dartington. He could not understand, at first, why the actors could not project their presence in the way he was accustomed to in Russia. He realized something was missing which the Russian soul and temperament did naturally. Through observation, he identified that what he and other Russian actors did instinctively was radiate their warmth and passion from a centre in their chest. This led him to experiment with how to teach this faculty to actors for whom it is not instinctive. Here are some of my experiments, as well as those developed by my teachers.

Heart-centre exploration 1 (partner work)

1. Throw and catch a ball or beanbag.
2. When you can do this with a sense of ease[*], throw and catch at varying distances.
3. Change from throwing and catching into giving and receiving. It is not necessary to invent scenarios to clothe the action. Simply exchange the ball or beanbag with the *intention* to receive or give it. Come quite close so you can permeate your giving and receiving with an intimate quality.
4. Let go of the beanbag, but continue to exchange your gestures. Pay attention to any changes in sensation when you *give* instead of throw and *receive* instead of catch. Where do you experience them in your body?
5. Alternate between throwing and catching and giving and receiving, and at different distances, observing any shift in your sensations.
6. Share your observations.

Heart-centre exploration 2

1. Warm up 'giving and receiving'.
2. As you move around, improvise the following scenarios with an imaginary recipient:

   - give a precious gift to a beloved friend
   - give a drink of water to someone who is ill and thirsty
   - give money to a beggar
   - give hope to someone who has lost all hope
   - give encouragement to someone who lacks confidence
   - give a genuine compliment to someone.

Notice the progression from giving an object to giving a *quality*. Allow time to imagine each situation and improvise the action. Pay attention to sensations that arise in the act of giving and where you observe their source in your body.

---

[*] See chapter 5, page 234.

Heart-centre exploration 3

1. Improvise the same scenarios but now as the receiver.
2. Experiment with *handing* an object to someone or *giving* it, *taking* an object or *receiving* it. Do the sensations differ? Where do you observe them in your body?

When you give and receive, can you sense a warmth or flow of energy or glow in the centre of your chest; in the 'region of your heart'?

Heart-centre exploration 4 — for opening the heart

1. Reach out with a full-bodied gesture to a source of warmth and light; sunlight through a window, its reflection on the wall or floor, light from a lamp or candle, warmth from a heater.
2. Grasp the light or warmth with a gesture and draw it to you. Press it gently and firmly into the region of your heart. Shut your eyes and enclose the warmth and light within you.
3. Repeat this action several times until the region of your heart is permeated with the light and warmth.
4. Keep your eyes closed and direct the light and warmth from its source within your heart, to radiate first into each shoulder and each arm, right through to your fingertips, then through your torso and hips, down through each leg and into the tips of your toes, then up through your neck and head, permeating face and scalp and right into the centre of your brain. Follow the order that feels natural.
5. When your body is permeated by the light and warmth streaming from your heart, make a few simple movements. Keep your eyes closed at first. This will concentrate the energy. Can you sense the impulse for each movement stream from your heart? Can you sense that the power to organize your instrument into an integrated whole streams from your heart?
6. Now let the light and warmth stream from your heart into your eyes. It opens them, streams through them and out into the space around.
7. Move freely in the space with the sense your heart is a sun that permeates you with its light and warmth, transforming you into an integrated whole and spreading its rays into the world.
8. In the light that streams from your heart through your eyes, behold the world and your fellow human beings.
9. When ready, meet a partner and acknowledge them. What words flow from your heart: 'friend', 'love', 'warm'? Speak them. What are the qualities of your voice, when you speak from your heart?

Figure 13 – Heart-centre based on the image of Apollo

Heart-centre exploration 5

1. Stand before the picture of Apollo. See how the radiant sun in his chest streams into the world. Incorporate this image into warming up your own heart-centre.
2. Let your light and warmth radiate, like his, from the centre in your chest. Cup your hands around your heart. Imagine they protect a precious jewel or a flame from going out, or perhaps they are petals which enclose the centre of a flower.
3. Turn towards something in the space and open your hands so that the light and warmth stream from your heart and create a radiant path between you and the object. Walk a few steps along that path, aware of the sensations that arise when the impulse to move flows from your heart.
4. Open a pathway from your heart to someone unaware of your attention. Walk a few steps towards them on that path.
5. When you sense someone's willingness for a direct encounter, approach them. Create a path of light and warmth between you and walk a few steps towards each other. Open your hearts' flowers fully to each other.
6. When you are ready, let your hearts stream into your speech. Speak the words I AM, in a simple way. What is the quality of your speech when you speak from your heart?[37]

Heart-centre exploration 6

1. Prepare with the heart-centre explorations and explore the qualities of character or life-moments that suggest themselves.
2. Explore a character that interests you. Are there any moments in the play when the character acts or wishes to act from their heart in this pure way? Improvise such moments.

THE WILL CENTRE IN THE BELLY (WILL-CENTRE)

> *And I the strength of the strong*

Our will is the function most inaccessible to consciousness. Technology can translate into signals the transfer of energy from nerve cells to muscles that indicates consciousness is taking place, but those signals are not consciousness. We are entirely unaware of what translates the impulse to take hold of a glass of water and lift it to our mouth into the action of doing so.

When we work with impulse we confront the mystery of will. At first, an almost untraceable sensation appears on the edge between our consciousness and action. With practice, we learn to trust that such sensations come from an intelligence that cannot be foreseen by the rational mind, although with hindsight their wisdom will be vindicated. We learn this trust by saying 'yes' to the impulse before our reasoning can block it.[*] Work with impulse sensitizes us to the mystery and wisdom of our will. Meeting resistance to my will, makes me conscious of it. It is then I discover whether it is strong enough to meet the challenge.

Will-centre exploration 1 — the sensation of our will

1. Sit comfortably and imagine yourself doing something that requires a strong will: chopping wood, climbing in a challenging terrain, lifting a tree trunk or boulder that has fallen on a friend, etc.
2. Stand and incorporate the action. In your imagination, increase the degrees of resistance to your action and observe the equivalent increase of will aroused to meet the challenge.
3. Observe the difference in sensation between imagining that you are doing it, and doing it.

Will-centre exploration 2

Moulding and *wrestling* both require resistance and so make us conscious of our will.[†] If I wrestle only with my arms, I will soon be overcome.

1. Wrestle with a partner. Draw the power that you need up from the centre of the earth, through your feet and calves and thighs, then to circle through your hips and belly and from there stream up into your arms, empowering them.
2. When the strength that moves through you balances the strength moving through your partner, separate from each other and pour that strength into the gesture of the warrior.

You can use this archetypal-gesture to access the forces of your will.[‡] From this starting point grows a set of explorations that isolate the will-aspect of our soul's activity, so that we can recognize it and apply it consciously in different contexts.

Will-centre exploration 3

Let the following steps unfold as you gain confidence with each.

1. Incorporate the gesture of the warrior.

---

[*] See 'Yes, Let's!' on page 18.

[†] See chapter 1 (Moulding) and chapter 2 (Wrestling).

[‡] See *archetypal-gesture*, chapter 4.

Figure 14 – Will-centre based on a warrior 1

2. Sense the energy circle from the centre of the earth up through one leg, through the centre in your belly, down through the other leg and back again into the earth.

3. Intensify the circle of energy and as it moves through you, move within it, gently at first, until it picks you up and lifts you into walking, running, leaping and landing once again in your warrior-gesture. As it does so, sense it also circle through your arms.

4. Imagine you are a martial arts master. As you move around the space defend yourself from left and right, behind and front, above, below. Check you are in touch with the forces moving through your centre that empower you.

5. Create a warrior dance.

6. Create a warrior dance with a partner.

7. Separate from your partner and move around the space, sustaining the sensation this arouses as you walk, run, carry out an ordinary action. Build a sequence of such actions powered from that centre in your belly.

8. Leap into your 'warrior' gesture and as you do so, release your voice. What is its quality? What sounds emerge organically? Try speaking words like 'strength' or 'power'.[38]

9. Let these will sensations, mediated through the centre in your belly, remind you of moments in your life or of characters you have observed. Investigate a character that interests you. Is the character predominantly someone who functions out of will?

10. Perform an action of the character while sustaining the will sensations channelled through the centre in your belly and empowering your limbs.

11. Perhaps the character does not predominantly function out of will, but yet there is a moment where their will is strongly active? Warm-up your warrior gesture and sustaining the sensations that arise, improvise that moment.

Further aspects of the will
Indian mythology identifies three divinities connected with aspects of the will:

> Brahma — the Creator
> Vishnu — the Preserver
> Shiva — the Destroyer

We, too, can be inspired if we recognise the gods at work in one or other aspect of our will. Such inspirations will enrich the way we see and work with the characters that we create.[*]

---

[*] See chapter 4 for the section Archetypes.

Figure 15 – Will-centre based on a warrior 2

These three aspects of our will live unconsciously in our metabolism. Firstly, food must be *destroyed* by chewing before it can be swallowed. Once in the stomach and digestive tract, it is further broken down by forces which, in everyday awareness, I have no ability to consciously control. Nor have I any conscious control of the forces which re*create* my body and *maintain* the new creation.

We know that body temperature must be maintained if we are to function healthily. The many chemical reactions taking place throughout our body require heat and our digestion also generates enormous quantities of heat. Of this, we remain largely unaware unless we are unwell. The element of *fire* is fundamentally connected with our will – we even use physical activity to warm ourselves when we are cold. We shall now explore the relationship of fire to the expression of our will in the continuous cycle of creation, preservation and destruction.[39]

Will-centre exploration 4

1. Warm up with radiating.
2. Direct the fire into a movement sequence which embodies these three stages of the will in:

   - the digestive process
   - the *destruction* of a tree from which you *create* a wooden sculpture, violin or table and then *care for* it.

3. Identify the archetypal qualities within your actions.
4. Create a full-bodied archetypal sequence embodying this cycle.
5. Let the sensations that arise inspire you to explore a situation or character where one or more of these three aspects of the will reveals itself.

Will-centre exploration 5

1. Warm up with your full-bodied archetypal sequence.
2. Identify the movements and sensations at each stage.
3. Extract them and create out of each discrete stage of the cycle, the dances of Brahma, Vishnu and of Shiva. Each dance should culminate in a full-bodied gesture that embodies that divinity.

I have suggested that what Chekhov calls *the imaginary centre in the chest* is connected to that field of energy called in spiritual tradition the *heart chakra*. In the designation of the seven major chakras, counting upwards from the *root chakra*, the heart is number four. My investigation of the will centre, leads me to suggest that, in this case, we are not dealing with a single chakra.

The centre in the belly suggests to me the physical location of the *sacral* or the second chakra, connected in tradition to our sexuality and, thus, to our creative forces. This is located in between the *root chakra* and our *solar plexus;* each of which mediates other attributes of will. According to tradition, chakra three (the *solar plexus*) is connected to the work of our digestion. The *root chakra*, in addition to its other functions, directs its forces through our limbs, enabling us to find expression in the world. Thus we might imagine that through the centre in the belly, we mediate what flows through the three lower chakras and thus everything that streams through us as will.

THE THINKING CENTRE IN THE HEAD (HEAD-CENTRE)

> *I AM the reason of the reason endowed*

I have sensations of myself in action. Yet even when my motivation for that action is a conscious choice, as in the example quoted earlier of raising a glass of water to my mouth, I have no awareness of *how* I make this happen. The fact that I can act and be unaware of what I've done, proves that the working of my will can be unconscious. Macbeth, for instance, does not know that he has brought the bloody daggers from the place of Duncan's murder.

In the realm of my emotions, on the other hand, I can have some degree of consciousness. I can learn to control or transform them. I can push them into my unconscious so that I am not aware of them but I can lift them into consciousness again. Although Lady Macbeth succeeded for a time in suppressing her compassion so that she could will her husband to carry out the murder, in the end it broke through her 'armour':

> Had he not resembled my father as he slept I had done it. Who would have thought the old man to have had so much blood in him?

Thinking, however, differs from both will and feeling because without fully conscious activity it simply cannot happen. I am not referring to the endless stream of uninvited thoughts that occupy our minds much of the time. Their visitations we do not consciously control without the mental discipline to do so. But, the activity of thinking that we exercise when we wrestle with a problem, examine the evidence and discover a solution, give birth to some quite new idea or thought — this is only possible when I am present, utterly awake and active in my own thinking process.

I observe intelligence in every aspect of my body's functioning. Yet, if I observe myself when I am truly thinking, as opposed to 'having thoughts', I recognize my head to be the centre through which I channel my intelligence. It is where I experience my thinking.

Figure 16 – Head-centre based on the Charioteer

Figures 17 & 18

Head-centre exploration 1

1. Place chairs or other objects randomly around the working space.
2. Darken the space until there is just enough light to dimly show the presence of some, not all, of the objects but not enough to see them clearly.
3. Find your way around the space. Observe that when you try to see in the dark, it is as though you try to pierce the darkness with your vision. Express this full bodily. Observe how the focus of your consciousness shifts to your eyes and to the centre just between them and above.
4. When you are ready to recreate this body of sensations restore the light to the space and move around it as though you are still in the dark. Find a full-bodied gesture which expresses how you send out rays of light from that centre in your head to pierce the dark.
5. Recall the expression: I see. How we use it as a metaphor for understanding; how when we think we try to pierce or penetrate the darkness of ignorance. I see = I understand. Speak the words, *I see*, co-ordinating and releasing them with your full-bodied gesture so that the words pierce the space like a clear ray of light.
6. Practise throwing darts and extract from the process a full-bodied sequence of gesture which you can use to access this centre.
7. Revisit the javelin explorations in chapter 2. Integrate that work with the sequence of actions evolving from step 6.

Head-centre exploration 2

1. Warm up your warrior-gesture, aware that your consciousness and energy is centred in your belly.[*]

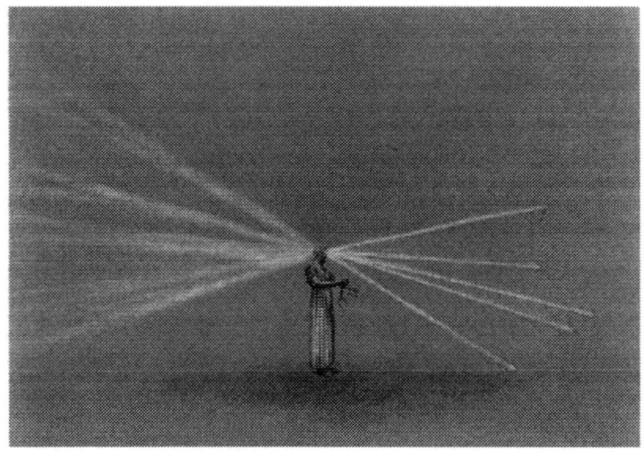

Figure 19 – Head-centre connected to the stars

2. Contemplate the image of the charioteer. Organize yourself to meet his gaze.
3. Observe your focus lift as you sense your consciousness stream upwards from your belly to your head to radiate from the centre in your brow.
4. Imagine that clear light, streaming through your gaze, light up the world. It is the light which lights our universe,

[*] See Figure 14.

Figure 20 – The Charioteer

the light of stars, of the intelligence which thought us and which now thinks through us when we think.

5. Imagine a star which is your own. Reach up behind you and grasp its light. Direct it through the centre in your brow to stream into the world. This is the arrow or javelin of light with which you pierce the dark of ignorance.

6. Pay attention to the contrast in sensation between the energy of light channelled through the centre in your head and the energy of warmth channelled through the centre in your belly. As the light from the universe streams through the centre in your head out into the world, adjust your body to support it. Sense your whole instrument rearrange itself to be a vessel for this new activity.

Head-centre exploration 3

1. Work in a group of three. A to incorporate the gesture of the charioteer, B and C the unseen horses.

2. Wind two sheets or cloths that are strong and large enough to support your weight. 'Harness' the chests of B and C, so that A can hold the 'reins' — loose enough to allow flexibility, yet firm enough for A to exercise control.

3. B and C try to escape control and move off in their own directions. A bring them into harmony so that you can move as a team. A to discover how much strength and sensitivity you need to gain control. The three of you must sense your way into each other's will and find the energy required. Too much resistance blocks cooperation. Too little will not activate A's necessary forces.

4. A aims to control the horses with strength imbued with ease and inner stillness.

5. Take turns to be the driver and acquire the necessary body of sensations through experience and mastery of physical resistance.

6. Recreate that body of sensations on your own, using your imagination. Bring 'those horses' under your control. Improvise the actions and resistances, until you sense the energy condensed into the driver's stillness. Do not confuse the ease and restfulness with which you stand and hold the horses with inactivity.

7. Practise until you can access at will this full-bodied sensing of activity-in-stillness. This sensation helps us differentiate having passive thoughts from creative thinking. The latter, called by Steiner 'living thinking', only happens when we activate our will within our thinking.

Head-centre exploration 4

1. Warm up the head-centre. Direct your gaze to something distant. Examine it. Send a clear ray of light towards it, pierce it with that ray of light and then move towards

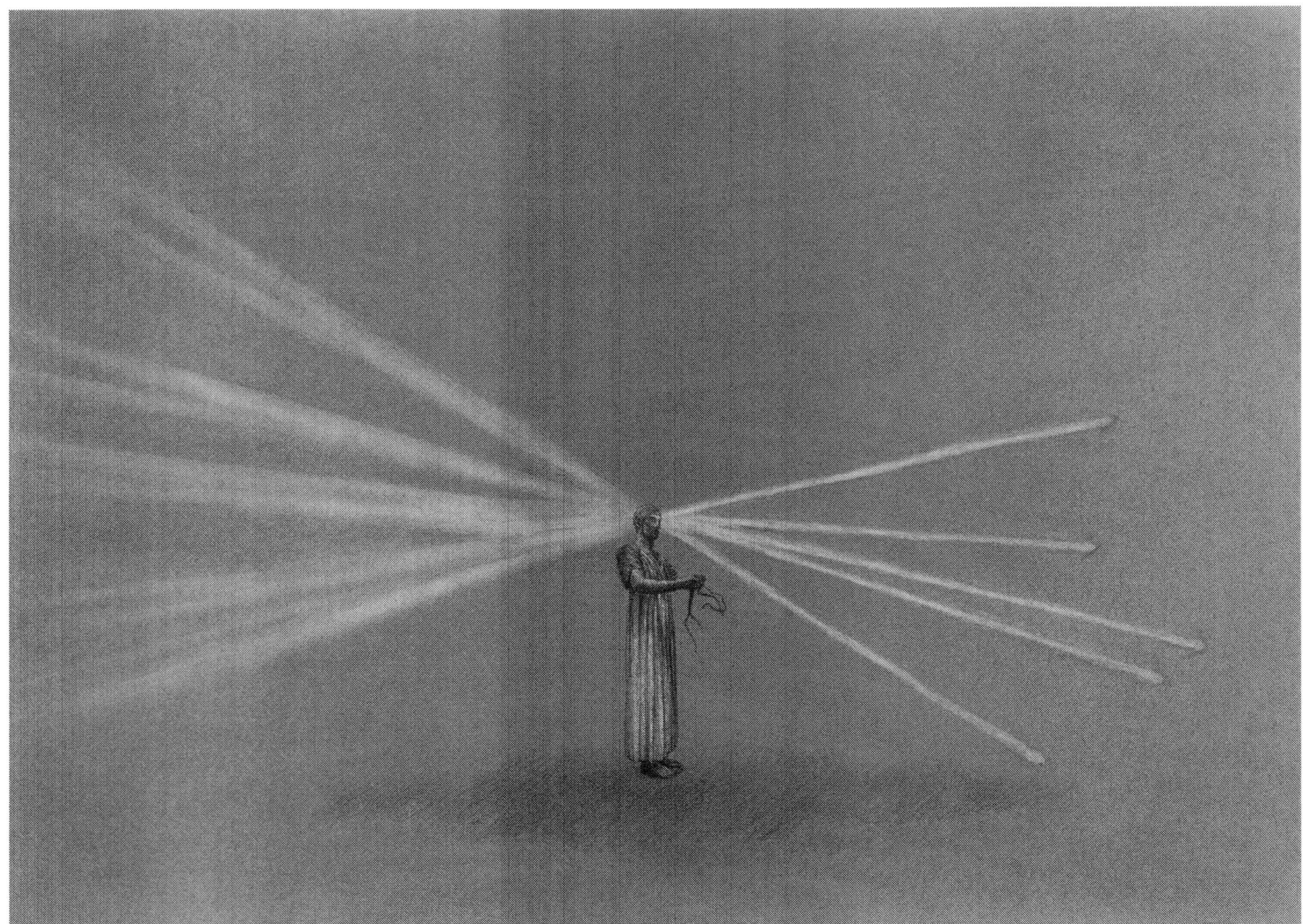

Figure 21 – Head-centre connected to the stars

it on that path of light. Pay attention to the 'body of sensation' that arises when you move along that path. How does it differ when your energy and consciousness stream through the centre in your heart or belly?

2. Walk, then run, sustaining this sensation and this consciousness.

3. Sit, kneel, and improvise some everyday activities, sustaining the sensation that your consciousness is centred in your head.

Head-centre exploration 5

1. Warm up the head-centre. Move around the space. What sorts of characters suggest themselves? How do you behave if you receive your impulses predominantly through the centre in your head?

2. Explore moments in life that arise.

3. Experiment with characters. Do they function strongly or predominantly from this centre? If not, is there a specific moment where they do?

4. Explore words that express this 'head' or intellectual quality: 'clear', 'reason', 'understand'. Observe your voice's quality when speaking from this centre in your head.[*]

The sculpture of the charioteer shows the connection of our head to our capacity to be a conscious, thinking human being. His clear gaze, so utterly awake, penetrates the world with conscious light which streams not only from his eyes but through the centre of his brow. When we take into account both function and location, how could this centre not be connected with the *brow or* sixth chakra, often referred to as the *Third Eye* and situated in-between the fifth and seventh chakras referred to as the *throat* and *crown?* And if it is, might it be our conscious work with the centre in our head that enables us to mediate what streams through the three upper chakras?

TRANSITIONS BETWEEN THE THREE CENTRES

Once we can work with each archetypal centre, we know how to shift from one centre to another as the situation or the character demands. We can also sense when a character functions predominantly in one centre or the other or is balanced. The ability to move between and to combine the centres adds to the repertoire of tools that access in objective ways the inner states required.[†]

---

[*] The relationship between the thinking-centre in our head and speech is explored in chapter 3 and *The Integrated Actor*, chapter Relationship of our threefold instrument to character and style.

[†] See also *The Art of Speech*, chapter 3, for connection between the centres and speech; see *The Integrated Actor*, chapter, Relationship of our threefold instrument to character and style, which deals with epic, lyric and dramatic styles.

Different styles can be developed by playing with these three archetypal centres. The naïve simplicity of heart appropriate for much of the mediaeval repertoire can be quickly accessed by working with the centre in the chest. In contrast, the style appropriate to comedy of manners, or a character skilled in the quick thrust and parry of words and wit, can be accessed through the centre in our head.[*]

When we can integrate the three different ways of functioning we have some sense of how the Ancient Greeks experienced the world, who were constituted so their thoughts and emotions were fused with their actions. This would enable us to better understand a character like Oedipus, for instance, born in such a different time and culture.

In contrast, many human beings at this time in our western culture experience fragmentation. Steiner suggests this is because, since the fifteenth century, our emotions, our thinking and our will have separated and pull us in different directions. Hamlet is perhaps the first character exemplifying this. A renaissance figure who stands at the dawn of modern consciousness, he was lover and poet (feeling), warrior-duellist (willing) and scholar and investigator (thinking). His dilemma, that he could not integrate all three, is surely what speaks to us so deeply, prophetically revealing to us, as he does, our modern soul condition.

3-centres exploration 1

1. Warm up each centre.
2. As you move, alternate the centres until sensations arising from the one combine with those arising from the other two.
3. Out of this combined source of impulse, experiment throughout the range of movement (10–1). Your psycho-physical awareness may suggest moments in your life when you have functioned strongly in this way, or suggest a character that does, or one that functions only in their head and will – who is awake, clear in their thoughts and powerful in action.
4. Improvise situations in which a head-will character carries out a deed requiring clear and calculated thoughts and the will to enact them. For example, someone sets off an explosion underneath a bridge in order to exact revenge; someone manipulates 'the system' to make a fortune, etc.
5. As you behold the consequences of your action, can you sense that there is something missing; the function that weaves between thinking and will, without which we cannot be entirely human? Now open your heart and allow yourself to feel what you have done.

---

[*] For a thorough exploration of stylistic application, see *The Integrated Actor*, chapter, Relationship of our threefold instrument to character and style.

3-centres exploration 2

Hamlet has returned from England, determined finally to face his uncle Claudius. Unaware Ophelia has drowned, he comes upon a gravedigger who is preparing her grave. A skull is thrown up from the earth. The gravedigger tells the prince it is the skull of someone Hamlet knew; the court jester Yorick who had played with Hamlet often when he was a child. Let the body of sensations aroused by working with each centre reveal different facets of this old relationship.

1. Place a beanbag in front of you; this will serve as Yorick's skull.
2. Warm up each centre.
3. Focus on the will and its centre in your belly.
4. You are Hamlet, the warrior, man of will. You have come back to Denmark energized and resolved to meet your destiny. Your will sensations determine what you do, how you move as you approach the 'skull', pick it up and speak:

   Alas, poor Yorick! I knew him Horatio. A fellow of infinite jest.

   Sustain your focus on this centre and let it show you how to end the scene.
5. Shift your focus and warm up the centre in your head. This time it is Hamlet, the investigator, scholar and philosopher who approaches Yorick's skull.
6. Shift your focus and warm up the centre in your chest. This time it is Hamlet, poet and lover, who approaches Yorick's skull.

THE THREE CENTRES AND THE CHAKRAS

In suggesting that the three centres are connected with the chakras, I do not imply that the path of preparation for an actor suggested in this book has the same purpose as an esoteric training which would open up the chakras and unfold their higher faculties. Although related, this is a separate path with its own responsibilities and stringent disciplines.[40] It is certainly not to be embarked upon by anyone who has not made an absolutely conscious choice to do so. I draw attention to these things to suggest a fruitful avenue of further research and to demonstrate the richness that even our most basic understanding of the chakras can bring to what we mean by the centres and how we work with them; and to indicate the deeper mystery contained in thinking, will and feeling. Thus, we arrive at a conception of the centres as physical locations where we field what streams between and through the seven major chakras:

- The head-centre acts as a connecting place for what streams from the chakras of the *crown*, the *Third Eye* and the *throat*. It is the location for channelling the upper chakras.
- The will-centre in the belly corresponds in function and location to what is called

Figure 22 – The 7 chakras in relationship to the 3 centres

the *sacral chakra*. It could likewise be regarded as the centre for channelling what streams through the lower chakras; the *root*, the *sacral* and the *solar plexus*.

- Through the centre in the chest, which corresponds in function and location to the *heart chakra*, we have the possibility to mediate and harmonize what streams from both directions.

Chekhov's work towards the theatre of the future was to plant the seeds for a technique that could train the actor of the future. It is inconceivable that training processes by which an actor of the future will evolve could be separated from the processes by which the human being of the future will evolve. Steiner stressed the importance of developing the chakra of the heart. He observed we can be truly human only when our hearts mediate between our thinking and our will. From our consciously developed hearts streams what is noble in our human striving. Chekhov translated this into a language and a process for the actor. To make it accessible to anyone, regardless of philosophical/spiritual orientation, he called it, not the 'heart' but the actor's *centre in the chest*.

Through our explorations, we begin to sense that it is Love we channel through this centre when we work with it in such a conscious, archetypal way. This Love becomes our template, the foundation of our feeling life. Without this as a reference to which we constantly return, we run the risk of being torn apart by the emotional extremes that many characters require us to invoke.

When the heart-centre fulfils its task as mediator, will and thinking also function healthily. Will, without heart, leads to power without morality. Thinking, without heart, is cold and calculating; clever, even brilliant, but empty of humanity. Equally, feeling needs our thinking and our will. Without this tempering, our hearts can lead to sentimental wallowing, emotion that is powerless to act, passion that is uncontrolled and inability to make a healthy judgement.

Chekhov's approach enables us to healthily access the sensations needed by characters whose soul life is unhealthy or destructive; equally, to access levels of soul-health and maturity we may not yet have mastered or experienced ourselves: the characters of Cordelia from *King Lear*, Marina and Cerimon from *Pericles*, and Benedictus and Maria from Steiner's *Mystery Dramas* come to mind.

Chekhov called the sensations, feelings and emotions that are not dependent on the actor's subjective inner life but are called forth within a greater context, 'artistic'.

We have imagined that the centre in our belly, through which our will initially is channelled, is connected to the larger universe through the forces at the centre of the earth that stream as will through our instrument. By imagining we grasp the stars, channelling their rays through the centre in our head, we experience our thinking is connected to the cosmic thought that permeates our universe. And our heart? Could love exist on earth to warm our hearts if there did not first exist a heart much greater that, Shakespeare-like, embraces everything? If we cannot yet believe it, we can imagine it. We can open the petals of our heart to embrace ever wider circles until the utmost we can encompass is in turn encompassed:

> Because the Holy Ghost, over the bent world broods
> With warm breast and with ah! bright wings.

sonnet, G M Hopkins

Imaginary-centres

I have called these three centres archetypal because no matter how differently specific personalities may think or feel or act, it is these centres that allow us to be human beings. We have explored how to access their functions in their most ideal and archetypal sense. If we want now to find the way to access the soul life that belongs to the infinite variety of human personalities with all their particularities and eccentricities, sometimes glorious and sometimes terrible, we can use what Chekhov called 'imaginary centres'. In this chapter we shall learn how to imagine and incorporate some easily recognized distortions of the archetypal centres. This will lay the basis for working with imaginary centres in the next chapter.

We begin by working with a variation on the heart-centre which I call the undefended heart. With this as the healing template to which we can refer, we can safely explore the various distortions which occur on our long journey to become a human being.

Imaginary-centres exploration 1 — undefended heart

1. Stand and imagine deep within the centre in your chest, in the region of your heart, a flower of great beauty. When it opens, it allows the world to enter in and can, in turn, stream out to the world. When it feels the need to be nurtured from within, its petals close.
2. Let your hands be the petals of the flower. Beginning from the smallest and most delicate opening let your petals open fully to the world. Now, let them close again in order to digest and integrate what streamed in and out.
3. Try this process several times, sometimes opening towards an object in the space, sometimes to another person. This meeting may be indirect, or when you are ready, meet and open your heart-flower to each other.
4. Identify the feelings and emotions which arise from an open, undefended heart: tenderness, compassion, trust, joy, peace, courage, a consciously maintained and willing vulnerability. These are your template for a healthy soul. With practice, you will easily be able to return to them.

Imaginary-centres exploration 2 — undefended heart — gesture into speaking

In order to explore the quality of speech arising from an undefended heart we create our first full-bodied gesture as a pathway that can guide and shape our speech.

1. Build on *undefended heart exploration 1* and let your heart open fully to the whole earth, streaming out through your arms and hands into a full-bodied gesture that

embraces the whole earth … then do the same to the heavens, then the world of other human beings.

2. Once again we return to Hamlet's speech and use these gestures to explore his state of soul before the events unfold that change his life forever. Experiment with speaking the words from Hamlet's speech that relate to each gesture.

I embrace the earth:

This goodly frame the earth …

Figure 23 – Undefended heart 1

I embrace the heavens:

> This most excellent canopy the air, look you, this brave o'erhanging firmament, this majestical roof, fretted with golden fire...

Figure 24 – Undefended heart 2

I embrace humanity:

> What a piece of work is a man, how noble in reason, how infinite in faculties,
> in form and moving, how express and admirable, in action how like an angel,
> in apprehension, how like a god: the beauty of the world, the paragon of animals; …

Figure 25 – Undefended heart 3

Imaginary-centres exploration 3 — defended heart (partner work)

1. Imagine the 'slings and arrows of outrageous fortune'. Identify with your partner what some of these might be. Concretize the image and express these slings and arrows in a series of full-bodied gestures in which A aims and projects directly at B's heart. B respond with full-bodied gestures that defend your heart against A's gestures of attack.
2. Reverse roles.
3. Work on your own and explore the gestures that defended you from being hurt.
4. Identify some of the emotions that arise from your defended heart. For example: fear, shyness, caution, anger, hatred, jealousy, anxiety, suspicion, lack of trust, defence, attack, retaliation, etc.
5. Share your findings with your partner.

Imaginary-centres exploration 4 — defended heart — gesture into speaking

Use *exploration 3* as the basis for approaching Hamlet's experience after the loss of innocence. Where once he trusted, now he defends his heart from everyone and everything.

Figure 26 — Defended heart 1

Figure 27 — Defended heart 2

How does the quality of speaking change when we meet the world with the gesture of defending our heart?

I defend my heart against the earth: . . . seems to me a sterile promontory . . .

I defend my heart against the heavens: . . . why it appeareth no other thing to me than a foul and pestilent congregation of vapours . . .

I defend my heart from my fellow human beings: . . . what is this quintessence of dust?

Imaginary-centres exploration 5 — alternating gestures into speaking

Since we are just beginning to explore how full-bodied gesture creates a pathway that shapes and guides our quality of speech, continue to work at level 10 of gesture.

1. Put the speech back together as you move between the full-bodied gestures for undefended and defended heart as a way of exploring the conflicted state of Hamlet's soul.
2. Experiment with the range of gesture 10-1 and whether you can sustain the quality of gesture in your speech when the outer gesture is diminished.[*]

Having surveyed the spectrum of experience connected with our undefended and defended heart, still using the heart as our focus, we can explore Chekhov's process for working with *imaginary centre.*

A note on hygienic practice

Before and after each incorporation, consciously return to the archetypal centre in your chest (head or belly, whichever is appropriate). Take time to access the healthy expression of that function of your soul. Hygienic practice thus becomes a habit you build into your process.

The heart

Think of expressions and images that convey the damage or wounding that can happen to our hearts:

---

[*] These explorations provide just a taste of the work with full-bodied gesture explored more thoroughly in chapter 4. The relationship between speech and gesture is the theme of an entire chapter in *The Integrated Actor.*

a broken heart
a breaking heart
a heart torn in two
heart of stone
wooden heart
cold or frozen hearted
pierced to the heart; by cupid's arrow, grief or sorrow.
sick at heart
to have a splinter in one's heart
heart-ache
heavy-hearted
heart-sick
wear one's heart on one's sleeve

Use these expressions as a basis for creating an imaginary centre. The suggestions provided are not intended for a single session.

Imaginary-centres exploration 6 — process for creating an imaginary centre

1. Choose an image. Stand and imagine it so strongly that your body responds.
2. Sustain the sensation that arises and carry out some simple actions.
3. What characters, or moments in their lives, suggest themselves?
4. Return to base.

The head

Think of expressions and images that convey the distortions and one-sidedness related to our thinking. For example:

a foggy brain
a sharp brain or mind
a razor-sharp intellect or wit
a head filled with cotton wool
a head in the clouds
a head crowded with unwanted thoughts
feather-brained
bird-brain
brain turned to mush

Using the process described above choose one of these imaginary centres and incorporate it.

The belly

Think of expressions and images that convey the distortions and one-sidedness related to our will. For example:

a fire in the belly
to have a belly full
a belly full of writhing snakes
jelly belly
yellow-bellied
to be gutsy/have guts
to have a gut full
to be gutless or to have no guts, a gutless wonder

Choose one and follow the steps to create an imaginary centre.

In chapter 4 we shall see how much further Chekhov was prepared to go in imagining how centres can inspire an actor's creativity.

Imaginary centres in practice

In developing the characters in Beckett's *Waiting for Godot*, we explored each one's relationship to the three centres. My character was Lucky. Through improvising with the other characters, images arose which subsequently formed the basis of my character. I discovered that his relationship to thinking was sporadic; moments of startling clarity breaking through a fog of confusion and inability to hold onto the mass of frayed and tangled threads which filled his head. The image that arose of the centre in his head was the eye of a needle through which he constantly attempted to direct the frayed ending of a thread. At times he would succeed and draw a clear thought through, at other times his efforts were in vain.

Further explorations revealed that Lucky had long since passed beyond the point of exhaustion and only fear of punishment could make him act. He would then make monumental efforts to obey his master but soon collapse again. The image that revealed itself was cranking up the engine of an old vintage car. It spurts and sputters into action momentarily before its power fades. I imagined such an ancient engine in my belly. Only by supreme effort could I crank it to the point where I could take a step or carry out an action before collapsing once again.

As for Lucky's heart! Exploring interaction with his master, Pozzo, revealed a complicated co-dependency; an ancient love betrayed that now had turned to hatred. I felt his heart was being eaten by resentment and jealousy. An image came of a tiny sharp-toothed and ferocious creature gnawing at his heart.

I decided to work with each of these in turn until I knew that I could confidently move between them and in any order. Each one would predominate at different times. Then there were moments where each of them could play their layer through the others. The absence of the easy-to-recognize benchmarks of a life, from which we are accustomed to build the gestalt of a character is a feature of absurdist drama. In this case the complex layering of centres gave me a solid basis for the character of Lucky. In addition, the full-bodied exploration this entailed provided the intensities that this expressionistic style required.

Animals

Chapter 2 has taught us that our bodies are expressive instruments when we work with that subtle ether which imbues physicality with life. In fact, what we refer to as our *body* both emerges from and disappears again into the unseen continuity of life. This continuity of life is what human beings share with plants. By the cultivation of attention in our physical activity, we train ourselves to be aware of the sensations which inform us of this life.[*]

Our explorations have brought us ever closer to the spectrum of emotions we commonly associate with 'soul'. As we train ourselves to recognize and freely move within their range, we find we are exploring what we share with animals. Of course, we project on animals, just as we do upon our fellow human beings. But the fact that we project our emotions onto others does not invalidate our observation that when, for instance, a dog or cat looks at us, we sense precisely what they 'feel'. The mood of soul we share seems unmistakable. Here follow some expressions which reflect our sense of this:

busy as a bee (or ant)	*predatory as a vulture*
gentle as a dove	*savage as a tiger*
faithful or devoted as a dog	*dogged*
scared or timid as a mouse	*nervous as a rabbit*
contented as a cow	*mad as a bull*
stubborn as an ox	*cunning as a fox*
wise as an owl	*quiet as a mouse*
mischievous as a monkey	*brave as a lion*
slippery as a snake	*voracious as a wolf*

In many of these (and you can think of many more), the adjective conveys as much an *action* as a mood. In this sense we could say that animals are actors. What they 'feel', they do. It is no surprise then that actors have long found a rich source of inspiration in observing animals, incorporating them[†] and applying the aspects of personality that arise to human character. Yet there is a fundamental difference between the animal and human soul.

The animal, fixed in its specific form and gesture, is limited to acting out its single ray. A human being, on the other hand, who is fixed in one specific state of soul, is regarded as unhealthy. What makes us human is our flexibility, our capacity to

---

[*] See chapter 2, page 75, and also chapter 5 of *The Art of Speech*.

[†] Regarding incorporation, see chapter 4.

exercise a choice. We are capable of investigating and identifying with the behaviour of each ray in the spectrum; those mentioned above and many others. The I AM or spirit can stand outside a situation, see a range of possible responses and choose what is appropriate. Although the study and incorporation of animal behaviour is not specific to Chekhov's training for the actor, I include it here because it is another demonstration of the psycho-physical relationship and is enriched when seen in this holistic context.

Animals exploration 1

1. Observe different animals in daily life, a sanctuary or zoo or on film. Imitate their movement and behaviour as accurately as you can. Observe the changes in your soul. What sensations or emotions are aroused when you move like a monkey or elephant or cat?
2. Play with these sensations and emotions as they suggest moments from your life or the lives of others or remind you of specific human beings you have seen or met.
3. Move back and forth between the animal, and human behaviour emerging from the animal. Experiment with degrees of metamorphosis between 'pure' animal behaviour and its human counterpart. Enjoy the extremes that emerge from working full-bodily.
4. Create a character at the extremity of 'animal' but who is recognizable as human.
5. Create a character in whom the 'animal' is more subtle.
6. Consolidate the essence of your animal within a human character. Improvise that character doing simple things; sitting, standing, reading, eating. Begin with solo actions that allow you to focus on sustaining and finding impulses within your 'body of sensation'.
7. Let those impulses inspire a more complex situation and interaction with another character.

Animals exploration 2

1. Identify the animals that are connected to aspects of yourself and other people that you know.
2. Observe those animals in detail.
3. Incorporate them and explore their behaviour, moving between 10–1 in bodily expression.
4. Identify the 'animals' in the behaviour and personality of a character that interests you.
5. Apply the steps in *Animals exploration 1 and 2*.

6. Improvise moments from a play, playing the character as an animal, taking its qualities to an extreme before experimenting with them in a human form.

Layering

Work with an animal not only leads to rich discoveries about a character and its interaction with another but also provides us with a tool to strongly delineate the features of someone who differs from ourselves. To build a character predominantly from such a single choice would however only be appropriate when working with a broader style; one requiring 'types' or caricatures.

Complex characters require a richer texturing, of which work with a specific animal is but one of many layers to be integrated. A student creating the title character from *Richard III* was inspired with Shakespeare's own description of Richard as a 'bottled spider'. This image did, indeed, contribute a terrifying shape and dimension to the character, but there were aspects which the qualities of 'spider' did not address, that needed to be accessed differently and layered into Richard's 'spiderness'.

In the following example, I layered animals with the archetypal centres. I needed to differentiate ten characters for my solo presentation of *King Lear*. Nearly always, Shakespeare's language shows us what to do. The three daughters, Goneril, Regan and Cordelia, tell us in which centre their souls predominantly function.

> *Goneril*:   We must *do* something and in the heat.

I found that if I layered 'python' with the archetypal centre for the will, I sensed someone inside me who enveloped and then crushed her victim.

> *Regan*:   We shall *think* further on it.

I experienced Regan as a ferocious cat who scratched and clawed whatever threatened her. When I layered this with the archetypal centre in the head, I sensed someone inside me, different from Goneril, who defended her territory, not by engulfing her rivals, but by tearing them with razor sharp words.

> *Cordelia*: What shall Cordelia say? Love and be silent …
> Alas! I cannot heave my *heart* into my mouth.

Beginning with the archetypal centre in the chest and then the undefended heart, my exploration of Cordelia led me not to an animal, but to the universal human; the face of the sphinx. I sensed inside me someone who transcends the one-sided tendencies of animals. Is it possible that the greatest master of our language, did not understand the implications of the words he gave to her? Shakespeare could not be more explicit expressing who it is that speaks in the moment when Lear returns to consciousness in the tent and recognizes her.[*]

Lear: I think this lady to be my child Cordelia.
Cordelia: And so I am, I am.

Using 'animal' in practice

A female student working on the male character, Yasha, in Anton Chekhov's *The Cherry Orchard*, directed by Suzanne Kersten, expressed her experience of using 'animal'.

Yasha

The actor is hungry, crouched under the table with animal eyes, calculating the danger. She is a wolf and she is trapped. She lopes. Sits. Sniffs at the air. She straightens, an unravelling of moments; the animal spine reorients itself to the upright.

Now she is a man with a wolf's heart.

Sinking back into animal nature, the man-wolf lopes about the studio faster and faster, seeking escape but there is none and the wolf howls. She feels the wonderful release and pity of that howl and knows now Yasha has arrived and the wolf inside Yasha is predatory in a new way; unfurls into the human shape — young, lithe, dangerous.

The sexual predator approaches the director because Suzanne can cope with Yasha and so the actor does not fear blurred lines. Yasha with his wolf's heart makes crude passes at the sophisticated Suzanne. She fends him off. He laughs and retreats further into his servant's suit; coat and leather boots to keep him warm in the frozen Russian winter. The brim of his hat conceals an avaricious eye.

Inside Yasha with his wolf's heart beating she steps into the play and the lines flow off the page into her mouth and she speaks with his mouth and the wolf's howl wails, silent now, no longer release but the implosion of his heart until only the ragged hole remains.

He will devour the girl and leave the carcass for the vultures to pick over after the revolution. Off to Paris with him, slavish after his mistress; he bares his teeth and fetches her pills.

Yasha broods, hovering in the background while Suzanne walks here and there, checking sight-lines.

'Break time,' announces the stage manager and the actor steps out of Yasha, lays down the wolf's hide folded neatly and shakes herself. Shakes them away. Smiling, heads to the kitchen for lunch, already chatting with the other players.

And Yasha?

Like a good servant, he waits.

And if his hand should stretch out to stroke the wolf's rough pelt?

No one will blame her.

Clare Strahan

---

[*] Refer to *The Integrated Actor* for a comprehensive exploration of the Lear characters.

Animal forms as gestures

Compare the human baby's helplessness with the ability of many newborn animals to perform the actions necessary for survival. The human body matures into its capabilities over many years. Even then, in comparison to animals, it remains a jack-of-all-trades who has mastered none. We cannot swim as well as swimming animals, nor run as fast as running animals nor dig as well as digging animals nor build as well as building animals. Yet we can swim and run and dig and build. Because the human body is, comparatively, so incapable, we use our thinking to extend our capabilities.

In contrast to this vast adaptability across the spectrum of behaviour, animals are limited, precisely by their perfect specificity, to embody perfectly their one ray of the spectrum. Human attempts to embody forms and gestures, voices of specific animals, remain comparatively shallow, yet, only human beings can be flexible enough to try and in doing so discover some, at least, of what we share with them.

There are animals whose forms determine that they stay attached to earth, others that they are at home in water, others in the air, some whose forms are flexible — enabling them to move between the elements. Whether it has wings or fins or claws, its form is a crystallization of intelligence that enables it to be at one with its environment without necessity to think. We might say its thinking is *not able to be thought by* it but *is* it. Its consciousness is what we mean by *instinct*. It's composed of action, sensation, emotion and intelligence so fused that they cannot be divided. This means that no part of their consciousness is free to observe and therefore become conscious of itself.

Human beings, while possessing certain instincts, have the potential to be *conscious of their consciousness*. Consciousness that can *be conscious of itself being conscious* arises only when within the course of evolution, our thinking, feeling and our will begin to separate. Until this separation makes self-observation possible, we, like animals, live instinctively. As in the animal, our instincts are composed of intelligence (as yet unconscious of itself), will, sensation and emotion fused as one.

On the long journey to becoming human, we can remain unconscious in parts or all of our instinctive life, but this does not change the fact of our potential which comes about because we have a form that does not fix us in any one possibility. We cannot be as perfect as the animals in their specialized abilities. It is our very imperfection, though, that drives us to make those things we do not do so well, conscious, so we can find out how to do them better. Likewise, we can transform our instincts and raise the source of our behaviour to the level of conscious motivation and ideals.

Such considerations arise out of Steiner's research into human evolution. They provide a broader, deeper context within which actors may appreciate the contribution of the animals both to their craft as actors and to their own becoming.[*]

---

[*] These thoughts in relation to artistic style are developed further in *The Integrated Actor*.

Feelings or emotions

I should like to make a clear distinction between what we vaguely and often interchangeably refer to as our feelings and emotions. A deeply relevant example from the history of theatre should suffice to clarify the way I mean to use these terms.

The 'Revenge' or 'Blood' tragedy, now a staple of the film industry, has been a major item on the theatre menu through the ages. The struggle to achieve a transformation of the instinct to retaliate or take revenge is a central theme explored by Shakespeare through the journey of his plays. Connected with the instinct for revenge are such states as anger, hatred, rage, anguish, grief, desire to hurt, to name a few. I will use the word *emotions* to refer to these; states of soul arising from our bodily, instinctive nature, generally when we *react* to circumstances.

On the other hand, the forgiveness which Hamlet struggles to achieve without success, but Desdemona offers to Othello with her dying breath, and Cordelia to Lear, shows what emotions can become when the I AM works to transform them. These transformed emotions I will refer to as our *feelings*.

Feelings are distinct from our emotions in that they are willed consciously. The range of what I choose to call *emotions* can be ennobled and transformed into a different range of *feelings*.

Emotions, then, are those affects that are unexamined or remain unchallenged or yet untransformed within our consciousness. Feelings are developed through our active agency, working to transform the raw material of our emotions. This transformation is not to be confused with suppression or repression.

It may be helpful, as a starting point, to list examples:

Emotions: fear, terror, desire, longing, anger, irritation, hate, resentment, cruelty, revenge, anxiety, jealousy, salacious curiosity, sadness, grief, arrogance, pride, envy, boredom.

Feelings: compassion, interest, forgiveness, kindness, equanimity, serenity, courage, love, reverence, gentleness, tenderness, humility, hope, trust, patience, generosity, peace, faithfulness.

You may observe that many of the states listed here as emotions arise from a defended heart, while what are listed here as feelings are expressions of an undefended heart.[*] Emotions are expressions of the more instinctive end of our soul's spectrum of experience. As such, they have the tendency to govern us unless we

---

[*] See pages 159–163.

actively engage with our potential to govern them and thus achieve true feeling. At the instinctive end of the spectrum, emotions reflect the soul's tendency to constantly swing back and forth between what were referred to earlier as 'antipathy and sympathy'.[41]

Emotions enter our soul through the gateways connected to our bodily experience and the sense of self derived from that; feelings arise when our spirits are active in our soul. The undefended heart exploration on page 160, is a tool which enables us to consciously choose love as a healthy starting and concluding point of working with emotions.

In his search to find a healthy way for actors to access the whole range of emotions, Chekhov distinguished between the raw emotion which remains dependent on the actor's subjective state of soul, and what he called *artistic feeling*.

Qualities and sensations

The commonly accepted approach to access truthful emotion was formulated first by Constantin Stanislavski (1863–1938). Variously called 'personal emotional recall' or 'affective memory', it requires actors to reproduce a situation or moment in their own lives when they experienced the 'same' emotion their artistic instinct tells them that a character must 'feel'.

Chekhov acknowledged the genius of Stanislavski and his debt to him, but saw how emotion called forth in this way tied a character to the actor's personal biography, not allowing it an independent life, and encouraging the actor to always play him/herself. He knew first hand, the unhealthy consequences of a conscious excavation of his own subjective, emotional material; how it could play havoc with the 'permeable membrane' of an actor's sensibilities and blur the boundaries between the sense of one's own self and the character.

He discovered that if we trust, instead, that the soul's experience is carried as *sensation memory* within the body, and move with the quality required, then *the body* will 'remember' the sensation. Movement will release sensation from a well of deep response buried in the cells themselves; a response more potent than any feeling or emotion we can consciously try to recall; a response that has its source in something universal, something like the soul-life which all human beings share.[42]

I play a sad character. Instead of being sad myself, or *trying* to feel sad, or trying to reproduce a moment in my life when I was sad, I trust my body knows how to move *sadly*. I focus now on *moving sadly* until every limb and muscle, every cell of me is moving with this quality. Then, almost without realizing, I become aware of a particular sensation permeating me. It is sadness. I have not tried to 'feel' it, nor had to squeeze it from my actor's soul in some self-conscious way. I invited it and it has come to visit me.

The sensation that arises when I *move sadly* has an objective truth. It is not my *idea* of sadness. Nor is it limited to my remembering a circumstance that may have no relevance to my character's experience. Because I focus on the way I *move* rather than the way I *feel*, the sensations that arise permeate my instrument. This means I can control the use I make of them and radiate their substance to my fellow players and the audience.

Here is a way to practise this process. If we name the quality with which we wish to move in the form of an adverb it facilitates the sense of 'doing' it. Here is a selection of qualities:

sadly	*cautiously*	*anxiously*
suspiciously	*trustingly*	*threateningly*

confidently   *arrogantly*   *dominatingly*
nostalgically   *regretfully*   *despairingly*
hopefully   *compassionately*   *wearily*
exhaustedly   *enthusiastically*   *frustratedly*
tentatively   *joyfully*   *sneakily*

Quality & sensation exploration 1

1. Stand in a state of 'neutral availability'.
2. Move your right hand with the chosen quality. For example: sadly.
3. Move your whole arm sadly. Lift it above your head, then lower it, sadly.
4. Repeat the process with your left hand and arm.
5. Move your left foot sadly, then your right.
6. Let the sensation permeate your legs, and move them sadly.
7. Move your whole body sadly.
8. When you sense your whole body permeated with sensation, alternate between the levels (10–1). If the sensation weakens in any part of your body, focus again on moving that part sadly.
9. Sustain the sensation and carry out some simple actions: sitting, kneeling, standing, lying down, picking up an object, handling it, opening and closing doors or windows, adjusting drapes, etc.
10. Say a simple word like 'yes' or 'no' or 'maybe'.
11. Return to full-bodied movement, then to standing. Consciously decide to end. Release the quality in whatever way frees you from it: shake it off, stretch, etc.

Quality & sensation exploration 2 (partner work)

When you can move through the whole process confidently, in a range of qualities, work with a partner.

1. A work with a quality and B observe.
2. With gentle touching, B indicate to A whether some part of A's body is not penetrated with the chosen quality.
3. Swap roles.
4. Share your observations.

Quality & sensation exploration 3 – neutral mask

Repeat *explorations* 1 and 2 with a neutral mask. We can easily rely on our face to communicate emotion and be unaware that the rest of our body is not engaged. Wearing a neutral mask acts as an objective barometer. Whatever quality permeates our instrument is magically transmitted through the mask. If, however, we rely on our face to express a quality, the lack of engagement of our body is exposed and the mask 'expresses' nothing. Neutral mask encourages the whole instrument to be a countenance.[*]

Quality & sensation exploration 4

While following the steps for explorations 1–3, different moments or events from life may suggest themselves, or a moment from the life of a character. Such moments are released organically within your body of sensation and become artistic impulses which inspire your improvising and rehearsing. Do not stray outside the field of the sensation you are working with. Focus on continuing to move according to your chosen quality.

Quality & sensation exploration 5

Apply this process to a character.

1. Identify a quality appropriate at a specific moment in a scene, or one fundamental to the character.
2. Warm up your quality and let the sensation that arises be the impulse to explore your character and situation.
3. Once you can access single qualities, identify a sequence of qualities within a speech or scene and practise conscious transitions from one into another.

When I move with a specific *quality*, my body releases in my soul the *sensation* of that quality.[†] This leads me to experience the feeling or emotion in a way that Chekhov called 'artistic'. An emotion accessed in this way presents itself with *ease*. The attempt to permeate our whole instrument imparts to it a sense of *form* and *beauty*. And because it is not separated from our instrument, but integrated with it, it is imbued with an aspect of what Chekhov called a *sense of the whole*.[‡]

---

[*] See the role of discus throwing in the section on the Greek gymnastics in chapter 2.

[†] The integration of *quality and sensation* with the activity of speaking works very beautifully with the exploration of vowels described in chapter 1 of both *The Art of Speech* and *The Integrated Actor*.

[‡] See chapter 5, The Four brothers.

Atmosphere

Feeling and emotion also manifest as *atmosphere*. The stage depends on atmosphere to come alive. It's also important in film, but not the task of actors to create it; there sound effects and music accompany the images and editing manipulates them to produce the atmosphere that impacts the souls of the audience. On stage, atmosphere can only be achieved by the actor. Music, lights and set contribute, but we know that the cleverest and most spectacular effects on stage are empty if the actors cannot radiate an atmosphere.

Imagine these places; each exudes an atmosphere that we can sense and almost touch:

an old ruined castle
the house you grew up in
particular rooms in the house you grew up in
a hospital emergency ward
a dental waiting room
a cathedral
a busy railway station
a pub
a forest, peaceful in the moonlight evening
a forest, dark and terrifying in a storm
the seaside
a graveyard

Through these imaginings, we are aware that place has a soul. Although human beings contribute to, and can create, an atmosphere, it does appear to have a life outside of us and an effect upon us. We know how we react when we walk into a place with an atmosphere; it is larger than what comes from an individual soul.

An event can also generate an atmosphere. Imagine the atmospheres connected with a christening, a wedding or a funeral, an accident, a birth or death.

When atmosphere is present on the stage, we are gripped by the performance. Without it, the stage seems empty and what happens on it, boring. Events take place, the actors may be very busy, but the space is not charged. Technology cannot create an atmosphere, though we use it to try to make up for the lack of it. What has no soul cannot create soul. Atmosphere cannot be recorded on a camera because it is not physically perceptible. Soul can only be perceived by soul.

If the stage is to be charged with it, actors need the skills to create, sustain and then transform an atmosphere. Chekhov suggests the following process:[*]

- Imagine the atmosphere is a presence entering the room.
- When you sense it all around you, respond to it.
- Continue to imagine it outside you in the space, and to respond to it.

These steps require us to be simultaneously conscious of ourselves as centre and periphery, in order to create in both at once.

Atmosphere exploration 1

1. Imagine the room around you filling with some physically discernible sensations, for example: black smoke seeps into the room; the air is filled with gentle rain; buffeted with heavy stormy wind and downpour; the walls drip with dank humidity and the air smells of decay and mould.
2. Imagine and respond to each one in turn.

Atmosphere exploration 2

1. When you can imagine a physical sensation and respond to it, imagine the room filling with different qualities of soul. Imagine sadness, fear, the sort of tension you can 'cut with a knife' seep into the room, through windows, cracks, underneath the door. Or peace, anticipation, joyous expectancy.
2. Imagine and respond to each one in turn.

Atmosphere exploration 3

1. Observe atmospheres in different environments. What sense impressions, feelings or emotions seem to fill each space and help to weave its atmosphere? Observe your psycho-physical response.
2. Back in your rehearsal space, recall each atmosphere and following the steps described, recreate it.
3. Recreate atmospheres from your past which made a strong impression on you.

Atmosphere exploration 4 (group work)

1. Choose some scenes in plays that have strong atmospheres. For example: the battlements of Elsinore at midnight; the great hall in the House of Capulet as the

---

[*] See chapter 4 of Chekhov's *To the Actor*.

guests arrive; the orchard in the moonlight under Juliet's balcony; the heath where the weird sisters first confront Macbeth; the chamber in the castle where Macbeth and his wife prepare the murder of the king.

2. As a group, build up a description of the many different sense impressions and emotions that contribute to this atmosphere.

3. Follow the process of imagining it slowly fill the space, then respond and move in it together.

4. Speak some text within the atmosphere.

Atmosphere exploration 5 (group work)

Divide into two groups; each group decides on an atmosphere and in turn creates it, while the other watches and identifies it.

Atmosphere exploration 6

Speak simple words within each atmosphere that you create: 'yes', 'no', 'maybe'.

Atmosphere exploration 7 – working with text (group work)

Choose texts that suggest strong atmospheres, create each atmosphere and when you sense it round you, experiment with speaking words. Here are a few examples:

> Break! Break! Break!
> On thy cold grey stones O sea,
> And I wish that my heart could utter
> The thoughts that arise in me.
>
> Tennyson, *In Memoriam.*

> How sweet the moonlight sleeps upon this bank!
> Here will we sit and let the sound of music
> Creep in our ears. Soft stillness and the night
> Become the touches of sweet harmony ...
>
> Shakespeare, *Merchant of Venice.*

Atmosphere exploration 8 – working with text

1. Make use of the processes in explorations 1–4 to create the atmospheres suggested by these texts. Speak each text within its atmosphere.

> The winter evening settles down
> With smell of steaks in passageways,
> Six o'clock.
> The burnt out ends of smoky days.
> And now a gusty shower wraps
> The grimy scraps

Of withered leaves about your feet
And newspapers from vacant lots;
The showers beat
On broken blinds and chimney-pots,
And at the corner of the street
A lonely cab-horse steams and stamps.
And then the lighting of the lamps.

The morning comes to consciousness
Of faint stale smells of beer
From the sawdust-trampled street
With all its muddy feet that press
To early coffee stands.

TS Eliot, *Preludes*

Here is no water but only rock
Rock and no water and the sandy road
The road winding above among the mountains
Which are mountains of rock without water
If there were water we should stop and drink...
Sweat is dry and feet are in the sand
If there were only water amongst the rock...
There is not even silence in the mountains...
But dry sterile thunder without rain
There is not even solitude in the mountains
But red sullen faces sneer and snarl
From doors of mud cracked houses

TS Eliot, *The Wasteland*

And now there came both mist and snow,
And it grew wondrous cold:
And ice, mast-high, came floating by
As green as emerald.

And through the drifts the snowy clifts
Did send a dismal sheen:
Nor shapes of men nor beasts we ken—
The ice was all between.

The ice was here, the ice was there,
The ice was all around:
It cracked and growled, and roared and howled
Like noises in a swound!

S T Coleridge, *The Ancient Mariner*

1. Choose other passages of poetry or prose that evoke strong atmospheres.
2. Work with a partner to create each atmosphere in turn. How does the atmosphere affect your meeting? Exchange the practice dialogue: *I didn't expect etc. . . .*
3. Work with a group and create each atmosphere. How does it affect your interaction? Where the atmosphere is based on text exchange the words within each atmosphere.*

---

*See chapter 6, Ensemble.

Incorporating objects: stick, ball & veil

We know that when we incorporate an animal,[*] we experience a different inwardness; a rich immediacy of bodily sensation delivers insights from a realm of inspiration that we cannot access through the intellect.

Now we explore the potential of an object to stir our inner life. Incorporating objects is another way to release a range of inner states, which liberate us from the repertoire of our familiar selves.

As with an animal, when we incorporate the shape and qualities of any simple object, we concentrate a single aspect of our souls. This creates a boundary within our range of responses and on its own, leads to the one-sided sorts of characters, or caricatures appropriate to plays which require a broader style. However, when integrated with our other choices, such extremities contribute a layer to more subtle and deeply textured characters.

To illustrate the range of possibilities, Chekhov chose three objects: stick, ball and veil. Their contrasts open a doorway into three fundamental types of character which bear some resemblance to the thinking, feeling and the willing types considered earlier, but now in eccentric and glorious distortion.

Incorporating objects exploration 1
Follow the process with stick; then ball; then veil. The order does not matter.

1. Pick up the object (stick, ball or veil) and play with it. Explore its shape and qualities, the different ways it moves, is moved, its functions, etc.
2. Still playing with the object, incorporate its qualities.
3. Let go of the object and focus on 'becoming' it.
4. Explore the range of qualities and functions you observed. Don't be afraid to make this as extreme as your own body can allow. The more extreme the outer shape, the more intense the inner body of sensation; how it 'feels' to be *inside* such a body.
5. Relish the characters your body of sensation inspires in you; perhaps they seem exaggerated or extreme, but you are exercising the capacity to change your inner life by metamorphosing your outer shape.

When I was training in New York, the wildest, most exaggerated characters appeared in the streets around me on a daily basis. They were unconscious of being anything but 'normal' and the crowd of New Yorkers were oblivious to the fact that there was anyone remarkable amongst them.

---

[*] See page 168.

Incorporating objects exploration 2

Once you are confident in working with the object, use your imagination to remind your body of the object's qualities.

1. Warm up, incorporating one of the objects and developing its 'character'.
2. After experimenting with your character in imaginary situations, take him/her to a real supermarket to do the weekly shopping. Let your character decide what 'you' put into the trolley. Sustain your character as you go through the check-out.

Incorporating objects exploration 3 (group work)

1. Warm up. Incorporate your object of choice and with whatever character evolves begin to interact with others.
2. Improvise. What happens when stick, ball and veil types get together?

Incorporating objects exploration 4 (group work)

1. Warm up to each object and divide into groups of three.
2. Each explore each choice in turn so that the three types of 'character' are always present in the space together. After some open-ended interaction, improvise specific situations: a reunion of old class mates in a restaurant, being trapped in a lift, etc.
3. Swap roles until each member of the group has had a turn at each character-type.

Incorporating objects in practice

My solo performance of *King Lear*, required me to create ten characters; three women, seven men. I knew from initial feedback that, overall, the characters were working well, except I could not differentiate sufficiently between the two older men, Lear himself and Gloucester, both central to my artistic vision of the play. Chekhov's tools had helped me excavate the depth of their psychologies and certain aspects of their physicality were present, but the key to identify their different shapes eluded me. Then, I was inspired to work with stick and ball.

Incorporating these two simple objects was not what I would have guessed would provide the missing element for such important characters; but clarity of shape was needed by an audience in scenes where dialogue between the Earl of Gloucester and the king alternated frequently, sometimes in quick succession.

It enabled me to make the quick transitions not only with outward clarity but with a clarity of inward definition, not shallow but profound. And this is what I had not bargained for: the body of sensation arising in response to taking on those outer

shapes — stick for Lear and ball for Gloucester — when exposed to the other preparation, underwent an unexpected transformation. The resulting interactions of the
many layers led to revelations in my understanding of the characters and of their
journeys. These choices fed into and reorganized the other elements into a truthful
whole.[*]

A galvanising integration of our pre-existent work on a character by the addition
of another choice confirms its rightness. The inspiration we receive when the
choices we have made begin to 'work' increasingly becomes our benchmark for
artistic progress in a role. It's what we begin to expect and rely upon from
Chekhov's legacy.

Relation to speaking
Incorporating objects leads to increased flexibility within our psycho-physical practice
and awareness. Full-bodied engagement allows us to play with voice and speech
extremities without caricature or harm to our instrument. If vocal character is to arise
healthily and not be forced into the voice by distortion, then the vocal organs must
achieve their necessary tensions not by manipulating them in isolation from the whole
but from their participation in a totally attuned instrument.[†]

Incorporating objects exploration 5 – Speech-exploration
We can enjoy discovering what sort of voice emerges from extreme body shapes. Allow
stick, ball or veil to organize your bodily awareness, and investigate which region of
your vocal instrument awakens.

1. Warm up with your choice of object.
2. Speak a few simple words and pay attention to which of your speech organs are
   stimulated to be active; lips, teeth, tongue, hard or soft palate?
3. What tendencies of voice or speech emerge?
4. Which consonants and vowels suggest themselves?
5. Repeat steps 1–4 with the other objects.

Incorporating objects exploration 6 – Speech-exploration
Stick, ball and *veil* inspired the following Speech-explorations. They require full-bodied
preparation as a strong foundation for creating vocal character. Use the steps of
exploration 1 to warm up each in turn.

---

[*] An exploration of the character creations for *King Lear* can be found in Book 3.
[†] See *The Art of Speech.*

Stick

Warm up 'stick' before you speak. Use staccato exercise *flick a stick* to warm up your voice.[*] Then experiment with:

> See me! splintered from a tree.
> What a thin stick I be!
> Straight and true.
> Some say my feeling's weak,
> I let my reason lead,
> Elegant, stiff and cold
> It's up to you.

Ball

Warm up 'ball' before you speak. Vary the number and speed of bounces according to the size of ball.

> Round and warm/small
> I'm a ball.
> I can roll down the hall
> Or I can bounce, bounce, bounce, bounce … etc.

Veil

Warm up 'veil' before you speak.

> Soft as silk, I'm a veil
> Wafting everywhere.
> I wave to you my darling — over there!

Incorporating objects exploration 7

1. Can the archetype of stick, ball or veil be layered into any of the complex characters you have created?
2. If one suggests itself, after your full-bodied preparation, allow your sensation body to inspire you. Let your stick, ball or veil tendencies weave in and out of your other choices until they integrate with the existing character.

Working with other objects

Apply this process to any object. Play with it, get to know its qualities and incorporate them. Once you have 'become' the object, pay attention to the inner life released within

---

[*] See page 110.

its outer form. Perhaps it suggests a character or an aspect of a character. Allow it to develop. Any object can inspire artistic impulses, but here are some to start you off:

knife	*sword*
feather duster	*comfortable armchair*
stiff backed chair	*toothbrush*
hose	*torch/flashlight*
needle	*sponge*
sparkler	*fire-cracker*

Once you are secure in your ability to sustain the level of sensation aroused by full-bodied preparation, experiment with levels (10–1). Can you radiate the inwardness aroused by incorporating sword or feather duster, for example, without revealing how you have achieved it (your actor's secret)? Improvise some meetings between characters and play with, *'I didn't expect to see you here today . . .'.*[*]

---

[*] See page 93, Expansion and contraction exploration 7 – working with text.

The Sphinx

We have considered the Sphinx in both its forms: distorted monster and benign. We have explored the archetypal centres in relation to thinking, will and feeling and considered the connection of our human soul to souls of animals. With this in mind let us look again at the Sphinx.

Lion

We could express another difference between feelings and emotions by saying that emotions happen, but feelings must be *won*. Our I AM transforms emotion into feeling by consciously developing the chakra of our heart. This ennobling of our heart forces has sometimes been imagined as the transformation of the lion from the beast of prey to the noble king who rules the forest wild. The lion-king, not ruled by but ruler of emotion, can at last lay down beside the lamb.

Shakespeare hints at this in *A Midsummer Night's Dream* when Bottom offers, if he is allowed to play the lion, to roar 'as 'twere any nightingale', so as not to terrify the ladies. Blake depicts this transformed lion, weeping 'tears of gold', in his poem 'Night' from *Songs of Innocence*. CS Lewis in *The Chronicles of Narnia* has given us the lion, Aslan; he too demonstrates the awesome power of emotions which could tear the soul to pieces but are transformed into moral power by the I AM.

Bull

We can connect our capacity for action with the bull aspect of the Sphinx. The sexual potency, for which the bull is celebrated, relates to the creative power of the will, the Brahma aspect of the godhead. The maddened bull ('mad as a bull') wreaks destructive havoc and relates to the Shiva aspect of the will. Hathor, the nurturing Egyptian goddess, the sacred cow of India, the eternal cycle of digestion and the cosmic milk that nourishes, relate to the Vishnu aspect of the godhead; the maintainer and preserver. The ox has been valued for its steadfast will channelled into earthly labour. Yet the will can also sink into the lethargy, embodied in the limbs of the hippopotamus as depicted in the image from the *Egyptian Book of the Dead*.[*]

Vladimir and Estragon in Samuel Beckett's *Waiting for Godot*, demonstrate the hippopotamus aspect of the will; limbs sunk beneath the muddy waters and reeds of meaningless existence, where life is absurd and any action futile, they can scarcely find the will to move. The final moment of the play reveals them still paralysed by the same desperate boredom as the opening scene reveals. Their final words: '*Yes, let's go*'. The final stage direction: They do not move.

---

[*] See illustration on page 14.

Yet the hippopotamus can also be a savage killer. Eugène Ionesco, in his play *Rhinoceros*, depicts the destructive forces of the will not harmonized and integrated with our thinking and our feeling functions. Without a human face, they charge unconsciously through city streets, trampling the civilized veneer of our society, recruiting everyone to join the herd mentality.

Eagle

In *Love's Labour's Lost*, Shakespeare depicts the kingdom of the brilliant mind, a world where intellect and wit hold sway. Determined to banish any possibility the heart should enter learning's territory and thus obstruct its single-minded intellectual pursuit, the King of Navarre decrees that *no woman shall come within a mile of my court . . . on pain of losing her tongue.* In *Titus Andronicus* Shakespeare shows us the reality of that atrocity when Lavinia's tongue is cut out. How easily the intellect can ignore the horror and pass such a glib decree.

Fortunately, in *Love's Labour's Lost*, Shakespeare lets us witness the absurdity of what the four earnest seekers after truth intend. They cannot long exist without the love their clever heads dismiss as interference to 'true' learning and almost before the ink is dry on the agreed conditions of their vows, their hearts 'betray' them. In a master stroke, Shakespeare indicates a truer learning which includes the heart. Berowne, the cleverest of the four, is issued a challenge by his love: if he would marry her he must spend a year in a hospice and demonstrate that his intelligence and wit can serve the sick and dying.

In this play, Shakespeare explores the challenges we face when we value our intellect exclusively. With its centre in the head, the thinking function of our soul has been embodied in the eagle aspect of the sphinx. Its wings enable it to soar above the earth, surveying vistas and perspectives from a distant height that cannot be seen below. From there, aided by extraordinary clarity of vision, it can hone in on a tiny detail, on anything that moves, then plummet from the sky to swoop with unerring accuracy on its prey. Its sharp beak and claws can then dismember and dissect the living creature.

How awesome are the eagle's attributes! How terrifying is its singular pursuit of the vulnerable and its power to demolish what cannot withstand its onslaught. How much in need of love to balance and redeem its powers! How blessed when our brilliant minds can have a human face. Then can we agree with Hamlet when he says, 'What a piece of work is man, how noble in reason . . .'

The human face

These images serve as inspiration for an actor's process, providing rich material for improvising and exploring how to draw upon these forces in the service of our art.

They enlarge the mythic context within which we understand and work not only upon specific characters, but also our development as actors. We can layer archetypal centres with explorations of these archetypal beasts. We can explore, by working with our actor's centre,[*] the Sphinx's human face; the I AM that integrates the beasts within us.

---

[*] See pages 119 and 157.

Right and left: understanding and emotion

In recent years there has been much research and discussion about 'left and right brain'. It's now clear that, contrary to what was thought for many years, our brains demonstrate remarkable plasticity. Nevertheless there is a tendency for different functions to be centred in the left or right sides of our brain, which results in a fundamental difference in functioning between the left and right poles of our psycho-physical constitution.[43]

Rudolf Steiner pointed out that actors and directors need to cultivate a sensitivity to left/right polarity.[*] What an audience experiences when a scene is acted on their left or right will be significantly different. An event experienced in left or heart space (right brain function) will engage their feelings and emotions. An event experienced in right space (left brain function) will engage their interest and understanding.

Actors can develop an organ to perceive such nuances, enabling them to sense, for example, where to place themselves on stage or in relation to another character. Is it more important at this moment in the play for an audience to connect through their emotions or to comprehend? Bertolt Brecht, another influential figure in the theatre of the last century, was centrally concerned with this question.[44]

If we want to play creatively with the possibilities of left and right and not impose them dogmatically, we need to cultivate an instinct for how these two poles of consciousness affect relationships in space: between the actors, the characters, and between the audience and actors.

Right & left exploration 1 (partner work)

Try these simple experiments enough and you will cultivate awareness.

1. Walk past each other, alternating left and right and observe whether you respond differently on either side.
2. Expand your interactions, and exchange *I didn't expect to see you here today*, etc., changing sides, observing your responses.[†]

Right & left exploration 2

Choose a moment of emotional intensity either from a text you are working on or improvised, and play it on each side of an audience of colleagues. Invite and share responses.

---

[*] See Steiner's *Speech and Drama* lectures.

[†] See page 93. Also the gestures and dynamics suggested in chapter 5 provide many examples to play with.

Right & left exploration 3

Choose a moment that requires our understanding either from a text you are working on or improvised, and play it on each side of an audience of colleagues. Invite and share responses.

The 12 senses

Steiner invites us to think of twelve gateways to perception (senses) including the commonly regarded five.[*] Without turning this into a dogmatic scheme, we can recognize how fundamental to our explorations of the body are the senses of life, movement, touch and balance. How often we call upon sensations of resistance (touch) to experience our body. How often the sensations of movement, life and balance inform us that our bodies are not lifeless lumps enclosed in bags of skin, but living forms.

We do not ordinarily connect sensations mediated through these senses to the feelings or emotions we commonly associate with our souls. And yet our language indicates that at some instinctive level we recognize that these more physical sensations are intimately bound to our life of feelings and emotions. We speak of being moved, deeply moved or of the power to move another's soul. We speak of touching someone's soul or an experience that touches us, of someone's heart made hard or soft. We sense how grief or sorrow drains the life from us while joy renews it. We speak of someone who is balanced or unbalanced in relation to the mastery of their emotions and integration with their will and thinking.

These expressions reflect the powerful connections between this first group of senses and our feeling and emotion. Yet the correspondences they draw attention to, though profound, are not specific. When we move on to the second group of senses (smell, taste, sight and warmth), the range of correspondences explodes. It leads us into such a rich and detailed exploration of what we normally refer to as our soul that we must agree with Stanislavski who recognized that sensory recall was a powerful tool for training actors to access emotion.

Across cultures and traditions, texts describing mystical experience demonstrate the intimate connection of physical sensation to experiences of the soul and spirit. The language of *The Song of Solomon,* for instance, has permeated souls connected to the Judaic-Christian stream throughout the ages with this fusion of sensation, feeling and emotion.

From the Song of Solomon

Hearing	The voice of my beloved!
Movement	Behold he comes,
	leaping upon the mountains,
	bounding over the hills
Balance	Behold. There he stands behind our wall

---

[*] See the Terms of reference, page 44.

Warmth	For lo the winter is past,
Life	the flowers appear on the earth …
Thought	Upon my bed by night
	I sought him whom my soul loves;
	I will seek him whom my soul loves.
	Have you seen him whom my soul loves?
Sight	You have ravished my heart with a glance of your eyes
	with one jewel of your necklace
Smell	How sweet is your love, my sister, my bride!
	How much better is your love than wine,
	and the fragrance of your oils than any spice!
Taste	Your lips distil nectar, my bride;
	honey and milk are under your tongue;
Smell	the scent of your garments is like
	the scent of Lebanon …
Touch	O that his left hand were under my head,
	And that his right hand embraced me …
	I had bathed my feet.
	How could I soil them?
Hearing	Hark! My beloved is knocking …
Word	His speech is most sweet …
'I'	This is my beloved, this is my friend

The Song of Solomon (an abridged excerpt)

Taste, smell, warmth and sight

Shakespeare's language is so filled with words employing these four senses to communicate emotion that I can find no better way to make my point.

Taste[*]

Metaphors of sweet, sour and bitter indicate the deep connection between our taste sensations and emotion; we speak of someone as a sweet or sour or bitter person, of our own experience, our tears, our memories, our present state of soul. We speak of someone else as the 'salt of the earth'. A sense of failure tastes like ashes in our mouths, while success tastes sweet. We also recognize how too much sweetness cloys.

Orsino from *Twelfth Night*:

If music be the food of love, play on:
Give me excess of it, that surfeiting,
The appetite may sicken and so die.

---

[*] See also *The Integrated Actor*, chapter, Relationship of our threefold instrument to character and style.

Leontes from *A Winter's Tale* as he beholds the statue of the wife he thinks is dead:

> For this affliction has a taste as sweet
> As any cordial comfort . . .

Macbeth, on the other hand, has *supp'd full with horrors*, and tells us he has *almost forgot the taste of fears*.

The angel in the *Book of Revelation*, handing John the scroll to eat, instructs him that as his soul digests its wisdom:

> [It] will be bitter to your stomach, but sweet as honey to your mouth.

Smell

Closely allied to our sense of taste is smell. They often work together, smell informing us whether we want to taste or not. In the following examples, we cannot help but notice how our sense of smell is connected with feelings of morality.

Claudius from *Hamlet*:

> O, my offence is rank. It smells to heaven.

Shakespeare, *sonnet*:

> Lilies that fester smell far worse than weeds.

Lady Macbeth from *Macbeth*:

> Yet, here's the smell of blood still. All the perfumes in Arabia will not sweeten this little hand.

Othello stooping over Desdemona before killing her, *Othello*:

> I'll smell it on the tree.
> O balmy breath, that dost almost persuade
> Justice to break her sword...

Regan from *King Lear*, after blinding Gloucester:

> Go and let him smell his way to Dover.

In this last example, a depth of horror at the violation of the moral order is aroused in the hearer almost as a consequence of the unadorned crassness of that tiny verb 'smell'. It shocks us, forcing us to recognize with Gloucester the evil threatening to suffocate the earth.

Warmth

Our sense of warmth informs us of the temperature outside us or within our bodies. It registers emotions equally on its thermometer, informing us if someone is a warm or cold-hearted person or of their emotional temperature in a specific situation.

Juliet from *Romeo and Juliet*:

I have a faint cold fear that almost freezes up my sense of life.

Leontes, in *The Winter's Tale*, first registers his obsessive and unfounded jealousy as a rise in temperature. Is it his own or what he thinks he witnesses within his wife, Hermione?

Too hot, too hot!

And, at the end of the play, when the statue of Hermione appears to waken, it is not just a body come to life Leontes celebrates and kisses, but her soul he senses.

O, she's warm.

We also 'burn with passion' and depict the damned in hell as burning in everlasting flames of torment. No less that hell of icy wasteland where the soul whose heart has frozen languishes in regions no warmth can penetrate. Claudio from *Measure for Measure*:

Ay, but to die, and go we know not where;
To lie in cold obstruction and to rot;
The sensible warm motion to become
A kneaded clod; and the delighted spirit
To bathe in fiery floods, or to reside
In thrilling region of thick-ribbed ice ...

Sight

If I see something with my own eyes it must be true! Yet, no other sense can so deceive us and tempt us to confuse appearance with reality.

Tell me where is fancy bred,
Or in the heart or in the head?

It is engendred in the eyes,
With gazing fed; and fancy dies
In the cradle where it lies ...

From a song from *Merchant of Venice*

Our sense of sight is often linked with our confusion over which emotions we can trust. Romantic love can seem so real because it is intense and yet it often proves ephemeral. In *A Midsummer Night's Dream*, Shakespeare depicts it as the consequence of juice from the flower known as 'Love in Idleness' being rubbed into the victim's eyes. This causes man or woman to fall in love with the semblance or appearance of the very first person who should come along, conforming it to what their soul desires. Shakespeare compares such love, bred in idleness, or without the active agency of s/he who loves, to love which is muscular, which works to reach true vision of the other and maintain it. That is the love:

> ... which looks on tempests and is never shaken.

Shakespeare, sonnet

We negotiate a path between the sight of that which is illusory, the emotions that deceive our sight, and the dishonesty that prevents us seeing what is true. Lady Macbeth calls on the dark to hide her attempt to kill the king. It is not only heaven but herself that she does not want to see what she is doing:

> That my keen eye see not the wound it makes
> Nor heaven peep through the blanket of the dark
> To cry: Hold! Hold!

And, as Viola from *Twelfth Night* discovers when she pierces Olivia's defensive veil of arrogance, we can also see the truth behind appearances:

> I see you what you are. You are too proud.

Though having eyes we can be blind and thus misled, yet being blinded we can learn to truly see. Lear to Gloucester in *King Lear*:

> A man may see how this world goes with no eyes.
> Look with thine ears.

Sight can separate us from reality or, piercing through the veil, reveal a deeper truth. But breaking through the semblance of material perception can jumble up our senses, leaving us disoriented. Bottom feels this strongly when he wakes up from his vision of the elemental beings working in the world of nature.

> The eye of man hath not heard, the ear of man hath not seen, man's hand is not able to taste, his tongue to conceive, nor his heart to report what my dream was.

A Midsummer Night's Dream, Shakespeare

When we consider the senses through which we can perceive the spirit: hearing, word, thought and I, Shakespeare indicates that we cross the threshold between soul and spirit when we shift from sight to hearing. Lorenzo from *Merchant of Venice*:

> Look how the floor of heaven
> Is thick inlaid with patines of bright gold.
> There's not the smallest orb, which thou beholds't
> But in his motion, like an angel sings,
> Still quiring to the young eyed cherubin.
> Such harmony is in immortal souls
> But whilst the muddy vesture of decay
> Doth grossly close us in, we cannot hear it.

These rich examples of sensory experience awaken our appreciation of the depth such work contains. What actors traditionally do with sensory recall, building on the work of Stanislavski, enables them to accurately reproduce the minute physical particulars that make a naturalistic style believable. The above consideration of the senses expands the field of sensory recall, enabling us to deepen and enhance our practice.

Bridge to chapter 4

Dr Dysart, the psychiatrist in Peter Shaffer's drama *Equus*, contemplates the mystery of why the boy sent to him for treatment for the crime of blinding horses in a stable, acted as he did.

> It asks questions I've avoided all my professional life. A child is born into a world of phenomena all equal in their power to enslave. It sniffs — it sucks — it strokes its eyes over the whole uncomfortable range. Suddenly one strikes. Why? Moments snap together like magnets, forging a chain of shackles. Why? I can trace them. I can even, with time, pull them apart again. But why, at the start, they were ever magnetized at all — just those particular moments of experience and no others — I don't know. *And nor does anyone else.* Yet if I don't know — if I can never know that — then what am I doing here? I don't mean clinically doing or socially doing — I mean fundamentally! These questions, these Whys, are fundamental — yet they have no place in a consulting room. So then, do I? ... This is the feeling more and more with me — No Place. Displacement ... 'Account for me,' says staring Equus. 'First account for Me!'

Dysart puts his finger on a central question for our time and for the actor. Can we, or any characters we play, be reduced to the sum of the disparate sensations and emotions we display? Or is there a 'someone' who organizes those experiences, *intending them*, and then forgetting that it did; attracting them into its field, endowing them with meaning quite specific to that self? Dysart's training had not taught him to approach this question. Yet the very limits that his training set to what can be allowed as *real*, produced the question that takes us to the threshold between soul and spirit.

We have explored the spectrum of experience connected to our soul, in terms useful to an actor. Our exploration has provided tools that enable us to access the souls of characters we play and enrich our understanding of their lives. Yet a further step is needed if the actor wants to know and reveal the character itself. Many would regard this as their central work, yet without the proper tools, the self of the character remains a nebulous identity that actors can at most hope their luck and instinctive talent will enable them to grasp and manifest. Once again, Chekhov offers us a reliable pathway by placing this highest goal of the actor's art in the context of spirit.

Spirit is not new to us. We have constantly considered how the I AM interacts with soul and body, since these are the garments it inhabits. No aspect of this methodology can be truly experienced without participation of the spirit. Now though, with Chekhov's guidance, we approach the spirit in its own domain and humbly investigate the origin and purpose of every sacred human journey. We have arrived at the mystery of character.

Chapter 4

Spirit

I am the Self
abiding in the hearts of all beings . . .
I am the source of the forth going
of the whole universe
and likewise the place of its dissolving.
There is nought whatsoever higher than I . . .
All this is threads on me
as rows of pearls on a string

Spirit and the creation of character

In his autobiography, *Confessions of an Actor*, Lawrence Olivier tells of a seminal experience early on in his career. He was frustrated playing Sergius in Shaw's *Arms and the Man*. He knew that he was just not 'getting it', especially after he received a particularly negative review. His friend, the great director Tyrone Guthrie, offered his honest opinion and Olivier invited his advice. Guthrie asked him if he loved his character. Olivier was startled by the question and realised he disliked the character intensely. Guthrie told him: 'Well, of course, if you can't love him, you'll never be any good at him, will you?' and Olivier wrote, 'I received the richest pearl of advice in my life.'

The tools we have worked with until now inform us of the complex interactions between soul and body which reveal many aspects of a character. But what is 'character'?

A human being is not a set of attributes. We are impressed by the skill with which a Rembrandt or a Leonardo depict myriad details; hair and eyelashes, colour of eye and skin, the structure of the cheekbones, etc. But what moves us is that through those details, a *being* looks at us. So too does a great actor convince us that a character is not a sum of cleverly depicted details, fragments of behaviour, but a self, a 'real' human being.

The capacity to sense this 'self' or 'I' of the other is no less a sense, than is our sense of smell and can be as consciously enhanced and trained as any other of our senses. To prepare a context for such training, we consider two seminal myths connected with the origins of drama in our Western culture. Both tell a story of death and dismemberment and the journey that leads to resurrection and to wholeness.[45] The first was celebrated in the passion play performed in Ancient Egypt at Abydos; the second in Ancient Greece at the mystery centre of Eleusis.

The Abydos Passion Play

The ritual enactment in ancient Egypt of the death and resurrection of Osiris is often cited in history of theatre textbooks as the source of Western drama.[46] Performed each year by priests within the Temple at Abydos, it was, in part, to celebrate the fertility resulting from the annual flooding of the Nile. There are no extant records of the text nor of what took place within the temple but the *Stela* of *Ikhernofret* does give some detailed information about aspects of the celebration in which the whole community participated.[47] In the progression within which sacred ritual evolved into the theatre, this passion of the god Osiris has widely been assumed to be the ancestor of Western drama.[48]

The enacted rituals told the story of the jealousy of the evil god Set towards his brother/god, Osiris. Set's determination to destroy his brother is an archetype enacted over and again, not only through the course of history, but in the content of drama through the ages. We need only think of *Hamlet*.

Set's first attempt is rendered unsuccessful through the faithfulness of Isis who rescues the body of Osiris, her husband/brother, and brings him back to life. Later versions of the story tell how Set tries again to kill his brother. This time he dismembers him, scattering the pieces of his body throughout Egypt. Once again, the goddess searches faithfully. She finds the pieces, assembles them and, through her healing ministrations, restores her lord to wholeness and conceives with him their child Horus. In some accounts, their son Horus, not bound to a linear experience of time, aids her in this search and then pursues the evil one to exact revenge upon his father's murderer.

The Mystery Drama of Eleusis

The myth that formed the basis of the ritual enactment at Eleusis, just outside of Athens, tells the story of the goddesses Persephone and Demeter and their relationship to the god, Dionysus. Once again, due to strict conditions that demanded secrecy from those participating, we have no records of what took place within the temple but it is assumed from what is known of the public rituals in which the aspirants took part, that what the priests enacted at the culmination of the Mysteries was the seed from which Greek drama would unfold.

Edouard Schuré, the Alsatian poet, history scholar, dramatist and mystic, felt inspired to write what he imagined to have taken place.[49] In 1911, Rudolf Steiner, who endorsed the integrity of Schuré's vision, supported performances in Munich of a re-enactment of his *Sacred Drama of Eleusis*. The central figure is the Goddess Demeter. We behold her desperate attempts to find her child, Persephone, stolen from Paradise by the Lord of Hades. Having tasted death, Persephone can only be redeemed by one who searches after wisdom, who can follow her down into the realm of darkness and return with her to paradise. There she is destined to be reunited with her bridegroom, Dionysus.

Some versions of the myth depict him as the son of Semele, a mortal mother in union with a god, his father Zeus. Thus in his first manifestation, Dionysus is experienced as both mortal and immortal. Sometimes pictured as a baby who at birth already challenged the supremacy of Zeus, his father and chief among the gods, Dionysus was dismembered by the Titans for his crime of hubris; the arrogance of those who regard themselves as equal to the gods and for which they must be punished. Yet Dionysus was prophesied to be the bridegroom of Persephone; the human soul needing to be rescued from the realm of darkness which the Greeks called Hades.

We see Demeter ascend to the highest realms to plead with Zeus. Through their union, a second Dionysus is conceived who, unlike the first, is not subject to mortality but will be the wholly immortal bridegroom of Persephone. To rescue her, Demeter initiated Triptolemos, Prince of the Royal Family at Eleusis, and sent him down to Hades to bring her daughter back into the realm of light, to be the bride of Dionysus.

According to tradition, Triptolemos became the founding parent of the Eumolpidae family, who guarded this initiation wisdom for 1500 years. As priests, they lived to channel the specific deity each one served. These deities, when invoked, no doubt gave the Mysteries the power for which the regular enactment of the cycles at Eleusis was renowned throughout the ancient world and which changed the consciousness of the aspirants. We know the successful neophytes departed with the certainty of immortality, and lost the fear of death.

We might well regard the preparation by the priest or priestess to channel the divinity they served as the origin of what an actor does today to create or 'build' a character. Many actors have a sense that they are 'channels' who 'receive' their characters and then express them through the instrument of voice and body.

The evolution of Greek drama, to its heights, took place within the comparatively short time that encompasses the first tragedies of Aeschylus and the comedies of Aristophanes. It is well recognized that the characters of early plays were gods or god-like human beings. Only later, characters became decreasingly divine, increasingly 'human'.

Dionysus, the god in whose honour drama festivals were held, embodies this mysterious paradox. In *The Bacchae* by Euripides, for instance, sometimes he manifests as human and sometimes reveals his divinity. Aristophanes used his comedy, *The Frogs*, to thoroughly investigate this paradox of Dionysus' true identity which lies at the very heart of our struggle to be 'human' and continues to bewilder and intrigue us through the ages. Hamlet expresses it like this, 'What should such fellows as I do, crawling between earth and heaven?'

In both myths, the god who was restored to wholeness existed in that wholeness before dismemberment. The feminine aspect embodied in the bride/mother remained faithful to that pre-existent Self. Her knowledge of this Self enabled Isis, patiently, to go in search of the pieces until she could reconstitute the whole. Her commitment to this Self gave Demeter the passion that convinced the highest god to grant it resurrection through their union.

The I AM

Dionysus, the Bridegroom, the I AM or Transpersonal Self

This 'Self' is the *being* great artists are able to reveal; the 'I' or 'I AM' that we can learn to sense. It is the sun, the immortal part of us, which is destined from its centre within each to radiate and permeate the mortal parts of us. Through the dramas of our lives, the I AM gradually integrates the fragments, transforming the sum of qualities into that wholeness from which we sprang and that is, as well, the goal of our exertions.

Recent streams of psychotherapy call this divine part of our nature that wrestles with the 'too, too solid flesh', the *transpersonal self*. This is the being that the Greeks named Dionysus, the true bridegroom of Persephone, our human soul. He works as guardian and guide within our depths and brings about the meetings and events that constitute the lessons which educate our soul and rescues her from Hades/hell.

Is not this very 'crawling between earth and heaven' the content of the great dramas? And though they may not be conscious that this is what they do, nor of how they do it, is not the ability to move us at this existential level what great actors always do instinctively and what makes them great?

We live now in a time when it is valid to enquire how to consciously approach this mystery. How can actors channel, consciously, our human struggle to evolve beyond the 'plant' or 'animal' within our nature and reveal the god?

An actor will be interested in every kind of character, from those who have forgotten the divine aspect of their selves and appear to have lost their way completely, to those who demonstrate the noblest and the highest of what a human being may attain. But at whatever point along the scale of possible development a character appears, as

Guthrie told Olivier, actors who cannot love their characters (as a bridegroom loves his bride), will never be 'any good at it'.

An actor may not 'like' a character, but the 'true bridegroom' is faithful to that soul as Cordelia is to Lear, as Solveig is to Peer Gynt, and as Shakespeare is, who 'marries' all his characters. Such actors create their characters with the same unjudging love of which the poet Dylan Thomas writes in *This Side of the Truth*:

> And all your deeds and words,
> Each truth, each lie,
> Die in unjudging love.

Spirit has been at work in the processes explored till now, transforming soul and body by it own activity into a vessel through which it can express itself more fully. Now we approach directly the training of that sense with which we can perceive the spirit. Clothed in specific qualities of soul and body, the actor works towards a character the audience can recognize as 'real'; a self who, unconsciously or consciously, is somewhere on the long journey to be fully realized; to become the 'piece of work' we call a 'human' being.

I AM exploration 1

Let us first affirm our sense of the one who integrates the sum of qualities and fragments into a whole.

1. Warm-up your heart-centre.[*] When you feel its warmth and light permeate your instrument, gently speak the words aloud, or silently within: I AM.
2. Meet a partner, open your hearts to each other and exchange the words: I AM.

With the 'I' of the actor as our starting point, we use the processes and tools described by Chekhov to cultivate our sense for the 'I' of a character.

---

[*] See pages 137–140.

Objectives

We observe how people look, what they say, that they behave in this way or that, that they tend to be depressed or optimistic, to manifest one of the temperaments, be aggressive, retiring, etc. Such qualities form layers of a richly textured character and can be achieved with tools explored already. But now the actor seeks to perform the deed of Isis; to gather the broken pieces into a gestalt, an integrity of self.

Super-objectives

I contact this core level in myself when I recognize that I come into this world with an intention. I want to experience and learn specific things and if I can make my purpose or objective conscious, I might express it thus: *I want to achieve compassion*, or *I want to learn wisdom*; *I want to make amends for past mistakes*, or *I want to learn the lessons I can only learn by having power* or *wealth* or *by being poor*. Chekhov calls an intention at this over-arching level, the *super-objective*. The super-objective identifies, within the largest context and perspective, the purpose of an individual's life. If we imagine levels or layers of objectives as a set of Russian dolls, the super-objective corresponds to the largest doll.

Other levels of objectives

Inside that doll nestle many gradually decreasing, smaller ones. As an individual's life unfolds, the super-objective translates into many more specific ones. *I want to dominate; make money; make you love me* or *be worthy of your love*; *I want to hurt you so that you experience my pain*; *I want to protect myself; to help you; work with you; be famous; to be president; be an actor, doctor or musician; to be with you; to pay you back; to marry you*, etc. These objectives become, in turn, even more specific. *I want to find that letter; hide this money; meet this person, avoid that one; give you this ring; steal that book; get to the bottom of what's going on*, etc.

Chekhov found a way to take Stanislavski's work with objectives further and considered this the crown of his technique.[*] He called it *psychological gesture* (PG).

PG is the key with which an actor can access and release the energy and emotional dynamic condensed in an objective. A successful PG gathers and organizes all aspects of a character, drawing them into its vortex. To identify, make conscious a character's objective/s an actor has to *think*. The intensity and nuances with which each objective is pursued depend on the *feelings* or *emotions* attached to it and the *actions* undertaken to achieve it.

---

[*] See chapter 5 of *To the Actor* and numerous references in *On the Technique of Acting*.

Psychological gesture

Chekhov gave precise instructions for creating a PG. Yet these were not intended as a formula to replace the actor's individual creative process — what Chekhov called the actor's *creative individuality*.

As with any other tool, the purpose of PG is to open a door to the actor's inspiration, then to provide a process by which that inspiration can be clarified, verified and consolidated in a form that is repeatable, yet capable of evolution. This is achieved if the process is firmly anchored in the psycho-physical technique/s which we can trust on the one hand to access our initial inspiration, and on the other, leave an open door to further insights and discoveries.

Knowing this allows us to explore Chekhov's process without fear that our creativity will be constrained. Therefore, although his formulation of PG involved the following components, we accept whatever our creative impulse offers as a place to begin. As soon as we apply the tools, we plunge into torrents of sensation whose waves we learn to ride; first creating then participating in what we have created.

(a) Through *thinking*, clarify your character's *objective/s*.
(b) Embody each objective in a *gesture* which expresses the *action* undertaken by the character to achieve the objective.
(c) Identify specific *feelings* or *emotions* connected with the character's objective. Apply the process of *qualities and sensations* to access them.[*] Layer them with the gesture.

Gesture

To explore what Chekhov meant by *gesture*, consider the balcony scene in *Romeo and Juliet*. Romeo is too far away from Juliet to touch her, yet inwardly his soul reaches out to her and outwardly his gesture does the same. In this example we see that the outer and the inner gesture coincide. But think of a situation in which someone says, 'I love you' but may mean any of the following: *I want to have you in my power/keep you off my back/push you away/inherit your fortune.* Or perhaps the text states that a character stirs a cup of tea, eats a cucumber like Charlotta in *The Cherry Orchard*, or opens a window. The objective or intention underlying the action might be: *I want to punish you/make you feel guilty/heal your pain/forget my loneliness.* These examples demonstrate more complex moments when we recognize the difference between the words or outer action of a character and the inner dynamics (the subtext) which inform, yet appear disconnected from or even in conflict with the text.

---

[*] See pages 176–179, Qualities and sensations.

For example, at the end of Anton Chekhov's *Cherry Orchard*, Varya and Lopakhin, pushed together and expected to confirm that they will marry, search for a pair of galoshes, look through the window, stare at the furniture, discuss the weather, etc. When we excavate this apparently trivial interaction, we uncover a subtext woven of such contradictory objectives as: *I want to disappear/I want to marry him or her/I want to know what it is I really want/I want to know what I should do/I want to keep my independence/I want someone to care for me, look after me/I want to please my mother or Lyubov/I want to end this whole excruciating farce,* etc. These objectives form a tapestry of invisible gestures and unheard dialogue which constitute the 'real' drama taking place, and which it is the actor's task to reveal.

The first step is to make the invisible gesture, visible. Such gesture is not to be confused with everyday naturalistic gesture. We perceive it only with a kind of 'x-ray' or clairvoyant vision that reveals the deeper life of gesture in our souls which is expressed when we speak of someone as a 'grasping' or a 'giving' soul, for instance, or as one who 'reaches for the stars'. Someone else is 'self-effacing', while another we describe as 'pushy'.

PG exploration 1

It will help to understand the language of these gestures if we identify their purpose or objective with a sentence which begins; 'I want to …' Whenever possible, complete the sentence with an active verb as this inspires us to be concrete in our search for a full-bodied gesture which expresses the objective. It's not important that we 'get it right' immediately, but that we engage in an ongoing process of refinement as we search to match our words exactly with the action which embodies them.

1. Create a gesture for each of these in turn: reaching for the stars, grasping, giving, pushing, and attempting to obscure/hide your face. Involve your whole body in the gesture to become a living sculpture.
2. Express your intention with the words: *I want to grasp/reach for the stars/give myself to the world/push my way through life/hide my face,* etc. Explore how words and movement interact and feed each other. Sometimes speak them inwardly, sometimes aloud.
3. Focus on one. Create the full-bodied gesture, then sustain the sensations as you let the outer gesture fall away and perform ordinary actions such as sitting, standing, opening the door, speaking 'yes' or 'no' or 'maybe'.

We begin to sense how a PG has the power to organize a character's behaviour; for a single word or phrase or line, a speech or scene, or even a whole play. It serves as a magnet, drawing to itself the other choices that we make, integrating them into the wholeness which actors call the *continuity of character*.

A PG is only powerful enough to consistently accomplish this if we first express it full-bodily. To do this, we need to understand Chekhov's concept of an archetypal-gesture.

Archetypal-gesture

Such words as 'embrace' or 'give' or 'hit' propel us instantly towards specific contexts or nuances of feeling and emotion which make it hard to resist the pull into the naturalistic and particular. Therefore, Chekhov suggests it will be easier to understand an archetypal-gesture if we explore such neutral verbs as *push*, *pull*, *lift* and *throw* because these allow us to investigate the very nature of a gesture, in itself.

PG exploration 2 – archetypal-gesture – to push

1. Explore the many different ways of pushing a partner and/or objects.
2. Work by yourself to reproduce the gestures from task 1, their qualities of tension and resistance. What do they have in common that makes them a *push*? What is the essence of *push*?
3. Condense that essence into a full-bodied gesture; a commitment in *space* of feet, legs, torso, hips, arms, hands, shoulders, neck and head.
4. Refine that gesture further into a progression in *time*; including

   (a) preparation to receive the impulse
   (b) beginning
   (c) middle
   (d) completion, which includes sustaining.

This final gesture in which *the essence of an action* is *gathered from the space* around, executed *full-bodily* and then *released back to the space*, is what Chekhov calls an archetypal-gesture. It awakens an inner sensation that we learn to sustain.

PG exploration 3 – archetypal-gesture – to push

These next steps develop the capacity to recreate a gesture inwardly and to radiate it into the space.

1. Perform the archetypal-gesture *push* until you are familiar with the strong inner journey of sensation that accompanies the stages of preparation, execution, completion and sustaining. On our scale of 10–1, this is level 10.
2. Sustain the same level of sensation aroused at level 10 while you reduce the outer gesture to level 5.

3. Now *push* at level 1 or 2, with little or no outer movement but *no reduction of sensation.*
4. Invite feedback from a partner or the class. Can they experience your *inner* gesture?

PG exploration 4 — integrating archetypal-gesture and objective — to push

1. Perform the archetypal-gesture *push* once again. Sustain the sensation aroused by the gesture and radiate it as you walk around the space.
2. When the sensation starts to fade, perform the gesture at level 10 again to reawaken the original intensity.
3. Radiate the inner gesture through different sequences of simple actions; sitting, standing, walking, etc. Return as often as is needed to the outer gesture level 10 to strengthen sensations of the inner gesture. With practice over time, the tiniest degree of outer gesture will arouse in your psychology the full power of the inner gesture and allow you to sustain it.
4. Perform the archetypal-gesture as you speak the word *push*, until the sounds the word is made of and the gesture integrate.

When through full-bodied physical expression we arouse intense sensations and radiate them in the space, this generates on stage (or in rehearsal space) a magnetic 'field' which both audience and fellow actors sense.

When we learn how to create and then to move and interact within such a mutually generated field, the soul substance that surrounds us is so tangible that it reveals the dynamics and subtleties of interaction that determine our relationship. We learn to sense and ride its currents and at the same time, shape them into an artistic form.

PG exploration 5 — integrating gesture and objective — to push (partner work)

1. Perform a full-bodied *push* while playing with the words, *I want to push you away.* Do this several times until naming the objective and expressing it in gesture are integrated.
2. Sustain the sensations as you move around, radiating the objective *I want to push you away.*
3. Meet a partner in the field created by your mutual objectives. Interweave your gestures in varying degrees of outer action, (10–1), working silently at first.
4. Introduce the sentence, *I want to push you away.*
5. Use it as a dialogue and improvise a short exchange. Stay entirely focused on radiating your objective/gesture. Can you sustain it when you meet another? Can you sustain it when you speak?

6. Sustaining your mutual objective, *I want to push you away,* play back and forth between steps 1–5.
7. Exchange your practice-dialogue *I didn't expect to see you here,* etc., in the field you generate together. Include reversing roles.

PG exploration 6 – integrating gesture and objective – to pull, to lift, to throw

Apply the above stages (explorations 2–5) to the actions *pull, lift* and *throw.* In the final stages, here are some of the possible objectives to sustain and radiate:

1. I want to pull you towards me.
2. I want to support you/this cause. I want to raise your spirits/lift you out of despair.
3. I want to throw this idea at you. I want to throw myself at you/on your mercy./I want to throw everything away.

A scenario may suggest itself but scenarios are not the goal. Stay anchored in the sensations generated by renewing of the outer and sustaining of the inner gesture/s. Focus on building the capacity to permeate the substance of the space with an intention/objective and thus to generate a field.

Practising transitions from the outer to the inner action develops 'inner muscles' that enable you to move from objective to objective as you let yourself affect and be affected by your partner.

PG exploration 7 – objective and dialogue (partner work)

1. Improvise with a partner, mixing the various objectives worked with in relation to the archetypal-gestures *push, pull, lift* and *throw.*
2. Move back and forth between the words which name your objectives and the practice dialogue: *I didn't expect to see you here,* etc.
3. Move through the four gestures in degrees from 10–1. The criterion for satisfaction with an inner gesture is the degree to which you can project it in the space. With practice, it will become instinctive to return to some degree of outer gesture when you need to re-awaken the original intensity of your objective.
4. Share feedback with your partner about your ability to permeate the substance of the space with your objectives, and to generate a field.

If we have experienced how *archetypal-gesture* can organize our inwardness by condensing an objective into a single act of integrated potency, we are ready to explore what happens when we layer archetypal-gesture with *quality and sensation.*

PG exploration 8 — integrating gesture with qualities-and-sensations

1. Warm up the quality *cautiously* or *tenderly*.
2. When you are permeated with your chosen quality, perform your archetypal-gesture for push, pull, lift or throw. Pay attention to the body of sensation awakened by *pushing tenderly*, or *throwing cautiously*.
3. Express the sensation in the form of an objective; a sentence beginning with the words, *I want to*...
4. Sustain your objective and carry out some simple actions.
5. Sustain your objective as you interact with a partner. When you sense the impulse to speak, begin by verbalizing your objectives to each other, letting your subtext be the text.
6. Sustain your objectives. Let your subtext disappear below the surface but permeate your practice-dialogue *I didn't expect to see you here*, etc.
7. Experiment with interacting in degrees of outer gesture, 10–1.

When I work with 'pushing tenderly', for instance, I identify the strong sensation it generates as the objective, 'I want to trust you.' For someone else, the same combination might result in the objective, 'I want to free you', for example. There is no experience or name that is the 'right' one. What matters is the potency it has for you. Be patient with the process of naming your sensation precisely. You need not 'get it right' at once. Try different words until you sense a perfect match between the sensation that results from combining quality with archetypal-gesture and the way you name your objective.

PG exploration 9 — integrating gesture with qualities-and-sensations
Now we are ready to expand the range of qualities and gestures we combine.

1. Make a list of actions, for example: slash, punch, twist, point, reach, stroke, slice, embrace, scrape, cover, penetrate, tear, caress, knead, scratch, poke, etc.
2. Make a list of qualities or use the list of qualities in chapter 3.
3. Select one at random from each list and observe what happens when you layer them together.

If we want reliable access to a powerful sensation, we must not bypass the stage of full-bodied preparation. Objectives not turned into concrete actions remain ideas. Only a full-bodied gesture forms the basis for a strong inner one. Only a strong inner gesture can be relied on to consistently transform the space and free the actor from dependency on 'feeling' the emotion.

PG exploration 10 — integrating gesture with qualities-and-sensations

1. Warm up a full-bodied action/archetypal-gesture.
2. Warm up a full-bodied quality.
3. Layer your archetypal-gesture with the quality. Explore this combination and then crystallize it in a single full-bodied gesture.
4. Sustain and renew the gesture until you can identify its inwardness as an objective: *I want to . . .*
5. You have created a PG that expresses an objective. Release the outer gesture and improvise a few simple actions while sustaining your objective.
6. Sustain your objective as you meet a partner. Let your interaction be determined by the subtext woven out of your objectives. Apply the practice-dialogue *I didn't expect to see you here,* etc.
7. Experiment with the range of bodily expression (10–1) and return to your PG if you sense the intensity of your objective weaken.

PG with qualities-and-sensations in practice

When choosing actions to integrate with qualities, don't necessarily combine the obvious. Powerful sensations can result from what the intellect judges an unlikely combination. On one occasion I created an archetypal-gesture from the verb, to slash. From a 'lucky dip', I chose the quality of 'tenderly'. My intellect objected but I did it anyway. The resulting sensation was a profound and unexpected revelation that I was subsequently able to incorporate to powerful effect in my performance of *King Lear.*

Now you know the combination of gesture and quality awakens a sensation you can identify as an objective, you are ready to explore the process in reverse. Begin by identifying your objective, then search for the combination of quality and gesture (PG) that will reliably enable you to access your objective's organizing power.

PG exploration 11 — identifying the objective first

Choose an objective, for example: *I want to dominate/I want to protect.*

1. Guided by your actor's instinct, experiment with qualities and actions until you find a full-bodied gesture that works for you — that awakens a powerful sensation that you want to *dominate* or *protect.* Take note of the precise quality and gesture that achieve this goal and consolidate them, so you can return to them at any time.
2. Having found the PG that expresses your objective, use it to access your objective and to sustain it while you improvise some simple actions.
3. Practise letting go and then returning to it.

4. Explore what arises when you meet a partner in the field created by the interaction of your two objectives.
5. Try the practice- dialogue *I didn't expect to see you here*, etc.
6. Does this PG with its objective apply to any character you are familiar with? Experiment.

Full-bodied gesture practised over time with different qualities and objectives expands the 'body' of our psycho-physical awareness. Our sense of how to move from PG to objective or objective to PG becomes instinctive. Increasingly, we trust the PG's engagement of all our faculties (thinking, will and feeling) to provide artistic impulses on which we can depend.

PG exploration 12 – identifying the objective first

1. Make a list of objectives, for example: *I want to understand you/what is going on, I want to protect myself/you, I want to hide my secret, I want to control the situation, I want to save the world, I want to expose the truth, I want to heal your pain, I want to make you suffer*, etc.
2. Make a PG for each objective you explore.
3. Work with a partner and apply your PGs to your practice-dialogue *I didn't expect to see you here*, etc.

PG exploration 13

1. Choose a character that interests you. Identify some of the character's objectives. Choose one and create a PG that embodies it.
2. Use the PG to explore a moment in the play or story of the character.
3. If the PG inspires words, either from the text or improvised, explore speaking them; do not force them but allow them to be born within the impulse.

How to name the objective

Some practitioners find it useful to begin the sentence identifying an objective with the words: *I want to...*, for example: *I want to push you away*. Some prefer to state it as an action: *I push you away*. For the former, the power of the PG to drive the dialogue or action is greater when the objective is expressed as something not completed and still to be attained. The latter find it helpful to express what they sense is happening.

Each serves a purpose, but in my experience, objectives differ from outcomes. If I have an *objective*, what I want has not yet been achieved. If it has been achieved, can it still be an objective with the power to motivate our action? Yes and no. An objective refers to what a character *intends*, unconsciously or consciously. This may or may not coincide with what the character is doing or accomplishing. In relationship to *pushing*, for example, someone whose behaviour pushes someone else away may have the opposite objective and be trying desperately to win the love or approval of the other character. Of course, we may be touching here on complex or conflicting layers of objectives.

In such a case, it is important to identify that *action* and *objective* differ from each other and that both are necessary. For it is their conflicting dynamics that create the potent field between the characters that brings their interaction to life.

Perhaps we can clarify the confusion in this way. My objective is always future oriented. How I go about achieving my objective is expressed in an action which I am doing NOW. For example: I identify that my character's objective in this moment is 'I want to control the situation'. Now I search for the action which expresses the precise way in which my character works to achieve that objective.

I CRUSH all opposition.

or

I PIERCE or SMASH through the confusion.

or

I STROKE or CARESS away any doubts or uncertainties.

I am convinced the spirit of this psycho-physical approach is undogmatic. What's important is that actors work with what inspires them, to contribute what is needed in the context of what is being shaped. Whether we adopt *I want to push* or *I push*, or a combination of the two, the spirit of our work requires that we put it into action and let this teach us what it will. What we want is something on which we can depend for access to artistic impulses.

Transformation of objectives

Within a speech or scene or play, a character may move from one objective to another and through different levels of objective, or be torn between conflicting objectives. If we want certainty that we can have a clear intention in each moment of performance and translate it into a sequence of precise and powerful, repeatable sensations, then we anchor this journey in a clear progression of PGs. It is a paradox that such certainty offers us not inflexibility precluding further insights and discovery, but a framework within which evolution can occur.

We develop this clear progression of PGs in rehearsal as we consolidate the journey of objectives of our character throughout the play. It is like a full-bodied 'dance' that *delineates* the structure of the inner journey each performance asks of us and, as well, *invokes* it. This underlying dance then manifests in what degree of outer movement

(10–1) is appropriate, according to the style of production. Whatever those require-ments, this full-bodied 'dance' is a potent way to warm up to a performance. To be quiet and make that same journey in your imagination just before the play begins, anchors your concentration in the character's pathway through the play.

PG in scene work

Imagine a whole scene or play rehearsed like this. Actors express their characters' evolving sequence of objectives to each other in full-bodied gesture; an unbroken stream of impulses arises within which they swim, navigate and ride the waves. Directors can work with them to shape a scene out of the complex web of energies and living substance generated in the space between them. Use the range of bodily expression (10–1) to explore the following scene work interactions.

PG exploration 14

1. A and B warm up a PG to express the objective: *I want to push you away.*
2. Approach each other and allow the interaction to unfold, sustaining the objective.

    (a) Explore in silence.
    (b) Use the sentence that names your objective, as your text.
    (c) Let your combined objectives become an evolving subtext as you explore the practice-dialogue: *I didn't expect*, etc.

PG exploration 15

A and B warm up a PG to express the objective: *I want to pull you towards me.*

1. Approach each other and allow the interaction to unfold, sustaining the objective.

    (a) Explore in silence.
    (b) Use the sentence that describes your objective as the text for your dialogue.
    (c) Let your combined objectives become an evolving subtext as you explore the practice-dialogue: *I didn't expect*, etc.

PG exploration 16

1. Warm up your PG. A: *I want to push you away.* B: *I want to pull you towards me.*
2. Approach each other and allow the interaction to unfold, each sustaining your objective.

    (a) Explore in silence.
    (b) Use the sentence that names your objective as your text.

(c) Let your combined objectives become an evolving subtext as you explore the practice-dialogue: *I didn't expect*, etc.

3. Swap objectives and repeat steps a, b and c.

PG exploration 17

1. Warm up your PGs. A: *I want to push you away.* B: *I want to pull you towards me.*
2. Approach each other and allow the interaction to unfold. Allow your partner's objective to influence yours until it changes into the other and you both move back and forth between them.

    (a) Explore in silence
    (b) Use the sentence that names your objective as your text
    (c) Let your combined objectives become an evolving subtext as you explore the practice-dialogue: *I didn't expect*, etc.

3. Swap objectives and repeat steps a, b and c.

PG exploration 18 – Hamlet

Assuming that the text, scene and characters have been explored as suggested in previous chapters, this exploration is for pairs or groups of three of any gender.

1. Unfold the interaction between Hamlet and Rosencrantz/Guildenstern within each combination of objectives described in *PG explorations 14–17*.
2. After playing with this silently, then using the sentence that names your objective as your text, you are ready for A (Hamlet) to speak the *I have of late* on page 283. B and/or C (Rosencrantz and/or Guildenstern) let the subtext arising from the interaction of your gestures determine how you listen to the prince.
3. Swap roles until each has had a turn to speak.

It may surprise you that the interactions arising from the interplay of just these two objectives can provide a satisfying sense of character which acts as a magnet, attracting any other layers you have explored.

Relationship of PG to language

Observe and enjoy the richly textured tapestry of interaction that evolves in an effortless, organic way when characters meet in a space charged with the dynamics, intentions and atmosphere created by PG. The underlying, shifting web of their objectives makes the subtext from which the text arises, tangible. The *speaking actor* then discovers that even heightened or poetic language can be a 'natural' expression of an inner journey. Because such texts are often spoken quickly, in an attempt to make them sound like the language that we use to express everyday experience, the heightened levels of experience embedded in the poetry are obscured.

We gabble words if we cannot sense the space between them is alive and filled with substance. When we work with PG, space is not an emptiness to be ignored and stuffed with syllables, but is charged with interweaving webs of energy. These 'lines of force' are *subtext rendered tangible*. When actors are in this field, they know that they can search for words instead of rushing through them, and that they find them threaded on those lines of force, hiding in those webs of subtext and relationship, waiting to reveal themselves.

PG also solves the problem of the actor/character whose turn it is *to listen*. While Hamlet speaks, Rosencrantz and Guildenstern do not simply wait their turn to speak again. We know they are engaged intensely with their own agenda. Actors using PG to embody their objectives and who listen in a consciously created stream of gesture, contribute no less powerfully to a moment than the one who speaks. Indeed, the character who speaks depends on the one who listens to discover what s/he wants to say and how to say it.

Super-objectives and the actor's creative process
The objectives suggested in the *Hamlet* PG explorations are not intended as pre-scriptive. They are opportunities to create a PG and apply it to a scene. PGs are invitations for the muse to enter our creative process. They provide us with a tool to consolidate what is revealed when we explore and deliver our creation from the vagaries of chance. Yet the creative process cannot be prescribed.

I might receive, in a single flash, an intuition of a character's super-objective. As I explore how to embody it in action, I may find a PG to organize my other insights and discoveries. With another character, I might search for that super-PG and objective through the whole rehearsal process without achieving certainty, but on the way I will discover much that contributes to the character; qualities and moments that compose his/her journey, and objectives specific to and active underneath the surface of those moments. I have experienced that when an insight of the super-PG and objective comes, it is as though before birth I look down on the earth and see what my character intends in coming here. It is the sacred seed from which a whole biography unfolds.

Some characters have lost their way. Their super-objective may have been forgotten for some or much of the journey. Nevertheless, it is this that leads us into the events and meetings necessary to fulfil itself. Our super-objective gives our life integrity and wholeness and makes sense of what, otherwise, seems absurd or meaningless. It provides the continuity by which we recognize that Lear, for instance, is the same character throughout the play. It is the same individual who shows such humility and wisdom in the final scenes, whose arrogance earlier led him to behave so stupidly.

The psycho-physical tools inspire creative impulses from a source deeper than our intellect can access on its own. Yet although they provide ways to circumvent intellectual analysis, the psycho-physical experience is deeply satisfying to that part of us that reasons and that rightly needs to know and understand.

Imaginary body, bizarre body

We have considered that the human body as an archetype, differs from the animal because it's less specialized form makes possible, relatively speaking, a *range* of soul experience and gesture.[*]

Nevertheless, the form of one specific human body, when compared with another, constitutes a certain narrowing of choice; albeit made at another level than we are conscious of in everyday reality. It may be experienced, in some sense, as a limitation. While I am one specific person, tall and skinny, for example, I cannot, at the same time, be a different one, perhaps short and fat. The choice to be one or the other embodies a particular objective which we might express: *I want to see/experience the world from this standpoint or perspective.* In this context, the physical attributes of an individual embody the mystery of destiny. The body is a quite specific vessel chosen by the spirit in order to accomplish its objective.

I may seek to change that body if there is something that I want or need which my present body cannot give me. I may decide to make my body fat or thin in order to protect myself. I may be convinced that a more attractive body or a different kind of nose will bring me happiness or love. I may be conflicted, sensing that I want to be a man and yet find myself inhabiting a woman's body. I may want to be much taller or much shorter than I perceive myself to be.

From this perspective, the body is a strong statement of *intention*. To develop the capacity to change or 'morph' one's shape has profound implications for the actor. Of course, we can wear a wig or false nose or a padded belly. Resorting to external means is sometimes necessary, but psycho-physical transformation is always our ideal. When we attempt, through imagination, to incorporate a body different from our own, we access the inner life of a character; a life of sensations that exclusively awaken in a quite specific physical 'container'.

Many great actors seem able to change shape. Chekhov was one of these and once again, he observed and made his own process conscious. Work with stick, ball and veil shows us the potential of incorporating qualities of objects.[†] Now we learn to work purely with the power of imagination.

If I imagine with sufficient concentration that I'm taller than my measurable height, I can so penetrate my own subtle life/etheric body with consciousness, that I appear taller to someone watching me. Or I can imagine being fatter, thinner or with huge pudgy hands or tiny feet, or long spindly legs or an enormous belly. My imaginations can become bizarre; that I have jelly elbows and a rusty knee, my feet are springs, my

---

[*] See chapter 3.
[†] See pages 184–187.

hands are claws, my head is filled with tiny metal wheels that spin or has become the head of a goat or chicken. The more bizarre the images, the more they provide opportunities for our imagination to break through the walls our intellect constructs. To choose the safe, familiar path to understanding character may prevent discovery of something new and unexpected.

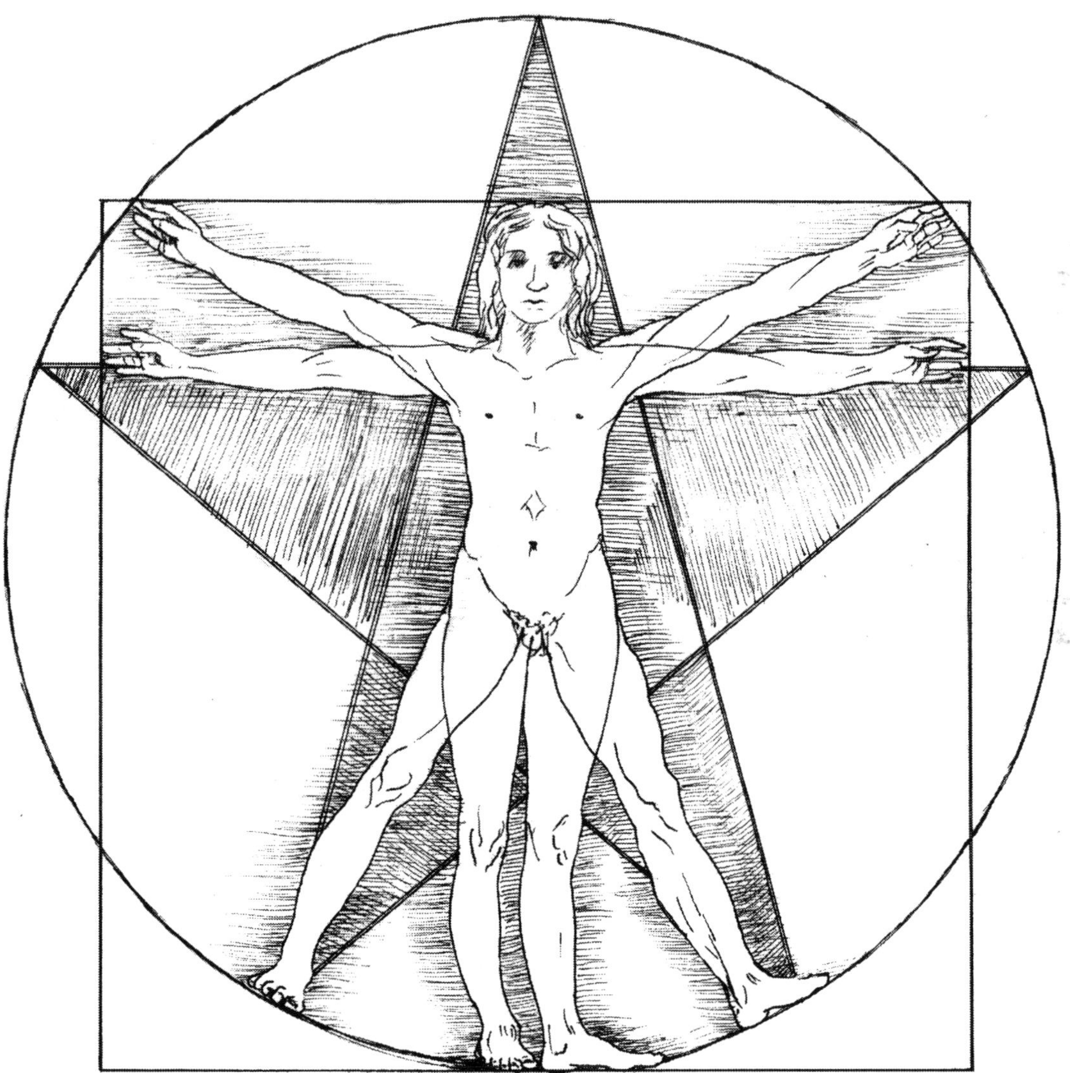

Based on the drawing by Leonardo da Vinci of the
'Human Being in a Circle: Illustrating the Proportions'

Figure 28

Chekhov's process to develop an *imaginary* body is more fruitful if we first become familiar with our own *habitual body* and with what Chekhov called our *archetypal body*.

Imaginary-body exploration 1 — becoming aware of archetypal and habitual body

Explore these steps without applying judgements of 'good or bad', 'right or wrong'. We want to sharpen our sense of a character's psycho-physical relationship with the body s/he inhabits.

1. Warm up *counter tensions.*[*]
2. Contemplate the illustrations of Greek sculptures on pages 79, 129, 131, 139, 150, and the one based on Leonardo's sketch: the 'Human Figure in a Circle' on page 221. These do not depict a specific personality or individual, but rather the human being in alignment with universal principles; what Blake referred to as, 'the human form divine', and help us gain a sense for Chekhov's term, the *archetypal body.*
3. Now see the figure of yourself stand before you. It has the qualities you recognize as you, yet you imagine it aligned with the cosmos.
4. Step into it, as though it is a garment. 'Try it on', grow into it until you fill its contours and are comfortable wearing it. Become aware of your sensations as you make the transition from your customary or habitual way of being in your body to inhabiting your archetypal body.
5. Move back and forth between your two 'bodies' until you can express the differences. For example: when I stand in my habitual body, I slightly lift and twist my left shoulder from the angle and position that it has in my archetypal body, or I hold my head higher or lower, or my shoulders are hunched. Perhaps I discover my habitual body to be pigeon-toed?
6. Work with a partner to clarify your observations.
7. Walk around, alternating your habitual and archetypal bodies. Expand your observations of the differences.

Our sense of archetypal body will be sharpened by practising Eurythmy and Bothmer Gym, or its recent evolution into Spatial Dynamics. An experience of archetypal body allows us to begin with a 'clean slate', as it were, being less likely to impose our own unconscious and habitual tendencies on any work we do.

---

[*] See pages 78–83.

Imaginary-body exploration 2 — creating an imaginary body
Steps 9–11 need not be attempted in the one practice period.

1. Stand in your habitual body. Imagine where you stand is one point of a triangle.
2. Look to a second point of the triangle. Picture your archetypal body standing there and step into it as though you step into a garment.
3. Step back to the first point of the triangle and into your habitual body.
4. Look to the third point of the triangle. See yourself standing there. It is still you but your body looks taller.
5. When you see that taller version of yourself, like a costume hanging there, step into it. Don't try to physically force your body to be taller, by standing on tiptoes or stretching your neck. Focus on imagining yourself within that taller body until you 'feel taller'.
6. When you are ready to sustain the sensation, move around the space. Don't be too complicated. What is it like to take a step, two steps, etc., for your 'taller' body to bend down, pick up an object, enter a room and look around, sit or meet someone shorter, etc.?
7. Check you have a sense of ease.[*] When you are ready to release your 'taller' body, return to its place on the triangle.
8. Step back into your habitual body and its place on the triangle.
9. Step into your archetypal body as you move to the third point of the triangle.
10. Take time to move from one point to another, transforming as you go into each of your three different 'bodies'. Pay attention to the different 'body of sensations' each awakens in you.
11. Repeat steps 1–9 with an imaginary body shorter than your own.
12. Experiment with other attributes: fat or thin, huge buttocks, tiny head. Don't attempt too much at once; one attribute at a time develops your capacity to change shape.
13. Work with a partner and assist each other with your observations. 'This is my imaginary body. Is this what you see?'
14. Mindful of the difference between 'indicating' and thorough penetration, prepare an imaginary body but do not tell what you imagine. Move across the space, inviting feedback from your partner. Can your partner 'see' the body you imagine?

---

[*] Chekhov's *sense of ease* is explored in chapter 6.

Imaginary centres

We explored the archetypal centres that provide the basis for our thinking, will and feeling and how to transform them in the one-sided ways in which we express these functions. Now we learn to channel consciousness through an imaginary centre that we can locate anywhere: upon or in or even sometimes outside of our body.

If I cut my finger or tread on something sharp, I have a clear sensation for a certain time, that my centre is located in my finger or my foot and has a quality of sharp jabbing pain which, at some point, transforms into a dull and throbbing ache. While it lasts, I sense how it's always there; I'm always mindful of its presence and it affects or even channels the rest of my experience or action. Such examples help us understand how a centre somewhere in our body with a certain quality is part of everyday experience.

When we fall in love, or are obsessed with a cause, we place our centre outside ourselves in the object of our love or obsession. Perhaps it shines before us with a mesmerizing glimmer that disappears only to appear again, always beckoning. Or it takes the form of an icy crag, forbidding, threatening, impossible to scale. Someone who is drunk or 'mad' is described, as being 'out of themselves'.

To be able to locate the centre in or outside of the body through which a character's consciousness is channelled, and identify its qualities from 'normal' through to unusual and bizarre is our next potent tool for creating character.

These first explorations remind us:

(a)   That to experience a centre with certain attributes is part of everyday experience.
(b)   How we function when our consciousness is focused through a centre.

Imaginary centres exploration 1

1. Imagine you have cut your finger or trod on something sharp. Improvise the moment, arriving at the point where you need to get on with your life with your wounded foot or finger.
2. Sustaining the sensation of the pain in your foot or finger, perform simple actions: walking, sitting, standing, reading, writing, etc.
3. Sustain the sensation of the pain in your foot or finger as you meet and interact with a partner.
4. Use your practice-dialogue:

>   A: I didn't expect to see you here today.
>   B: I didn't expect to see you either.

A:	How've you been?
B:	Fine!
A:	I've missed you.
B:	I've missed you too.

5. Try the other centre (foot or finger) or place it in a different part of your body.

6. Experiment with other centres, endowing them with different qualities.

Imaginary centres exploration 2

Wherever the centre and whatever its quality, the process is the same as for *imaginary body*. Don't rush into behaviour from your *idea* of a centre. Allow time for your imagination to really transform your 'sensation-body'.

1. Choose one of the centres listed below and imagine it until the sensations that arise so permeate your body that it begins to respond.

2. Here are some examples:

   - Imagine a red light bulb glowing at the tip of your nose.
   - Imagine a red light bulb in the palm of your hand.
   - Another time imagine it emits a healing power.
   - Change the location: place your centre in your foot (left or right) and imagine it is rotting.
   - Imagine that your foot is a saturated sponge which squelches water every time you take a step.

3. Change its quality. Your consciousness is still centred at the tip of your nose or the palm of your hand, for example, but instead of a light bulb, your nose or hand is rotting and emitting a foul odour.

4. Sustain your imagination of the centre and walk a few steps.

5. Perform simple movements: sitting, standing, kneeling, picking up an object, saying 'yes,' or ' no,' or 'maybe'.

6. Renew your imagination of the centre, then meet and interact with a partner. Exchange a few simple words and your practice dialogue: *I didn't expect*, etc.

7. If a character suggests itself from these explorations develop it further.

Further thoughts about the Self or spirit of the character

To know another human being, is to sense the essence that permeates and binds specific elements of this or that behaviour or reaction and apparent contradictions. Through this sense of the I,[*] we perceive when an actor does not only demonstrate a sequence of behaviours, but reveals the wholeness and being of a character to us.

This sense informs us of disorder or pathology when we witness behaviour that has no consistency or continuity; in extreme cases, a personality disintegrated into fragments. A certain 'logic' of transitions is how actors normally create the bridge between one thought or mood or action and another, enabling us to recognize behaviour or a character as 'normal'.

Of course, beneath what may appear to the sane mind as a splintered consciousness, a deeper, 'logic' is at work that issues from another level of the mind and makes connections based on other premises. A good script provides us with clues that enable us to excavate this deeper level and reveal the 'alternative logic' underlying the apparent lack of logic the character displays. Lady Macbeth's words in the sleepwalking scene reveal a splintered consciousness, hopping from one disconnected thought or image to another. Yet when we excavate those fragments we arrive at the wholeness buried underneath and which insists on itself even through her madness.

In chapter 3, I described my creation of Lucky's character from *Waiting for Godot* based on distortions of the three centres for our thinking, will and feeling. My conception of these was the fruit of that deeper excavation into Lucky's character and its symbiotic co-dependency with Pozzo. The interplay of these three centres revealed to me the depth of what takes place in Lucky's psyche, and the logic in what appears an incoherent babble when he speaks. It took me, as an artist, to the sacred place in which his consciousness is born, uncovering there the super-objective the character himself had long forgotten, but which at some level still doggedly worked on; to be in control as an *artist* of creating what the *character* increasingly could not control.

The wholeness or integrity of character is an organizing principle; like a skin that is invisible, this being or self or spirit is what holds the parts together. *Soul* is the realm where differences can manifest and play; one moment sad, the next happy. *Spirit* is what works to understand, make meaning, find balance, grow and develop further, not be swayed back and forth by the movement in the soul. In the language of mythology, it is Triptolemus, the hero who descends to Hades, rescues the soul, Persephone, and unites her with the Bridegroom, resurrected Dionysus. It is Isis who gathers and makes whole the broken body of Osiris.

---

[*] See, The 12 Senses, pages 44 and 194–199.

Visualization and incorporation

Imagine all the characters in all the dramas of the world. Somewhere in the realm of spirit, outside time and space some characters survive the centuries because their beings are eternal, they have a life and reality which we recognize and that is independent of the actors who portray them. Think of Hamlet or Malvolio. They wait to be invited to the earth. First, they wait for writers to behold them and draw them down onto the page. Then they wait for actors who, honouring the text, work back from the page, returning step-by-step to the place of their origin, weaving as they go, a garment made of soul and body suitable for them to dwell in. Then to reward such actors, grant them an encounter with the being of the one they serve.

Visualization and incorporation is another tool Chekhov has provided to train our ability to recognize the self of a character. He suggests that we invoke the character, invite it to reveal itself to us. If we open our imagination and create the right inner space, ask the right question, it may show us how it stands or sits or walks, what clothes it wears, what colours. Perhaps a moment from the play will flash into our mind and heart, or a situation quite outside the play's events reveal an unrecorded moment from the past of our character, or one still to be lived in the future. Where do such revelations come from? Can we trust them?

The spirit is the holographic level of the Self. The I AM is Alpha and Omega, beginning and end; a Presence, eternal and encompassing, beyond both time and space. So, what we invite might come from anywhere within that infinite continuum. Although what it reveals is but a fragment, that fragment is part of a greater whole; a whole that lies, initially, beyond our conscious mind.

If we give that whole, that being, the opportunity to show an aspect of itself and serve it faithfully by incorporating what it chooses to reveal, it may trust us with further revelations. When we ask a question, are we ready and willing to receive, without judgement, the answer that it gives, to accept what it reveals? Or do we impose our own agenda and interpretation?

A psychotherapist with a predetermined concept of why someone behaves in a certain way blocks the client's willingness to open up. We know how we react when we feel defined by someone else's context of reality; because we cannot trust that we are understood we feel unsafe and unwilling to reveal ourselves. So, too, the self of a character, retreats when it is approached by an actor with a preconceived interpretation. A character is more likely to reveal itself if our questions are born in an open mind and heart. When we have learned all we can from the text, we can ask to understand the greater mystery embedded in the clues the playwright has supplied.

Here is a sample of questions you can ask your character.

- Where do you spend most time?
- When do you first remember going/being there? How did it look then? How does it look now?
- Is there an object in the space which is significant to you?
- Do you have a special, secret place you go to when you need to be alone? When did you first go there?
- Is there some special object that is precious to you or is your secret that you keep in that secret place or somewhere else? What is it? Where do you keep it? Can you show it to me? How did it come to be in your possession?
- What do you like to wear? Do you have a favourite garment?
- Do you like to dance? What sort of music do you like? listen to? Is there a piece of music you particularly love? Why is it important to you?

Visualization & incorporation exploration 1

1. Sit, alert and comfortable, and close your eyes.
2. Invite your character to show you what it wants to, of itself.
3. Get up and incorporate whatever comes into your mind.* Copy it as accurately as you can. At this stage do not alter or add to it.
4. Sit again and invite a further revelation.
5. Stand and incorporate it.
6. Repeat this process for as long as inspiration comes.
7. Work through the moments once again, refining them into a sequence that you can repeat.
8. Perform your sequence for a partner and share feedback.

Visualisation & incorporation exploration 2

1. Choose a moment your character revealed and explore it further. What else does your character wish to reveal about the moment. Is it part of a larger event your character wants you to understand?
2. Dig deeper, with the different tools you have available, working in a full-bodied way. To mention just a few: can you discover a *PG* or *objective* invisibly at work within the action? Is there a *quality-of-movement* or a gesture of *expansion* or *con-traction* or a *tempo and dynamic* buried deep inside? Is there a *quality and sensation* you can penetrate more thoroughly?
3. Extract from your exploration anything that seems of value for your character, that

------

*See page 46.

you would like to keep. Consolidate what you have found in a full-bodied sequence that allows you to access your discoveries again.

Visualization & incorporation exploration 3

1. Ask your character to show you a specific moment in the play: how s/he behaves or performs a specific action. Follow the steps in exploration 1.
2. Ask questions of your character, such as those suggested earlier or any others that occur to you. Incorporate what is revealed to you.
3. Integrate what you discover with the processes described in *visualization & incorporation exploration 2*.

Archetypes

All the world's a stage
And all its men and women merely players.
They have their exits and their entrances
And one man in his time plays many parts.

Shakespeare, As You Like It

Imagine you are a king or queen. Of course, a specific king or queen has specific qualities, but the essence, the universal element of *king* or *queen* — do you have a sense of that? How? Where does it come from? Imagine now you are an orphan. How do you know what an orphan feels and looks like, how s/he behaves? Or a prophet, or a soldier, or a slave?

Chekhov understood that in the course of human evolution, the eternal spirit lives many times on earth. We could not possibly evolve to full maturity with knowledge gained from only one perspective; only a man for instance, or a woman; only a king and not also a beggar or a servant or a warrior; only a mother or father and never a child, a tyrant or a thief, a judge or priest or lover. The list of possibilities to gain experience and knowledge of ourselves on earth is as infinite and varied as the human race. And infinite are the roles that we can play and have played already. For do we not possess and know them all, somewhere inside us?

We access this rich realm of creative possibilities when we identify the archetypes within a character and learn how to work with them. Hamlet, for example, embodies the archetypes of prince, son, lover, poet, scholar, warrior, philosopher, friend, actor, tyrant, fool/clown, cynic, killer and destroyer, to name but a few.

Archetypes exploration 1 — visualization and incorporation
We begin this exploration with the tool of *visualization and incorporation*.

1. Sit, relaxed and alert. Close your eyes and visualize the archetype you have chosen to explore, for example: orphan. Accept whatever form your inspiration takes, whether it offers you a sound, an image or a smell, a momentary flash or something more extended. If nothing comes, approach it from a different angle, a different sense perhaps?
2. Whatever comes respond to it in action; if it was an image do exactly what you saw.

If it comes in some other way trust that when you engage your body, it will launch you into a stream of sensation.

3. Work further with the same archetype. Building on what went before, sit and invite a second image (if it is an image) or continuation of the first. Incorporate what comes.

4. Keep doing this until the inspiration ends. Sit again and play the moments back in your mind. Incorporate them into a sequence and refine the moments/inspirations into a perfect little 'work of art' with a beginning, middle and end.

5. While working, identify the psycho-physical vocabulary hidden in the sequence. Expand it into full-bodied exploration. For example:

- Is your chosen archetype *contracted or expanded* or does it move between?
- What seems to be the quality of *tempo and dynamic*? Does the archetype tend towards a certain *quality-of-movement*?
- Can you sense s/he behaves out of particular *objectives*? If so identify them and create PGs to embody them.
- What *qualities* with their *sensations* seem predominant?

6. Extract each tool and work it thoroughly into your body, letting the corresponding inner life unfold.

7. Take the fruits of this thorough exploration and incorporate them into your 'perfect little work of art'.

Having begun with what the archetype reveals about itself and used steps 5 and 6 to consolidate what we were shown, now we work the other way around, using steps 5 and 6 as starting points for our investigation.

Archetypes exploration 2

1. Choose an archetype to investigate.

2. Let your actor's intuition guide you to the tools that might be useful and explore them full-bodily. In the case of *slave*, for example, my sensation-body immediately tells me there is rich treasure to be mined by exploring *qualities-of-movement, expanding and contracting, tempo and dynamic, qualities and sensations, imaginary centres, PG* and *objectives*. Flashes of images weave in and out of all of them suggesting that *visualization and incorporation* will also be a useful tool.

3. Create a full-bodied sequence that consolidates what you have learned about 'slave' and refine it into a perfect little work of art.

Archetypes exploration 3

1. Make a list of archetypes and update it as more occur to you.
2. Use the processes suggested to explore as many of them as you can.

Here are some to add to the list: coward, hero, master, servant, peasant, aristocrat, miser, philanthropist, virgin, whore, Casanova, vampire, artist, poet, bureaucrat, mother, victim, martyr, etc.

All the basic tools to build a character are now available, yet how to know which ones will be useful to explore? We need to choose. What if our choice is wrong or we miss something, make a mistake? Wouldn't it be better to keep our options open? Yet, if fear tempts us not to commit to any choice, to stay within the realm of freedom where 'all things are still possible', our character will be vague and un-delineated. It cannot come into existence if it stays in the realm of potential; its glory lies in the *particularity* with which it incarnates into the earthly realm.

When we commit ourselves to a specific choice, even if it turns out to be 'wrong', we have time to change it. In addition, what we learn through our 'mistake' enriches the final work. Nothing is wasted and the so called 'wrong' choice brings us closer to the right one. As the Boyg tells Peer Gynt, the path of life is not a straight one. 'Round and about' is the way that we must go to be human.[*]

The realm of spirit is the realm of the creator. Even if we start with a vision that inspires, there is no fixed plan with a predetermined end, no path that does not have its surprises or discoveries along the way. Only when we have the courage to commit to the step before us do we discover where it leads, what we can learn from it and what the next step can be. When we work in this way, the character teaches us things we could not have planned before. And is it not our greatest joy to be surprised by our creation?

How to know which tools to try when we begin? By practising them all, we transform our instrument into a subtle body of cultivated sensibilities, making it an *organ of perception*.

These sensibilities function like antennae. A character approaches. The tendrils of our instrument begin to sense it on their radar. They wave and tremble setting up a field of attraction between their subtle pathways and the character. Within this field, the tools the character requires resonate, declare their relevance and announce themselves as portals to the chambers of sensation they are able to reveal. And the treasure that we find within each chamber contains the clue to the next portal we must enter.

---

[*] See *The Integrated Actor*.

Chapter 5

Art and Chekhov's 'Four Brothers'

The Four brothers

Art.

What is it?

> I will hear that play;
> For never anything can be amiss,
> When simpleness and duty tender it …
> Love, therefore, and tongue-tied simplicity
> In least speak most, to my capacity.
>
> Shakespeare, *A Midsummer Night's Dream*

> Nor do not saw the air too much with your hand, thus; but use all gently: for in the very torrent, tempest, and — as I may say — whirlwind of passion, you must acquire and beget a temperance, that may give it smoothness …
>
> Shakespeare, *Hamlet*

These words express two attitudes to our creative efforts. On the one hand, we honour the attempt whatever the results. On the other, what demands to be revealed requires a more transparent rendering, only possible by mastering the skills inherent in the art through which we seek expression. Commitment to such mastery is what distinguishes the artist from those content simply to express themselves.

To be obsessed with one extreme condemns us to the tyranny of a merciless aesthetic and to be satisfied exclusively with the other is to blunt our sensibilities on mediocrity. Both extremes can lead to self-absorption, work that is too personal, that does not allow us to evolve. Yet there is a context in which each perspective is appropriate and which we can learn to recognize.

In our postmodern culture, we hardly dare approach the mystery of art itself. What is it? Can we investigate its principles and finely tune our actor's sensibilities to recognize what makes our work artistic? For thematic reasons, I have placed this chapter in the culminating section of this book, yet what is here explored may be applied at any level of training and indeed, worked with from the start. We can cultivate the sense for art in every stage of the process instead of viewing it as something 'stuck on' at the end.

The psychologist, Maslow, derived the principles of humanistic psychology from studying healthy, high functioning and individuated human beings; in contrast to branches of psychology derived from a study of pathologies. So Chekhov, in his search to understand the principles of art, studied great works, great artists and the great actors he was privileged to watch. He asked what makes us call them art and artists? Is it something we can learn, or are their qualities to lie forever shrouded in the mystery of what we call an artist's genius or gift; a shrine not to be approached consciously?

Chekhov observed that great works of art possess the qualities of *ease, form, beauty,* and of *wholeness,* affectionately naming them the Four Brothers. He suggested exercises to cultivate the actor's sense for these.[*] Rather than repeat what he has written, we explore the context of his explorations.

THE SENSE OF EASE

> *Understand, that whether a being is powerful or splendid or filled with vigour,*
> *it comes from only a tiny part of my brilliance …*
> *I stand and hold up this entire world with only a little part of myself …*

When babies learn to crawl, stand and walk, they focus with utmost concentration. It's hard work, requiring all their commitment and engagement. Yet there is joy and playfulness when the task is tackled at the right time developmentally and not prematurely forced. Once the skill is mastered, it's easy; so effortless that it's difficult to remember the struggle. Could we perform with such a sense of ease?

Four brothers exploration 1 – sense of ease

Observe great artists when they work: musicians, actors, dancers, etc. Notice the ease with which their technique serves their art. It has become transparent. We are no longer conscious of the effort the artist makes to play those notes or leap so high. It just seems easy. We know, however, that child prodigies excepted, such ease is achieved only after many hours of practice.

Four brothers exploration 2 – sense of ease

1. Lie on the floor. Make a simple movement with a sense of ease. For example, move your hand. Now imagine how it was to be a baby making your first movements, then crawling, standing, walking. Slowly incorporate this journey. Take whatever time your 'baby' needs to find out how, step-by-step, to conquer gravity.

---

[*] See pages 13–19 of *To the Actor* and pages 13–19 of *On the Technique of Acting.*

2. Compare this with the way you normally stand up and walk. So easy! No need to think about it, or struggle to overcome the challenges.

3. Identify the sensations that constitute this sense of ease. Do they remind you of sensations connected with *flying* and *levity* or any other tools? If you recognize them from precise activities already practised then you know how to consciously create a sense of ease.

4. Move around the space, full-bodily and then naturalistically, with a sense of ease.

5. Work with any psycho-physical tool *without* a sense of ease. Introduce a sense of ease.

6. Attempt something difficult. Introduce a sense of ease. Mould or radiate with a sense of ease?

7. Devise a movement sequence that is challenging. Practise it until you perform it with a sense of ease.

8. Pick up a chair and move with it as though it is your partner. Explore the possibilities your 'partner' offers you and dance together with a sense of ease.

THE SENSE OF FORM

> *There is no end to my divine form …*
> *they are threaded upon me as pearls upon a string …*
> *At the coming of day all those things which have form*
> *come from that which is formless; at the coming of night they are dissolved at random into that*
> *which is known as the formless*

I have an impulse. I need to express it in order to know more clearly what it is, and to communicate it to another. I will only successfully communicate my impulse if I find the right *form*. It could be a right choice of colour or a line here or there that reveals the impulse that little bit more clearly. It could be a shift of tempo or of key or pitch and I feel what the composer felt. Or the right nuance of expression in that word or gesture and suddenly the audience is in no doubt; they experience the character's experience. Performer, character and audience are one.

Four brothers exploration 3 — sense of form

These steps may be attempted over several sessions; steps 1–4 in pairs or small groups.

1. Listen to the different intervals within an octave. Describe what each one awakens in your soul.

2. Listen to a minor chord and then a major one. Describe your response.
3. Look at paintings and sculptures acknowledged as great. Describe your responses to the artist's use of shape and colour.
4. Describe your response to different forms of architecture.
5. Move around the space with a sense of ease. Imagine you're a tree. Sense the ease as energy pours through you, sending roots deep down into the earth, gathering your body up into the form of trunk and branch and leaves. Can you can hold this form without it going 'dead'? How do you keep the tree alive? Dissolve the form of the tree back into movement.
6. Condense your movement into a second form; another tree or something else alive. Again dissolve it into movement with a sense of ease until again into a form, and back again to movement with a sense of ease – flow into form into flow into form.
7. Examine what you do when you form, the sensations that arise? Can you differentiate between *activity that forms* and the finished form? Perform some simple movements with a sense of form; walking, running, kneeling, playing with an object, etc.?

Four brothers exploration 4 – sense of form

1. Create a dance that explores your own body's form. What does the human body's upright form make possible that the horizontal form of many animals does not allow?
2. Observe any difference in sensation when you move your arm:

   (a) with the palm of your hand up
   (b) with the palm of your hand down
   (c) with your hand in a fist

3. Relate your own form to the forms around you, moving in relationship to them.

Four Brothers exploration 5 – sense of form (partner work)

1. Create living sculptures with a partner; flow into form into flow, etc.
2. Wear a neutral mask. By bringing your attention to your body, you are not tempted to rely on your face, but must express what you intend through the forms your body takes. Create living sculptures to express particular experiences; 'joy' or 'grief', for example.
3. Show them to a partner. Does each form communicate what you intend? Clarify what does or does not 'speak' successfully.

Four brothers exploration 6 — sense of form — Speech-exploration

If you wish to explore the role of *form* in speech and language.[*]

1. Experiment with vowels, consonants and words until you sense the form they make. For example, compare the vowel /a:/ (as in st<u>a</u>r) with /u:/ (as in d<u>oo</u>m), the consonant b (as in bud) with l (as in flower), the word *bud* with *flower*:

   (a) inside your mouth
   (b) out in the space

2. Create and compare a simple statement, question, command and exclamation. Explore their different forms. How does form reveal intention?
3. Speak each example so that you reveal its intention.

Four brothers exploration 7 — sense of form — working with text

> In the vast unmeasured worldwide spaces
> In the endless stream of time
> In the depths of human soul life
> In the world's great revelations
> Seek the unfolding of life's great mystery

Rudolf Steiner

Speak 'In the vast—' with a sense for its form; how each line builds towards the climax of the final line.[50]

Four brothers exploration 8 — sense of form — working with text

Look at different forms of poetry; alliteration, sonnet, rhyming couplet, blank verse, prose, rhyming verse, free verse, sprung rhythm, epic, lyric, dramatic, etc. Explore the responses they evoke in you.[†]

THE SENSE OF BEAUTY

> Who, if I shouted, among the hierarchy of angels
> would hear me? And supposing one of them
> took me suddenly to his heart, I would perish
> before his stronger existence. For beauty is nothing
> but the beginning of terror we can just barely endure,

---

[*] When working with the speech-exercises in *The Art of Speech*, can you sense the *form* of each, and speak it with that sense.

[†] See *The Art of Speech* and *The Integrated Actor*, chapter, Relationship of our threefold instrument to character and style.

and we admire it so, because it calmly disdains
to destroy us. Every angel is terrible.

from the first of Rilke's Duino Elegies[51]

Since brass, nor stone, nor earth nor boundless sea
But sad mortality o'ersways their power
How, with this rage, shall beauty hold a plea
Whose action is no stronger than a flower? …
Or who (time's) spoil of beauty can forbid?
O none! Unless this miracle have might
That in black ink my love may still shine bright.

Shakespeare, sonnet

Can beauty be determined by objective criteria? This question has been debated since philosophy began; many of the images used in this book were created at that time. Plato tells us that what we now refer to as the classical idea of beauty arose from a longing in the soul to represent divine perfection in an earthly form, to retain a last remnant of connection with the supersensible. To have such images surround them consoled the Greeks for their loss of perception of the spirit. Plato also pointed out that we worship what is beautiful because it wakens our sense of the divine.

> Thus far I have been speaking of the fourth and last kind of madness, which is imputed to him who, when he sees the beauty of the earth, is transported with the recollection of true beauty …
>
> … but all souls do not easily recall the things of the other world; … they may have lost the meaning of the holy things they saw … few only retain an adequate remembrance of them; and they, when they behold here any image of that other world, are rapt in amazement; but they are ignorant of what that rapture means, because they do not clearly perceive.

from Plato's Phaedrus

But is a daisy less beautiful than a rose? And if we think it is, does that mean that the divine speaks less through daisies than roses? Chaucer did not think so, naming daisies as his favourite flower. And is the bawdy miller with a wart on his nose that he described less divine than Botticelli's *Venus*? Or the earthy nurse in *Romeo and Juliet* than her obviously 'beautiful' mistress? And Rembrandt's self-portraits? As he ages and his face moves ever further from the classical idea of beauty, is he any less divine, or if we see 'beauty' of a different kind, what is it?

And what of Van Gogh's *Boots*? Or can only Monet's *Water Lilies* be considered 'beautiful'? Are certain things objectively beautiful and others not? What about a 'beautiful' body housing a depraved soul; as Oscar Wilde explores in his novel, *The*

Picture of Dorian Gray? Or the 'beautiful' soul inhabiting an 'ugly' body? Joseph (John) Merrick, the so-called Elephant Man, for instance. We judge constantly on the basis of some deeply sensed barometer of ugliness and beauty. Because what activates that judgement differs for each of us, we cannot explore what we mean by beauty by examining the *cause* of our response. But we can examine the response. Is there some sensation that we recognize as a response to beauty, regardless of the cause?

When I observe a sunset that registers as beautiful on my 'barometer', I experience sensations of increased life and energy, connection to the universe, expansion beyond the sense of a separate self bound within a body, into a communion.

Let's say that something we find beautiful evokes sensations of connection to a realm beyond the boundaries and surfaces of 'everyday reality'. What evokes these sensations in one individual, culture or community may not evoke them in another, but it is the *presence* of these particular sensations that constitutes experience of beauty. If we have identified this accurately, then we can use our psycho-physical technique to evoke it consciously.

I can evoke this sensation if I stand and move my arms gently in the space and sense the subtle substance of the ether that surrounds me. I can sustain this sensation and move so that I stay connected with the sense that space is touching me and I am touching space. If I move in such a simple way I sense the boundary of my skin dissolve, my consciousness expand beyond the separation that it usually contains me in, to sense a *presence*.

Our eyes look at Van Gogh's empty *Boots with laces* and 'cool reason' tells us there is no one there. But our hearts sense the presence of the one who wore them, the sacred mystery of years of poverty and toil and faithful service to the earth, the being who inhabited those boots.

Beauty … beatific … beatitudes … Beatrice. These words, with their common root, remind us of something 'blessed' or sacred. Chekhov suggests that actors who are artists reveal beauty in whatever they portray; the sacredness within the ordinary and extraordinary. Such beauty is not the sentimental sweetness that avoids the toughness or ugliness of life. This sense of beauty enables us to recognize the gift or blessing, even in what is first perceived as difficult or ugly.

The *Book of Genesis*, chapter 32, verses 24–29, tells how Jacob wrestles all night with an angel and dislocates his thigh. As morning comes the angel asks that Jacob let him go. Jacob says, 'I will not let you go until you bless me.' To wrestle with the difficult and painful and not let go of it until it reveals its gift or blessing is connected with the artist's search for beauty. We only find it by wrestling with each moment until it yields up its meaning and its holy mystery.

Figure 29 – Van Gogh's Boots with laces

Four brothers exploration 9 – sense of beauty

What stimulates your sense of beauty? Clearly describe what happens in you when you feel what you call 'beauty'. What are the sensations, gestures, feelings, thoughts?

Four brothers exploration 10 – sense of beauty

Compare works of art; some that in the course of time have been acknowledged beautiful, some not. What is your response? Choose one that is beautiful to you and clarify how the artist has evoked your sense of beauty. Clarify what makes *you* call it beautiful. Choose one you *don't* find beautiful and clarify the reasons why.

Four brothers exploration 11 – sense of beauty

1. Layer the sensations you associate with beauty into your full-bodied archetypal movement.

2. Perform everyday activities like sitting, standing, walking, running, picking up an object – with a sense of beauty. Is this the same as trying to 'look beautiful'?

3. Explore performing these simple actions with a sense of beauty; slam a door, kick or smash something, throw something at the wall.

4. Improvise a simple situation which is difficult or painful, for example: kick a dog, pick a rose, then kick it with a quality of 'bitterly'. Wrestle to find and portray the gift or blessing in this action; a deeper level to its meaning. Does this involve your heart opening? Does this involve a sensation of expansion beyond your skin?

Four brothers exploration 12 – sense of beauty

1. Choose a character considered physically beautiful, for example: Olivia in *Twelfth Night*, Romeo, Juliet (or any other romantic leads), Cleopatra, Yelena in Chekhov's *Uncle Vanya*. What tools help you to avoid a stereotype? What tools would you use to create a character like Sonya in *Uncle Vanya*; *John Merrick* in Pomerance's *The Elephant Man*; *Cyrano de Bergerac* in Rostand's play of that name – all considered physically plain or ugly, but with a beautiful soul.

2. Create with a sense of beauty, a character who is ugly and/or behaves in an ugly way; Lady Macbeth or Richard the Third, etc. What does it mean to wrestle with the character and not let it go until it blesses you?

3. Work with a sense of beauty to create an ugly situation, for example: Regan and Goneril's humiliation of Lear; the blinding of Gloucester in *King Lear*; the stoning of the baby in the pram in Edward Bond's *Saved*.

Four brothers exploration 13 – sense of beauty – Speech-exploration

1. Choose a word you find beautiful or which expresses an experience of beauty. What makes it beautiful for you? What would it mean to speak it with a sense of beauty?

2. Choose a word you find ugly or that expresses an experience of ugliness. What would it mean to speak it with a sense of beauty, to wrestle with it and not let it go till you can reveal its blessing when you speak?

3. Work with everyday expressions and examples from dramatic texts or literature that you find beautiful or ugly. Can you express them with a 'sense of beauty'?

THE SENSE OF THE WHOLE

> *I am also the beginning, middle and end of beings*

What convinced Mozart that every note was necessary?

Emperor Joseph of Austria: It's clever. It's German. It's quality work. And there are simply too many notes. Do you see?

Mozart: There are just as many notes Majesty, neither more nor less, as required.

Peter Shaffer, *Amadeus*

Required by what? We behold a Greek statue with head, arm or part of a leg missing and yet it is as though we see the missing pieces, can still perceive it whole. We sense an organizing presence that evokes a different response from the one evoked when I see only separate bits and pieces stuck together.

Some people sense the separate moments of their lives are connected to a greater whole — the *meaning* of this 'whole' continues to evolve but the sense of it is always there. Others go from one moment to another, arbitrarily, without the sense that each has significance beyond itself. This is the world depicted by Absurdist Drama and its characters experience themselves in just this way. Yet an actor who strives to be an artist, shows the experience of disconnection from the whole exists within a greater whole.

Four brothers exploration 14 — sense of the whole

1. Tell yourself to carry out a simple action, then do it, for example: *I will sit.*
2. Add an action, then tell yourself that you will do the first action followed by the second and do it, for example: *I will sit, then stand.*
3. Add a third action, then a fourth, etc., for example: *I will sit, then stand, then turn, then kneel, then stand, then sit again, then raise both arms, then lower them.*

Four brothers exploration 15 — sense of the whole

1. Lie on the floor. Roll over.
2. Repeat with the intention to sit up. Sit up.
3. Repeat as far as *sit* because you intend to stand. Stand.
4. Repeat as far as *stand* because you intend to walk. Walk.
5. Repeat as far as *walk* with the intention of opening the door. Open the door.
6. Repeat as far as *open the door* so that you can leave the house. Leave the house.
7. Repeat as far as *leave the house* so that you can run for the bus so that you will not be late for work. Run for the bus.
8. Perform the whole sequence knowing that if you are late for work, you lose your job.

Four brothers exploration 16 — sense of the whole

1. Curl up on the floor and imagine you are a seed. Choose: what sort of seed? Imagine in as much detail as you can the plant you will grow into.

2. When you have a clear image of what you will become grow into it. Observe how each stage on the way is drawn towards the final whole or how that whole pulls each stage towards itself.

Four brothers exploration 17 — sense of the whole

1. Perform a simple action. Start by lying on the floor:

   - sit
   - stand

2. Shut your eyes. Sense each action as a sequence with a beginning, middle and end. When you sense the completion of *sit*, calling you towards itself, sit. Do the same with *stand*.
3. Do this with other simple actions.
4. Create a sequence in which you move from one action to another but only as each one is first gathered as a whole.

   - sit
   - stand
   - walk three steps and come to rest
   - turn
   - walk three steps
   - turn
   - sit down

5. Perform the sequence as a series of discrete actions that happen to follow one another. When you are familiar with what comes, can you begin to sense that you cannot act unless what follows causes what you do before; the final action is the impulse that initiates the first movement in the sequence and draws everything that follows to itself.
6. Perform the sequence with a sense of the whole.

Four brothers exploration 18 — sense of the whole

1. Perform each of the following as a separate, discrete activity: lift a chair, place it somewhere, sit on it.
2. Now do it knowing that each action is performed in order to facilitate what follows. *Because I want to sit there, I lift the chair and move it to that place.* What generates the sense of wholeness that unites the component actions is my intention to sit in that place.

3. Add deeper levels of intention. Observe how each new level creates a different whole that organizes the components differently.

   (a) I lift the chair, move it over there and sit because I need to find an answer to my problem.
   (b) I lift the chair etc., because if I can't solve the problem I will lose my job.
   (c) I lift the chair etc., because if I lose my job I will be forced to leave the country. If I am forced to leave the country, I will have to say goodbye to my beloved, etc. That is why I move the chair … etc.

   Observe how you adjust each action as the wholeness which provides its context changes.
4. Once again perform each action as a separate and discrete activity. Then perform them once again as an evolving sequence within an evolving context. Notice the sensations that accompany each different way. Can you recognize a 'sense of the whole'?

Four brothers exploration 19 — sense of the whole

1. Choose a character. Make a list of actions the character performs within a scene or in the play.
2. Work on each in turn with a sense of ease.
3. Perform each action with a sense of its connection to the one that goes before, and the one that follows.
4. Decide on the character's overall objective in the scene or play. Create a PG to embody that objective. Use your PG to create the sense of whole which determines how you carry out each action.

VARIATIONS

After you have practised on your own, share your work with a partner or the class, inviting feedback. Can your audience perceive a difference when you perform an action with or without a sense of the whole? How do you/they describe the difference? The sense of the whole can also include work with a partner or ensemble enabling us to sense how the impulse of each individual contributes to the greater whole.[*]

The four brothers — layering (one big happy family)

Exploring the *Four Brothers* singly we become aware that each contains an aspect and

---

[*] See *The Art of Speech*, chapter 5, for an exploration of the sense of the whole in relationship to speech and language.

awakens an awareness of the others and contributes to what finally becomes one instinctive act of sensing work that qualifies to be artistic.

Four brothers exploration 20 – layering (partner work)

1. Throw a ball or beanbag to a partner with a sense of ease. Then, one at a time, layer in a sense of form, beauty and the whole. As you introduce each one, sustain what went before.
2. Extend your sense of wholeness to include your interaction with your partner.

Four brothers exploration 21 – layering (partner work)

At each stage, observe each other and share your observations. As you layer each successive *brother*, can you perceive a difference as performer, as beholder of the sequence?

1. Choose a simple movement with a strong and definite dynamic, for example: the first stage of the javelin sequence on pages 131–133. Do it several times.
2. When you are confident, follow the impulse it provides to add a second simple movement; then a third, etc.
3. Practise the sequence until it is familiar.
4. Perform it with a sense of ease, then layer in a sense of form, beauty and the whole.

Four brothers exploration 22 – layering

Improvising may be dance-like and abstract, or naturalistic and evolve into an everyday scenario.

1. Apply each of the *brothers* as you move freely with an object, like a chair, or veil, for example. Build your capacity to layer each one in turn.
2. Add levels of complexity by sharing your object with a partner.
3. Share with two, then three, etc., until the whole group moves with a sense they form a whole with the object and each other.

Like Russian dolls, these layers can be practised in relation to a single word or action, a single sentence, single speech, a single scene, and even an entire drama. In the end, not one word would be spoken, nor single action be performed that does not contain the whole work, of which it is a part.

Chapter 6

Performance and the Threshold

With the mind clinging to me
and performing yoga, refuged in me,
how thou shalt without doubt know me
to the uttermost, that hear thou . . .

There Arjuna beheld a whole universe,
divided into manifold parts,
standing in one body of the Deity of Deities
Then he, overwhelmed with astonishment,
his hair upstanding, bowed down his head
to the shining One.

Artistic sensibility and 'stage-fright'

We have considered how artistic sensibility relates to the challenges and dangers on the path of evolution as our gateways of perception open to once again include nonmaterial realities. It's time now to examine in this context, the phenomenon commonly referred to as 'stage fright' which is considered by many who perform to be an inescapable condition of their work.

Even acclaimed and gifted actors can suffer it to such degree they feel their careers are not sustainable. Resorting to alcohol and other drugs to mask the terror or giving up performing for a time are no solutions. It is grudgingly agreed that actors must experience some form of 'nerves' in order to deliver 'good' performances. After all, the argument continues, fear is what produces the adrenalin that makes performance possible. It is the necessary evil without which actors cannot access the intensity and energy required.

This terror when confronted with an audience is experienced by many who in no way consider they are actors. In Laing's terms, they are firmly 'embodied' and function confidently in the so-called 'real' world of practical affairs but are still reduced to terror if they have to speak in public. The fact that such 'nerves' or 'butterflies' or 'stage fright' are not the sole prerogative of actors invites investigation. Is there something about standing up in front of others which contains the clue that we are searching for?

When we are looked at, our skin no longer serves us as a boundary that keeps us separate. Therefore, anyone who stands in front of any audience, of any size, in any situation, finds themselves effectively outside their body. As we observed earlier, we need special skills if we are to manage this condition and use the gifts that it bestows on us.

We actors *need* our consciousness to be outside ourselves: in the other actors, characters, the play's reality and audience. At the same time, unless we are firmly anchored in our instrument we cannot channel the extraordinary consciousness available as a consequence of our out-of-body state. For whether it be poem, story, character or audience whose consciousness we enter and allow to enter us, it must be channelled through a body and a voice that can express it on the earth.

Fear is our natural reaction to what is unfamiliar. It is a necessary safeguard, protecting us from what, if undergone without the necessary preparation, could damage or destroy us. Astronauts, for instance, training to live outside earth's atmosphere where they will not be subject to the law of gravity, need a lengthy preparation to withstand the changed conditions. This we take for granted. Might not actors then need a preparation (what in the *Bhagavad Gita, Krishna* called a yoga) if we are to function healthily in those realities available to us outside our bodies?

And for those whose talent derives partly from the unconscious disembodied state that Laing describes as being the consequence of trauma, such a preparation is not a luxury but a necessity. Because the self dissociated from its body does not have a firm sense of its own existence, it needs to be seen by others to confirm that it exists. But since its sense of existence depends on a witness, it's vulnerable to the judgement of that witness. The disembodied or dissociated self is caught in impossible and contradictory conditions; the threat of annihilation if it is not seen, and the threat of annihilation if it is.

Actors face the contradictory demands of being fully inside and outside ourselves, at the same time. Yet this is the exact requirement Steiner has described as necessary for the aspirant who would achieve healthy supersensible experience.[*]

---

[*] See pages 35–37.

Steiner and the threshold

Steiner spent his life learning how to consciously inhabit both the physical sense world and the 'worlds' accessible to other senses. He provided indications for making the transitions in a healthy way; calling this a conscious 'crossing of the threshold'. In the *The Threshold of the Spiritual World*, he describes how we can achieve sound knowledge in each realm.[*] He calls what we experience within the world of physical perceptions, 'this side of the threshold' and points out that to experience or know another being in this realm, we must receive that other into us. He warns that a self that is too fragile risks being swallowed by the presence of the other. Laing refers to the same phenomenon, with the term *engulfed*.

Healthy relationships are only possible 'on this side of the threshold', in 'this world', if we develop an awareness of the Self which is not dependent on confirmation from without to know its own existence. Only the I AM can *receive into itself another being without the loss of consciousness of its identity*. The capacity to do this is what Steiner points to as the mature stage of what we mean by 'love' and indicates that this is what we are on earth to learn.

In the condition of supersensible awareness which Steiner refers to as being 'on the other side of the threshold' we do not experience our bodies as boundaries that separate us from each other. There we experience 'the other' by merging or dissolving into it. 'Falling in love' is the everyday condition in which most of us have experienced this phenomenon. Again, Steiner warns that only when the sense of 'self' or I AM is sufficiently developed can we encounter other beings in this state without obliteration. Only the I AM is able to *stay conscious of itself within the other*.

Implications for the actor

Steiner's indications refer to conditions that will apply to everyone within the course of evolution. Yet by virtue of their calling and their 'gift', actors are constantly exposed to these experiences, and with little or no comprehension of the dangers will most likely undergo them without the necessary preparation. Finding that we have such gifts and vocation, some of us have plunged ourselves into intensities which inspire but also damage us.

There are fine actors who seem able to transform into other characters entirely. They submerge their own identity and merge with the character they play. There are equally fine actors who always play themselves; yet they allow the inner life of the character to inhabit and express itself within them. Some seem mature and balanced

---

See pages 35–37.

souls who have achieved that presence which is unassailable and allows them to accomplish what they do 'without a drama'. They are like the gymnast who completes a sequence of astonishing complexity and lands with perfect poise. We don't know the path they have followed to arrive at that maturity. Of these 'stable' actors, the popular media does not have much to say.

But it is full of stories that reveal the tragic lives of actors who have found no way to manage the nature of the risks they face. Whether they are actors of the first or second type, if the sense of self with which they do their work is the fragile false identity whose survival is dependent on being seen and recognized, they are at risk. This need can drive it to pursue artistic excellence; be approved of and acclaimed by audience or critics. It can also drive the fragile ego into self-destructive patterns, seeking confirmation in the public's disapproval, shock and curiosity.

If the self that stands before an audience is the false identity, constructed out of what we have been taught we need to be if we want recognition, adulation or approval, the fear encountered at the threshold of performance can be likened to the fear of facing execution. The remedy is to win through, like Oedipus and Lear, to the eternal, indestructible I AM.

The path suggested in this book supports a growing consciousness of this eternal presence. Every exploration calls upon the I AM of the actor to make choices and mediate the sensations, thoughts, feelings and emotions it evokes.

The next explorations address the need to strengthen our awareness of the threshold nature of our work, provide some necessary preparation to support healthy entry to the realms we inhabit, and support our path back to a healthy resumption of personal relationships and everyday responsibilities.

Crossing the threshold

Chekhov used Steiner's term, *crossing the threshold,* to express the shift in consciousness that actors make at the moment when we step from everyday reality into the creative space, the realm of inspiration, intuition and imagination. He was concerned that we approach this moment consciously. Two ways are offered here. They can be used to start a class, practice or rehearsal as well as to prepare for performance. Each approach might be appropriate in different circumstances.

Threshold exploration 1

1. Become aware of the space in which you work. Consciously create an imaginary threshold that separates the artistic and creative space from the world of everyday reality.

2. Step across the threshold into that creative space.
3. To strengthen your awareness of this threshold step back over it, returning to the world of 'everyday reality'.
4. Before you cross again, be mindful of the special nature of the space you are about to enter. Whether you think of it as *sacred*, whatever name you give to it, something extraordinary takes place when you enter it. In order to serve this possibility, you, the artist, offer up your ordinary self and are willing to leave your everyday concerns behind; the shopping, dramas, worries, conflicts, that have occupied your mind until this moment, have no place here. You are not required to 'deny' or suppress them. Acknowledge them before you take the step, but choose to focus on the task in hand. This may be to be present for a warm-up, for your fellow actors or your character or audience. In fact, it may be easier to step across the threshold and focus on the task in hand if you first acknowledge any pressing personal concerns and commit to deal with them at a time that is appropriate.
5. Acknowledge, aloud or silently, who makes this choice: I AM.
6. When you are ready, step across the threshold.
7. Give yourself time to sense the 'field'; the space now charged with different energy. Let it permeate you and affect how you engage with your task. I AM.
8. Try a few simple movements; walking several steps, sitting, lying down, turning over, standing. Move one arm and then the other. Let the consciousness that you are in the field/sacred space affect your actions. I AM. Be wary of 'acting' a sacred or special quality rather than discovering a depth of imagination that has power to transform the space.
9. Make a transition into the specific task of this rehearsal/exploration/class/performance/preparation, etc., and begin that work.
10. At the completion of your work, consciously step back across the threshold and re-enter the space of everyday reality. I AM.

A group who shares this perspective can share the process. In the absence of a shared perspective, individuals can carry out the process for themselves.

Threshold exploration 2

Sometimes it is appropriate to address and integrate our personal concerns with our artistic process instead of leaving them outside the working space. For example, a cast member's brother was seriously injured in an accident. Could our group ignore the implications for all of us, of this huge event? After much consideration, we decided to fulfil our obligation to perform that night. It is for such circumstances, that *threshold exploration 1* might be adapted in this way.

1. Acknowledge who it is who does this work. I AM. Contemplate the threshold that separates your work space from the world of your personal exhaustion, grief, rage, anxiety, etc. Acknowledge, with gratitude and wonder, the drama of your life. The work you are about to do is an opportunity to bless your pain and for your pain to bless your work.

2. When you are ready, step across the threshold and acknowledge who it is who takes this step. I AM. Enter the sacred space where all experience is honoured and becomes the raw material from which you make your art. Instead of stepping over your subjective state, go into it and penetrate it as an artist. Use the tools you have acquired; explore the weight of your exhaustion, your compassion, or the quality of grief. Become aware what quality-of-movement or tempo or dynamic, you are in. Are you expanded or contracted? What objective or PG suggests itself? Acknowledge who it is who does this work. I AM.

3. Continue to investigate and penetrate the state in which you entered until you are no longer the victim of it, but the creator. You are an artist, using voice and body to shape your experience, transforming it into a work of art. Suddenly a bridge appears between your subjective world and the task required. Instead of blocking your artistic work, the personal enriches it and in turn, the artistic process heals the personal.

It's important to maintain clear boundaries between therapy and art. But there are times when we need to build a bridge between the challenge of personal events and the demand to rehearse or perform. The boundary can be maintained if we understand that our purpose is not the exploration of personal experience for therapeutic purposes but to invite the artist into what is personal so that a transition can be made into the objective task. Making this distinction clear, limits and determines the scope of what unfolds.

Chekhov's *Golden Hoop* described later in this chapter, is another useful tool with which to begin or conclude artistic work.

Crossing the threshold in relation to an audience

The more precise our knowledge of technique, the greater our possibilities for focus. Technique, in one respect, is nothing but a range of choices, each one of which provides the opportunity to focus consciousness. To focus consciousness, I must be *present*.

Presence or possession

The path of mindfulness. To be present in the moment, in the now. This is the language in which many undertaking spiritual practice in our time express their goal of *presence*. I don't think it's coincidence that actors use the same word to name what they aspire to; to fill the stage and 'hold' an audience requires *presence*.

Some possess it to a powerful degree. It's commonly regarded as a 'gift', something one either has or has not, but those who have it are compelling. *So-and-so has such a presence*, is what we hear expressed.

Yet we observe in those who have this power, an ability to focus their attention and capacities in a way that takes us with them, in 'willing suspension of our disbelief', into the world that they create. Some of these have found a *conscious* path to this achievement. Many who possess it as an unconcious gift, as I myself once did, are the kind of actors who thrive on the experience of being *seen*. The larger the audience, the better because it is the mirror that reflects them to themselves, 'proving' they exist.

Such actors find it difficult to live without the sense of self mirrored to them by an audience. It becomes a drug they seek out constantly, to feel they are alive. At the same time, they live in fear, for that same self is threatened by empty seats or judgement perceived as negative. As with all attempts to substitute a 'drug' for the real experience of Self, the initial euphoria gives way to torment.

Steiner observed that fear at the threshold is *necessary*, to deter the unprepared from crossing. Yet actors make that crossing, over and again. They rarely have guidance with regard to *presence* on the other side of the threshold, where their consciousness must be outside themselves: in the play, the audience, their fellow actors, and characters. Without conscious presence, actors can only hope and pray that Dionysus does not abandon them — that at the crucial moment the god/character will possess them. But over this visitation they have little or no control, or knowledge of how to manage the energies evoked by such possession; energies that compel or electrify an audience but, when they depart, leave the actors spent, uncertain how to find their way back into life.

To achieve conscious presence on that other side, we need presence first on *this* side of the threshold. To command body, voice and soul as expressive instrument, invokes the presence of the Self that consciously inhabits a specific body in the world of time and space, yet is not limited to time and space: like Krishna, who knows Himself to be that Presence who is, at once, creator and creation.

Like Martha at the end of *Who's Afraid of Virginia Woolf?*, most of us are 'babies in this long tremendous way'. Nevertheless, by choosing to be actors, we are called to the journey and can take the first baby steps along the path to that Self which Chekhov also called our *creative individuality*.

Any of the processes described in this book can contribute to this journey if they are approached with this intention. Some, however, may be specifically adapted to develop conscious *presence.* These first four are extensions of the Greek gymnastics explorations and are recommended for use as preparation.[*]

Presence exploration 1 – running – I AM present in my body

1. Stand, then walk, slowly at first. Build your tempo till you break into a run.
2. When you reach top speed do not slow down first but stop 'in your tracks', and sustain the sensation of running at top speed. Inhabit and penetrate it fully.
3. Acknowledge the presence of the Self within you who commands that intense activity. Speak the words quietly but firmly. I AM
4. Repeat steps 1–3 and imagine you are standing in the wings, about to enter your imaginary stage.
5. Sustain your awareness of I AM, walk on stage and take in an imaginary audience. Sustain your presence in front of them. Address them if you wish. Begin a story with the words, *Once upon a time…* Sustain your presence as you exit.
6. In the wings again, make a conscious choice to release the sensation of the 'inner run'.
7. Repeat steps 1–4 and try step 5 with an audience of colleagues.
8. Invite feedback regarding your degree and quality of presence.

Presence exploration 2 – javelin – I project my presence

1. Revisit *Greek Gymnastics exploration 12–13.*[*] As you perform your full-bodied sequence, remind yourself who does this deed. Sense your presence in yourself and name it to yourself. I AM is the Self who projects its presence to the goal.
2. Observe the attention you project into the world when you commit to the throw, your interest in seeing whether you have reached your goal. Sustain that interest and attention and continue to project and radiate it to the world as you move around the space. Remember who it is that radiates. Sustain that interest and attention and behold the world and other people through its lens.
3. 'Switch off'. Return to normal consciousness. Continue moving round the space and observe the difference in sensation when you no longer consciously project your attention or your energy; your presence.
4. Repeat steps 1–2. Instead of 'switching off', sustain your radiating presence, enter your imaginary stage and radiate your presence to your imaginary audience and while you exit. Once in the 'wings' again, 'switch off'.
5. Repeat step 4 with a practice audience.

---

[*] See chapter 2.

6. Repeat steps 4 and 5. When you stand before your audience (practice or imaginary), make them your goal.

   (a) Perform your sequence of gestures in front of them.
   (b) Project your presence to the audience.
   (c) Aim at different sections of the audience.

Presence exploration 3 – javelin – Speech-exploration

1. Extend the exploration by releasing words with your gesture. Imagine the words are the spear that you project to the audience.[*] Build them up:

   > Fling … fling from … fling from forward …

And finally:

   > Fling from forward forth.

Presence exploration 4 – discus – I project my presence

1. Revisit Greek Gymnastics explorations 10 and 11.[†] Imagine the audience is the periphery that draws you out.
2. Acknowledge in yourself the presence of the one who performs the discus sequence. Project your presence to the audience as you release the discus.

Presence exploration 5 – gravity and levity

1. Revisit gravity and levity explorations.[‡] Acknowledge your I AM is the one whose presence can balance the polarities within you.
2. Sustain that presence as you enter your imaginary stage in front of an imaginary audience, engage with them and exit.
3. Sustain your presence as you practise with an audience of colleagues.

Explorations like these demand our presence and teach us that projection of attention, interest, and energy to an audience is a skill that can be practised. *Presence means to be present in what we do, fully focused in a deed or action.* It is not some mystic gift bestowed on some but not on others. Presence and projection of our presence can be learned. Test it out! Observe whether you experience anxiety when you relate to an

---

[*] See *Art of Speech*, chapter 3.
[†] See chapter 2, pages 130–132.
[‡] See chapter 2, pages 118–121.

audience as suggested. If not, you know that you have found the formula for eradicating 'nerves' or stage fright. The conscious presence of the Self in the creative act is true Self-consciousness. The next explorations add to the tools we can use to practise presence.

Krishna taught Arjuna: the energy at the source of life and the universe is one expression of the Presence that created and sustains all things and of which we are a part. Accessing that energy, learning to direct it consciously, is one way to experience that Presence in ourselves and make us conscious that we need to humanize that energy. We now learn to consciously connect it to the centre in our chest; our heart chakra.

Presence exploration 6 — presence radiated through the heart-centre

1. Warm up the centre in your chest.[*]
2. Acknowledge who is present in that centre. In the wings of your imaginary stage, speak the words: I AM (or whatever name you give that presence).
3. Walk on stage and radiate your presence from your heart to your imaginary audience.
4. Repeat step 3 with an audience of colleagues.
5. Observe that radiating from your heart to an audience is a precise activity that requires presence. It is not a sentimental, vague idea.
6. Integrate radiating from your heart with other *presence* explorations.

Chekhov called this mediating of our presence through the centre in our chest: *radiating and receiving*. He also uses the term 'radiating' as the *quality-of-movement* related to the element of fire (as described in chapter 1). We will understand why he used the same term in both contexts if we have experienced how radiating in the context of the *qualities-of-movement* requires our utmost activity. By referring to projection of our presence through the heart as radiating, Chekhov indicates that radiating from our heart into the world is not some wishy-washy, sentimental, vague emotion. It requires intense activity and energy *activated consciously and humanized*, that is: made human through the heart.

Presence exploration 7 — radiating and receiving (partner work)

1. Warm up radiating as in *quality-of-movement exploration 15*.[†]
2. Radiate the fire through your heart chakra out into the world. Work full-bodily. Reduce the outer movement (10–1).

---

[*] See chapter 3, pages 137–140.
[†] See chapter 1, page 64.

3. Sustain radiating inwardly, and walk around the space.
4. Meet a partner, stop and radiate towards them. Receive the energy that radiates to you from them.
5. Alternate radiating and receiving energy. Embody this exchange in gesture (10–1).
6. Throw a beanbag back and forth with your partner. Penetrate your action with the radiating and receiving energies.
7. Prepare in your imaginary wings. Enter your imaginary stage and radiate to your imaginary audience. Receive from them as well. Return to full-bodied gesture when you need to strengthen the original sensations.
8. Repeat with a practice audience.

Presence exploration 8 – giving and receiving (partner work)

1. Warm up giving and receiving.[*]
2. Move between levels 10–1 of outer gesture as you are able to sustain the sensation inwardly.
3. Meet a partner and exchange your gestures. Explore their transitions; how your gestures grow from one into the other.
4. Prepare full-bodied gestures for giving and receiving in your imaginary wings. Enter your imaginary stage and stand in front of your imaginary audience. Using full-bodied gesture, create a gesture-dialogue of giving to, and receiving from your audience. Or first receive from them, and then sense what you wish to give.
5. Repeat this with a practice audience. Create the following exchange with full-bodied gesture first and then allow the words to unfold. The actor enters and receives from the audience:

Audience:	I give you my attention.
Actor:	I receive your attention. I give this gift/these words/this story to you.
Audience:	I receive your gift/your words/your story, etc.

6. After practising the archetypal dialogue, replace, *I give you this gift/ these words/ this story,* with *Once upon a time . . .*
7. Allow the story to develop phrase by phrase, image by image as response within the dialogue of gestures. When you are able to sustain the sensations of presence and radiate them to your audience, reduce your outer gestures (10–1).
8. Test your quality of presence and adapt these steps. Improvise with colleagues/ classmates, situations, atmospheres where the audience is not so supportive of

---

[*] See chapter 3, pages 137–138.

your presence. Can you maintain it until they are ready to give you their attention and receive from you?

9. Share your observations.

These explorations specifically support the development of presence and the projection of it to an audience. We have slowed down and magnified the normally invisible process that takes place in a fruitful interchange between performer and audience. This enables us to practise presence at that threshold instead of abandoning ourselves and plunging unconsciously across it into the abyss.

Presence can be developed like any other skill, by practice. We awaken it by being conscious as a *self* performing any action. We learn to apply it in the contexts of the different relationships the actor's art requires.

An actor's relationships

In each moment of our work, actors are engaged in one or more of the following relationships. Every relationship presents us with the threshold between self and other and therefore the opportunity to practise presence.

(a) actor to character
(b) actor to actor
(c) ensemble – performing in a group
(d) character to character
(e) actor to audience

Actor to character

We build a conscious relationship to our character with the tools explored in chapter 4. These provide us with the means for staying present when, in Steiner's terms, we are at the threshold where either we must let someone else exist inside our skin without the loss of self or, without a loss of self, slip into the skin of another. To choose a tool, engage with the set of choices it provides and stay conscious as we constantly renew them, guarantees our presence.

Actor to actor

The health of relationships with fellow actors is often relegated to the realm of the unconscious, with interactions largely determined by instinctive antipathies and sympathies.

The time has passed, or may at least be passing, that supports a culture of collusion with dysfunctional behaviour. I observe each new generation of my students, increasingly demand integration, from themselves, their teachers and artistic models. It is not an expectation to be perfect, but a growing sense we need to be responsible for our behaviour that arises from unconscious aspects of the self (our subtext). It is not acceptable that in the name of genius or talent others should be held to ransom by our own or a colleague's inappropriate behaviour.

The courage to make our subtext conscious and to own it, is dependent on our cultivation of the super-text. The central pillar of healthy interaction is reverence for the I AM in oneself and the other. This is not to be confused with the propping up of the illusory self encouraged in our culture by glamorizing actors and the value placed on stardom and celebrity.

The explorations for *opening the heart* and *giving and receiving* remind us, in an unsentimental way, of the love that supports and underpins healthy interactions. To behold, consistently, the sacred flame in our own and others' hearts, provides a different lens through which to view the tensions that arise.[*] It is the template that allows us to distinguish actors from the characters they play.

We know how enriched we are by colleagues who receive from and give to us on stage. Such partners are not selfishly concerned to be 'the star', to upstage, or glorify themselves. The radiating presence we strive for in this work is not to gain power over other actors or an audience, but to serve the character and play.

Nurturing a conscious heart connection, always receiving what my fellow actors give to me and giving back to them, we cultivate the social aspect of the art of acting that goes beyond unconscious camaraderie and leads to *ensemble*.

Many actors long for a healthy working culture yet it is naïve to imagine that problems between personalities would simply disappear by such practices. I have been part of several floundering and failed attempts to build a conscious, healthy social culture as a vessel for artistic work. The difficulty in achieving this does not invalidate the striving and is, no doubt, part of learning how to do it.

In the meantime, such work as we have mentioned provides a context within which difficult relationships may be contained. In addition, many methodologies developed in the last fifty years move back and forth across the boundaries between psychotherapeutic practice and the actor's art, acknowledging how imagination and acting out help us understand our own subtext and transform our interactions.[†]

Ensemble

Many actors dream of working together for the long term with the same group. Over the years, a special substance develops; a sense of the 'being' of the group that is not just the sum of its parts but has wisdom of its own. Decisions are not made by individuals but by the being of the group. And yet, each individual is in no way an automaton, but conscious, present, fully functioning, attuned to and participating in the greater whole, a single cell within an organism. When we see such a troupe at work, it feels like nothing else and awakens the longing to be part of such a work.

To cultivate ensemble consciousness, we learn to stay present while our consciousness expands and merges with the other actors in the group. The following is one of many variations evolving from an exercise Chekhov called 'The Golden Hoop'.

---

[*] See chapter 3, The heart-centre.

[†] For example: psychodrama, drama therapy, playback theatre, gestalt, process oriented therapy, psychosynthesis, etc.

Ensemble exploration 1 — the Golden Hoop

1. Stand in a circle. Be present in yourself. Take time, in silence, to sense each member of the group in turn, until you carry the whole circle in your consciousness. Listen to the space between you. The group attunes itself to the impulse described in step 2. It does not arise from any individual's will. No one takes the lead and 'jumps the gun' either from inability to tolerate uncertainty, or need to control. Neither does anyone resist and block the impulse but responds to the subtle shift of energy.
2. Imagine there exists, in the heavens, a golden hoop, within which lie the treasure and potential of the work we are about to do. This golden hoop is another way to imagine the threshold that we consciously step over to begin and close our work. We invite it to the earth before we start and give it back to the heavens at the end.

Ensemble exploration 2 — Golden Hoop to open our work

1. The 'body' of the group reaches up, receives the golden hoop from the heavens and draws it down to earth.
2. Sense the space needed for your work, expand to encompass it and place the hoop on the floor inside the circle of your feet.
3. Step inside the circle and begin.

Ensemble exploration 3 — Golden Hoop to close our work

1. Gather around the hoop you brought to the earth at the beginning and become aware again, that the group is 'one body'.
2. Sense the impulse, then bend down and pick up the golden hoop that lies inside the circle of your feet.
3. Then, as one body, lift it high into the air and lower it to gather the impetus to throw.
4. Then, as one body, fling it upwards to the heavens and watch it disappear. Sustain your attention until the group finds the impulse to release it.

Ensemble exploration 4 — Golden Hoop variation

If we have used the golden hoop as a threshold, to begin our work, we could use it as a threshold at the end.

1. At the end of your work gather consciously within the circle you laid down when you began.
2. As an ensemble, sense the impulse and step outside of it.
3. Sense the impulse, lift the hoop and return it to the heavens.

Ensemble exploration 5

At first, agree on the transitions before activity begins. As confidence increases, the group can sense the impulse of what wants to happen next without prior consultation. The next steps need not be included in a single session.

1. Stand in a circle, still and quiet, sensing the presence of the other individuals, the group.
2. Gently move your arms and hands as though you are seaweed in the ocean.
3. Become aware that you share that ocean, move within and are moved by the same currents.
4. As the currents carry you, be aware that all the 'bits of seaweed' are equally affected.
5. As the group expands, be aware that even your most tiny, subtle movements affect the other members of the group, as theirs affect you.
6. Choose one person and move in response to them.
7. Keeping that one in your consciousness, include another. Now you move in response to what two other people do.
8. Add a third to your awareness, moving in response to three.
9. Keep including members of the group in your awareness until everything you do is woven inextricably within the whole. At some point you sense that the group is held, as though within a 'skin' woven out of your peripheral awareness.
10. Weave easily, sensing the pathways that connect you, as though the space around you is alive and you are clothed in it. It cushions each of you, enabling you to move with confidence. You develop antennae that sense the other parts of your 'body'. You know where they are and it is impossible for any part to obstruct or crash into another.
11. The group functions as a single organism, each individual the cell of an amoeba floating in the sea.
12. Without any single 'cell' taking the initiative, yet with each one ready to respond, the body of the group transforms from floating into flying into radiating, then to moulding.
13. This exploration can develop to include the other tools: staccato and legato, expanding and contracting, etc.

Ensemble exploration 6

1. Each individual move freely in the space.
2. Focus on another member of the group and relate your movement to theirs. Choose someone unaware of your choice.

3. Integrate your movement with theirs and then expand your consciousness to include and respond to a second person. Now your movement connects you with unseen threads to two other members of the group.
4. Then three, then four and so on, until you hold the group in your awareness when you move and just as you hold them, so too are the others holding you.

Ensemble exploration 7 – a variation

1. Move as an individual.
2. Signal your intention to connect and when someone accepts your offer integrate your movement as a pair.
3. Connect your movement to another pair and form a group of four.
4. Connect to another group of four, etc., until the whole group moves as one.

Ensemble exploration 8

1. Stand in a circle, attune to each other, sense when the whole circle is prepared, sense the direction the 'body' of the group will take and move as one.
2. Do this several times.
3. Work in this way incorporating other simple movements: sitting, standing, moving backwards, forwards, kneeling.
4. As a single organism, sense when it is time to end and complete the work together.

Ensemble exploration 9 – variations
Try explorations 1–4:

(a) Within specific atmospheres.[*]
(b) Once the character is built, with the group of characters who share a scene or play.

Ensemble exploration 10 – impulse

1. Build ensemble consciousness.
2. Each member (cell) of the group (body), in turn, initiates an impulse, to which the body of the group responds as a single entity. For example: I raise an arm, the group kneels in response, I turn, the group swings around to face me from the other side, I sweep through the middle, the group scatters to all sides. The initiator learns to determine and direct the ensemble's energy; to create a focus that does not impose but emerges out of the ensemble.

---

[*] See chapter 3, page 179.

Character to character

The goal of I AM to I AM can be healthily nurtured by *opening our hearts* to one another and *giving and receiving,* but is unlikely to embody the dynamic underlying the relationships and interactions most characters display. This provides us with an opportunity to practise complex layers of presence.

Our training has prepared us to be present with both initiative and receptivity, to be available as artist to fellow artist. This does not need to be discarded as foundation for our work together, even when overlaid and interwoven with choices we have made to build our characters; choices which deny the possibility of healthy social interactions.

For an actor to radiate towards and be receptive to another actor when the character expresses, for example, the objective: *I want to hurt/or punish you* requires multi-levelled consciousness. We build our capacity for such complex functioning in simple steps.

Character-to-character exploration 1 (partner work)

1. Warm up *presence* and *radiate* it through your *heart-centre*. Meet your partner in the field generated by this pure dynamic.
2. Complete your interaction and separate.
3. Each prepare a gesture of *contraction.*
4. Minimize the outer gesture, inwardly sustaining it.
5. Approach and meet through the lens of your contracted state. As you sustain your inner gesture of contraction, allow yourself to be affected by each other.
6. Stay aware of this in one part of your consciousness and in another recall the sensation of radiating and receiving. Find out how to sustain the contraction as you radiate your presence to your partner and receive what radiates from him/her from a 'place' beyond your gestures of contraction.
7. Experiment with levels 10–1 of interweaving gestures (radiating/receiving and contraction) in order to juggle and sustain both sensations. As an artist you radiate to a fellow artist and receive from him/her in return. As a character your gesture of contraction affects and is affected by your partner's character's contraction.
8. Focus on receiving what your partner radiates to you, even while your character is inwardly contracted.
9. Focus on radiating to your partner even while your character remains contracted.
10. Explore your interactions and exchange your observations.

Character-to-character exploration 2 — working with text (partner work)

Expand *exploration 1,* into your practice dialogue: *I didn't expect to see you,* etc.

Character-to-character exploration 3 — working with text — Hamlet
Apply these choices to the interaction between Hamlet and Rosencrantz and/or Guildenstern.

Character-to-character exploration 4
Practise complex meetings with a partner within prepared artistic choices based on unhealthy interactions, even violence. Your goal is to simultaneously exercise both levels of awareness: the artist's and the character's.

Character-to-character exploration 5

1. Choose characters whose mutual antipathies provide an opportunity to practise multi-levelled consciousness: Romeo and Tybalt, Goneril and Lear, Shylock and Antonio, Prospero and Caliban, Lady Anne and Richard, Ophelia and Hamlet, George and Martha, for example.
2. Make some simple choices that create a field in which the characters can meet and interact. Can you, as actors, receive and radiate the choices that generate the interactions of your characters?

Actor to audience
'Bums on seats!' 'Let's get out there and show the bastards!' These expressions are part of theatre language. The first reflects a perception of the arts as an industry, the second of the audience as 'enemy'. In either case, audience and actor are reduced to objects; each existing only to manipulate or be manipulated. Neither interaction can result in communion which is only possible when actors know that they, their characters, their fellow actors and the audience are expressions of the sacred Self.

Actor to audience exploration 1
Practise *opening the heart, giving and receiving* and *presence* explorations with an imaginary then a practice audience as preparation for performing. Use a full-bodied gesture to embrace the space, the audience.

De-roling
We have considered the importance of de-roling and how to build this as hygienic practice into all we do.[*] Now we conclude this practical part of the book with an example of a process to be used at the end of a rehearsal or performance, particularly if the content of the play and characters require actors to inhabit the dark and

---

[*] See Terms of reference, page 49.

destructive elements of human nature. It can be modified to meet the need of individuals, or a group that shares a common goal in this respect.

De-roling exploration 1 — individual

1. After the rehearsal/performance, create the full-bodied gesture that most completely embodies all your preparation for the character you play.
2. Release it.
3. Use any of the steps of *heart-centre explorations 4–5* to contact the centre in your chest and fill yourself with heart forces.[*]
4. When you have acknowledged your I AM picture in turn each of the actors with whom you interact in the play and radiate a stream of warmth and light towards each one.

De-roling exploration 2 (group)

1. At the end of the rehearsal/performance, the company gathers on the stage.
2. Repeat steps 1–3 of *de-roling exploration 1*.
3. Move around the space and meet each other actor in turn. Take time to open your heart to each other. Speak the words I AM to each other.
4. When the meetings are complete, stand in a circle and create a gesture to embrace the circle from your heart.

Through Chekhov's explorations, we cultivate awareness of the divine self in our colleagues, characters, ourselves and audience, however far we may fall short of our divinity. Like the doctor in *Macbeth*, who witnesses the torment of Lady Macbeth compelled incessantly to re-enact the murder she conspired to commit; he beholds her with the love of the bridegroom for his bride, *God forgive us all... My mind she has mated.*

For actors to develop such profound sensibilities in relation to artistic content, audience and colleagues in the different contexts that different styles demand requires more research and experiment with opening the heart, giving and receiving, and radiating presence. It is obvious that to tell a story requires a different form for the relationship between the audience and artist than that required when I play a character or recite a lyric poem. Sometimes a work involves a combination of the three — Shakespeare's *Romeo and Juliet* requires actors who can play characters who interact, relate events and speak lyric poetry.

In relation to styles of drama, some do away with the fourth wall convention. These

---

[*] See pages 136–140.

and storytelling require audience and artist to relate directly. Dramas obeying the convention require an indirect connection with the audience that is sensed through the lens of a character.

The goal of actors in developing their speech and body skills is transparency. When this is achieved nothing that the artist does, or does not do, obscures what needs to be expressed and the audience believes that they experience reality. Such reality is not to be confused with naturalism. On the contrary, the greatest artists make extraordinary levels of experience real for the beholder.

But yet, the elements of sensibility, technique and gift do not themselves make art. Artists invest their passion, are willing to surrender, jump off the edge, be vulnerable, pour their life blood into their creation. This is what makes us sensitive to judgement or criticism, for it is our very self that we offer and that now awaits the verdict.

How imperative it is then, that we cultivate awareness of the Self that cannot be annihilated. Only this grants the objectivity that enables us to separate creation from creator and fruitfully receive and offer the critical appraisal without which our artistry cannot mature.

Epilogue

Dionysus and the New Epidaurus

A new Epidaurus

At the origin of drama was the actor-priest. The priest's task was to mediate between the supersensible realities of our existence and human beings, like Oedipus, increasingly unable to perceive such realities directly. The actor too, through the characters portrayed, reminded audiences of the god-like nature of the human being and the consequences of forgetting the divine. We have explored the thought that humanity has just begun the long journey home to 'paradise' or direct perception of the spirit. Within this context, how might the concept of the actor/priest metamorphose for our time; whose ancient task had been to mediate between humanity and a world of spirit increasingly removed and inaccessible.

When we behold or meet a human being who does the work of conscious presence, Nelson Mandela for example, we are strengthened by hope for humanity. If an audience could sense such presence in the actors who appear before them on the stage, might it not inspire them with their own potential to stand firm in the chaos of perceptions that threaten to submerge us; those flung at us by the world of everyday appearances and those flung at us as we loosen from what once appeared 'this too, too solid flesh' and the stability of matter. And show them too their potential to illuminate and order that experience. Almost every textbook that considers the purpose and philosophy of drama points out that its function is to hold up a mirror to reality so that the audience can see themselves. Could we expand our definition of reality and of the self that is reflected back?

In classical Greek times, Epidaurus was a centre of enlightenment for those who sought the mysteries of healing. Dedicated to Asclepius, the god of healing, the sanctuary included, in addition to the hospital, a temple, gymnasium, and theatre in which dramas thought to be essential to the patients' therapy were acted by the priests and physicians. Another element of healing was the dream bestowed upon the patient by Asclepius. According to the practice, after the required preparation, the god would visit the patient during sleep and grant a vision of the remedy.

Could we imagine performances in which the god reveals to an audience a vision that would heal; in which the presence of the god within the actor could be sensed — waking dreams in which the audience beholds the journey of their own divinity acknowledged in the characters portrayed, the stories told. We may hope that from our work, a new Epidaurus will arise; a theatre where, appropriately to the world and times, human beings would come in search of healing. Chekhov knew that what he called the 'theatre of the future' would require *actors of the future*. To this end he bequeathed his methodology.

Baby Dionysus

Chekhov's words about this path: *we are all babes in this long tremendous way,* could equally apply to all humanity. The vast perspective of the evolution of the earth and the arrival on it of our species, Homo sapiens, serves to reveal the stage upon which the drama of becoming human can unfold.

The connection of this drama with the divinity the Ancient Greeks called Dionysus, is embodied in their recognition of him as the patron god of theatre. Theatre was the ritual in which his mysteries were brought into the open at a level judged appropriate for the uninitiated population by the guardians of culture at that time. The death and resurrection of this God was celebrated each year in the springtime drama festival where Dionysus was invoked.

The myths surrounding Dionysus suggest a complex, many-faceted divinity, as difficult to comprehend as our own humanity. They embody the contradictions inherent in our journey towards selfhood; the egotism of a self not yet mature and the trials endured to purge and purify that self until the greater Self, that we have called the Bridegroom, can emerge.

In his poem *Craving for Spring*, D H Lawrence invokes in modern form, the Dionysian energy of spring and reveals the connection of that god to our humanity.

> Ah come, come quickly, spring!
> Come and lift us towards our culmination, we myriads;
> we who have never flowered, like patient cactuses.
> Come and lift us to our end, to blossom, bring us to our summer,
> we who are winter weary in the winter of the world ...

What Lawrence refers to as 'our end' our 'blossom', is the birth and development within us of the indestructible entelechy of the eternal Self: the I AM. This is the Self the Ancient Greeks called Dionysus, the Egyptians named Osiris and the Indians recognised as Krishna.

The stage on which this drama is enacted is the earth. The vessel that has been prepared is *Homo sapiens*, whose unique attributes make possible that one day we may consciously participate in our evolution. On this stage, that Self will play many parts in many different dramas until it learns to recognize itself as Love.

Shakespeare also understood that we are little more than babies on this path: 'Love is a babe …' (*A Midsummer Night's Dream*) and, 'Love is too young to know what conscience is …' (*sonnet 151*). How better, then, to show the early stage of our unfolding selfhood, than as a babe?

We have considered the central part played by the Mysteries of Eleusis in the evolution of the art of theatre in the West. It's impossible to form a clear picture of how these mysteries were celebrated every year. Surviving fragments of accounts suggest that the greater Mysteries, which took place over nine days in the Autumn, culminated in the joyous and triumphant procession of the statue of the *Iacchus Child,* also known as *Bromius,* back to Eleusis from its temple in Athens. Scholars differ regarding the connection of these names and the beings they designate. Were they different aspects of the one being which was also called Dionysus or were they separate beings, and what was their significance?

The outer evidence will never yield definitive answers to these questions but we can continue to explore the meaning of these images and names to the psyche which gave birth to them, and in which they continue to evolve and resonate. What we know is that the Greeks expressed an aspect of the being they called Dionysus in the image of a baby. Here we see the god Hermes/Mercury holding and beholding the baby Dionysus (figure 30).

In its infancy the ego kicks and struggles, like a baby throwing tantrums when it cannot get its way. One version of the myth recounts how baby Dionysus, unable to wait until he reached maturity to ascend his father's throne, snatches power prematurely, hurling Zeus's thunderbolts and wreaking havoc in his unbridled egotism. His hubris was punished by the Titans tearing him apart; his dismemberment an image of increasing division in the human race, the price paid to become an individual.

Theatre is that art which most closely shows this journey of the Self to know itself. Drama came into the world to teach us the steps this little baby has to take to grow up and mature; to stand face-to-face with his divine, elder counterpart, here shown as Hermes/Mercury.

Hermes, able to travel between earth and heaven, is chosen by the gods to be their messenger. So too could actors be; grounded in the supersensible realities as much as those of earth, at home on both sides of the threshold and able to make the transits easily.

The gaze of Hermes, kindly and serene, teaches actors how to love their characters and their creations; to contemplate the little baby self in its first attempts at being human; its stumblings, failures, falls, mistakes, its tantrums and its terrors, its agonies, hopes, delights, endearing foolishness, its joys and discoveries. And as baby actors contemplate the Self we would become, we rest secure in its calm, unjudging presence, repose at ease within the Love which is itself.[52]

Figure 30 – Hermes/Mercury and the Baby Dionysus

We can trace the evolution of the sacred myth of Dionysus in the dramas through the ages. Albee depicts it for our modern soul, in *Who's Afraid of Virginia Woolf?* The character of Martha reveals the sacred moment when, as modern human beings, we cease projecting our divinity outside ourselves. Martha has created a holy dream child who will never come to visit. Out there, ever absent, safely distant, he remains forever perfect.

Uncorrupted, ever worshipped and adored, ever split off from her darker side, he never threatens the reality of what has yet to be transformed and integrated. At last, but not before a struggle to the death, she finally accepts the dream that kept her in denial of the journey she must make, has shattered. Perhaps what seemed death throes were, as they were for Oedipus, the pains of birth as well: the agony of labour to bring to birth the god within. In her final lines, Martha takes her own first baby steps upon the path that leads us back to paradise, to transform and integrate her shadow as she goes.[53]

> *George*: [*puts his hand gently on her shoulder; she puts her head back and he sings to her very softly*]: Who's afraid of Virginia Woolf, Virginia Woolf, Virginia Woolf…
> *Martha*: I … am … George …
> *George*: Who's afraid of Virginia Woolf …
> *Martha*: I … am … George … I … am …
> [*George nods, slowly.*]
> [*Silence; tableau.*]

Dionysus comes of age

Two thousand years of horrifying history have burdened the Christian churches in the West with heavy karma, like a toxic cloud that permeates the world. As a result, although we can speak the names of Krishna, Dionysus or Osiris without faltering, acknowledging the role they play, even today, within our psychic depths, it is more complex and delicate to speak the name assigned by Christianity to the being whose mission was to bear cosmic love into the depths of earth. We are sensitive to the anomaly that:

> One came forth of gentle worth
> Smiling on the sanguine earth

[but]

> His words outlived him, like swift poison
> Withering up truth, peace and pity.

Then, like Prometheus in Shelley's lyric drama *Prometheus Unbound,* who sees a vision of a youth:

> With patient looks nailed to a crucifix

We say:

Figure 31 – Bacchus/John the Baptist

Thy name I will not speak.
It hath become a curse.

The first line of Albee's *Who's Afraid of Virginia Woolf?* is, *Jesus Christ*, uttered by Martha as a drunken curse. Yet this is the name in Christian mystical tradition of the true Bridegroom of the human soul, the one at work within us to bring us to our fruit and flowering.

St John the Baptist/Dionysus

The famous painting in the Louvre, based on a drawing by Leonardo da Vinci of St John the Baptist, hints at the mysterious connection between Christ and Dionysus. The painter has transformed the original image of the Baptist into Bacchus/Dionysus. The god, who to the Ancient Greeks embodied the arrival on the earth of selfhood, beckons us with the gesture increasingly reserved in Christian art for John the Baptist. It directs attention away from itself towards the greater one to come; He who replaced Dionysus as the god of theatre, when, in the 10th century AD[54], the drama, lost from Europe in the centuries following the dissolution of the Roman Empire, was reborn within the Easter Mass in the Benedictine Abbey of St Gall in Switzerland. The angels seated on the empty tomb greet the women who have come to mourn the body of their Lord.

> *Angels*: Quem quaeritis? (Whom do you seek in the sepulcher, O followers of Christ?)
> *Answer by the Marys*: Jesus of Nazareth, who was crucified, just as he foretold.
> *Angels*: He is not here. He is risen. Just as he foretold. Go, announce that he is risen from the sepulcher.[55]

From this liturgical insertion, sung in Latin by the priests, drama evolved once again, step-by-step expanding in its scope, spreading throughout Europe into the vernaculars; inviting congregations to become audiences sharing a more complex mystery of incarnation. Liturgy developed into characters and earthly interactions that revealed the living presence of a god within who continues to evolve through each cycle of humanity's becoming; requiring forms no longer tolerated or contained within the churches or theologies defining right and wrong in static liturgies, whose mysteries were no longer understood. As the scope of this drama widened to encompass the mystery enacted in the temple of each human being, so theatre reflected this, evolving outside the churches into the greater temple of the earth. In these stages we sense the evolution of the drama of Eleusis. For the hell from which Persephone must now be rescued is not somewhere else, but here. As Mephistopheles tells Faustus, who asks to understand where Hell is:

> *Mephistopheles*: [indicating all around] Why this is hell, nor are we out of it.[56]

Figure 32 – Priests enact the trope within the Easter mass

And as the hands of Dionysus/John the Baptist indicate, if the One to whom he points, invisible to earthly senses, is to transform our experience on earth, he must first have penetrated to the heart of it. This is the fulfilment of the prophecy that Hermes made to Prometheus, 1500 years before:

Hermes [to Prometheus]: Look to no ending to your agony
until a god shall freely suffer for you,

will take on him your pain and in your stead
descend to where the sun is turned to darkness;
the black depths of death.

Prometheus Bound, Aeschylus

The significant works that contribute to our western theatrical tradition may not have been *consciously* inspired by this perspective, but these words of Seneca point to the connection:

> It is not necessary to raise one's hands to heaven; there is no need to request a verger to give us access to the ear of an image, as though that would secure a close attention to our petitions. God is near you, with you always, within you. There is, I am sure, a divine spirit within us, which keeps watch and ward over all that is good or bad within us … No man is good without the presence of God; who can rise above the accidents of fate except by his help? From him comes the prompting to high and noble deeds. In every good man there dwells 'what god we know not, but a very god'.[58]

It may never be possible to find the outer evidence that proves Seneca had contact with the early Christians. Scholars are divided as to whether his purported correspondence with St Paul, is genuine. But whatever outer evidence might prove or disprove about Seneca's connections to the early Christians, he speaks of the One the angels said could not be found by looking there. Nor will outer evidence ever prove the identity of the One who has continued to evolve in the dramas springing from that first Easter Sunday morning seed.

But we know the plays of Seneca, rediscovered and translated during the Renaissance, formed the basis of revenge tragedy. We know that this became and still remains today, the staple of our entertainment. We know that Shakespeare wrote his plays, in part to find the way from *Titus Andronicus*, a world without forgiveness, to the vision of humanity made whole in *The Tempest*. We know that every drama ever written or performed reveals the tragedy of being stuck in the cycle of revenge or the comedy that awaits us if we could forgive.

Our Western theatre lineage

This collage of images reminds us of the mysteries which actors serve no less today than in the past; making clear the thread of our lineage. Tracing the pathway from their birth in the temple at Abydos: Osiris the risen Lord springing to new life in the harvest every year: reborn at Eleusis, revealing to the neophytes, in the ear of grain, the mystery of death and resurrection. These preparing for what would be enacted on the earth at Golgotha. Then, disappearing from our sight to reappear again in European churches in the Easter enactment of the mass. The eternal drama

Figure 33 – Our Western lineage

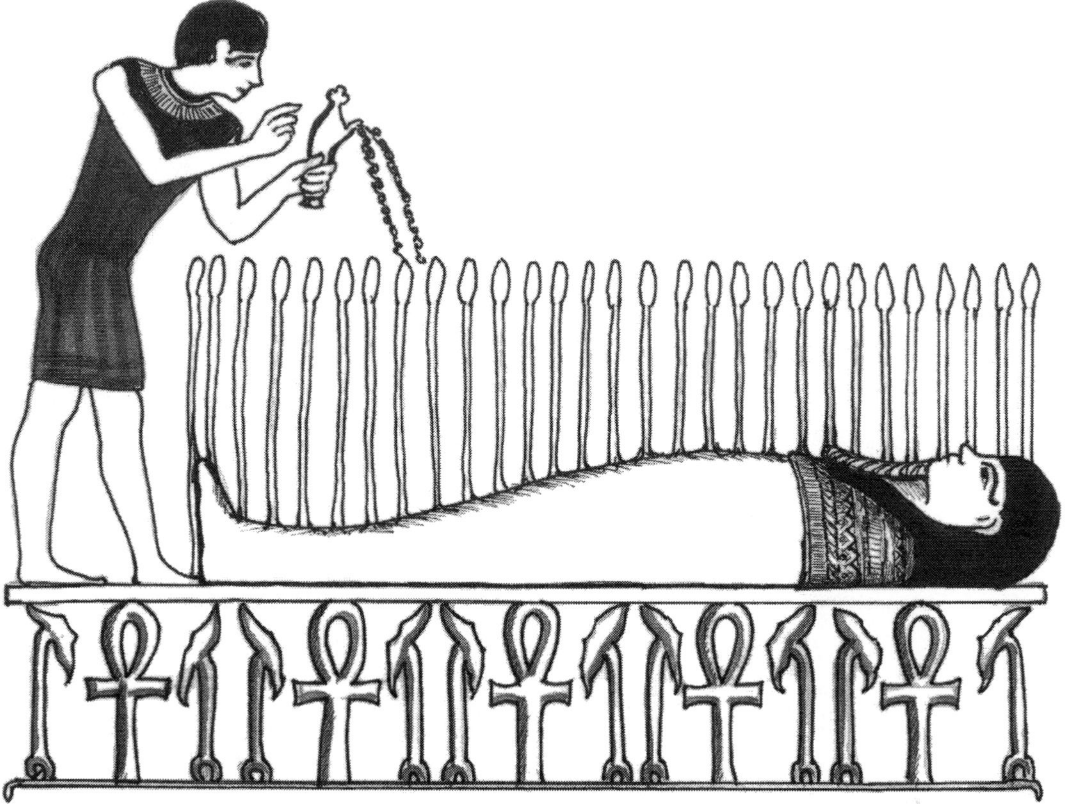

Figure 34 – Wheat sprouting from the body of Osiris

of that self who dies to be reborn in all cycles of humanity's becoming, is celebrated in this much-loved hymn, sung to the anonymous traditional French melody of the 15th century.

> Now the green blade riseth from the buried grain
> Wheat that in dark earth many days has lain
> Love lives again that with the dead has been;
> Love is come again like wheat that springeth green.
>
> In the grave they laid him, Love whom men had slain,
> Thinking that never he would wake again,
> Laid in the earth like grain that sleeps unseen:
> Love is come again like wheat that springeth green.
>
> Forth he came at Easter, like the risen grain,
> He that for three days in the grave had lain
> Quick from the dead, my risen Lord is seen;
> Love is come again like wheat that springeth green.

Figure 35 – Demeter bestows upon Triptolemus an ear of grain

When our hearts are wintry, grieving or in pain,
Thy touch can call us back to life again,
Fields of our hearts, the dead and bare have been;
Love is come again like wheat that springeth green.

with words by JMC Crum

It would be naïve to claim that the work of becoming fully human, which the alchemists referred to as the Magnum Opus, could be accomplished solely by such a training as this book describes. But Steiner and Chekhov invite us to consider that we cannot separate the journey to become an actor and an artist from the journey to become a human being.

Bridge to Book 2 — *The Art of Speech*

opening of St John's Gospel

A way of looking

You are digging in the earth. You strike a piece of stone. Excitedly, yet carefully, you brush away loose earth. There is a fragment from an ancient carving. It is covered with strange markings, utterly incomprehensible to you. Yet it is clear the markings have been carved with an intention to communicate. They are words. You may not yet be able to decipher them but you have no doubt that they can be deciphered. It would be perverse to insist those figures, carved with such clear intention, are arbitrary marks, formed by chance that has no purpose and no meaning.

Just so, would it be to look out into all that we perceive — the intricate order of the stars and planets, of a leaf formation, the wisdom concentrated in each creature, great and small, the geometry even of a tiny flower — and not see that each thing is a word. Each word expresses meaning and is created to express that meaning. Each word, in its turn, connects to greater wholes; sentences, paragraphs, whole treatises. The universe is one great book. There is nothing that is arbitrary.

To cultivate our sense of these connections means we draw our inspiration for artistic feelings from the greatest work of art, the universe itself. Within its macrocosmic counterpart our individual artistic journey can be nurtured and enriched. My focus in *The Art of Acting* has been to investigate what the actor's art could be when it draws its inspiration from that macrocosmic counterpart of our creative process; exploring and explicitly expressing some of the realities at the foundation of Michael Chekhov's psycho-physical technique.

In *The Art of Speech*, I focus on that other aspect of the actor's instrument; our voice and speech. Rudolf Steiner contributes to an understanding that the elements of voice, speech and language belong no less to these realities. I hope to make a bridge between the actor's art and the art of Speech, between our human words and the cosmic Word to which St John refers.

APPENDICES

Appendix A

Shakespeare, *Hamlet*: Act 2, scene 2

> *Hamlet [to Rosencrantz and Guildenstern]:*
> I have of late, but wherefore I know not,
> lost all my mirth,
> forgone all custom of exercises;
> and indeed,
> it goes so heavily with my disposition
> that this goodly frame, the earth,
> seems to me a sterile promontory;
> this most excellent canopy the air, look you,
> this brave o'erhanging firmament,
> this majestical roof, fretted with golden fire:
> why it appeareth no other thing to me
> than a foul and pestilent congregation of vapours.
> What a piece of work is a man,
> how noble in reason,
> how infinite in faculties,
> in form and moving, how express and admirable,
> in action how like an angel,
> in apprehension, how like a god:
> the beauty of the world,
> the paragon of animals;
> and yet to me,
> what is this quintessence of dust?

Appendix B

Michael Chekhov's original preface for *To the Actor*.[*]

Preface

This book is the result of lectures and lessons which I have given in my teaching work; of my experiments as a director and actor; and of my observation of the work of great exponents of the art of the theatre in many countries. I conceived the idea of such a book many years ago, and since have had the happy opportunity of verifying its fundamental principles in Russia, Latvia, Lithuania, Czechoslovakia, France, Poland, Germany, later in England and, finally, for the past few years in the United States.

In 1936, Mr and Mrs Leonard Elmhirst and Miss Beatrice Whitney Straight founded a theatre studio at Dartington Hall, in Devonshire, England, and I was invited to be its director. So the Chekhov Theatre Studio came into being. In 1939, the Studio moved to Ridgefield, Connecticut, where it has continued its work of training American actors and has achieved its aim of creating an acting group which has presented productions in New York and has toured the entire eastern part of the United States, being urged to do so by idealistic cultural aims. Much of the material in this book has been crystallized during the years I have worked with this group, and I am deeply grateful to Mr And Mrs Elmhirst and Miss Straight for their confidence in me and for the unique opportunity given me to work upon my ideas for the theatre.

To enable my readers to cope more easily with the construction and the general thought upon which my method, as a whole, is based, the following must be said.

In the last four to five decades, within the big stream of the development of science, art, philosophy and religion, one can clearly distinguish a new movement arising, the tendency of which is directed toward the <u>unification of science, art and spiritual knowledge</u>.

The initiator of this movement, Dr Rudolf Steiner, through his encyclopaedical knowledge, his sharp, clear thinking and his outstanding spiritual faculty, was able to give concrete practical advice to scientists, philosophers, artists and other specialists who wanted to develop, to refresh and to widen their professional knowledge.

Cold, analytical, materialistic <u>science</u>, being more and more deprived of its original artistic freedom on the one hand, and of its spiritual content on the other, once again absorbed its lost inspiring values in a new form. It became artistic and synthetic.

---

[*] This preface formed part of the original 1942 manuscript. It was copied by the author from a copy in the possession of Diedre Hurst du Prey, who worked with Chekhov in composing it. It has been reproduced here, in an identical form — with underlinings of words, etc., as they originally appeared — by kind permission of Pierre du Prey.

The Arts, having preserved their free and inspired nature, have received a strong foundation of clear, disciplined thinking, and were also able to widen their spiritual horizon. All vagueness, all floundering in the realm of certain branches of art, (and especially in theatrical art), was expelled from it. Concrete knowledge took its place.

Spiritual life gained also from the artistic and scientific inflow into its realm. Old-fashioned mysticism lost its meaning under the influence of Dr Rudolf Steiner's concrete spiritual investigations.

Because of this interplay of the three main branches of human cultural activities, (science, art and religion), the new methods and new contents became evident in natural history, psychiatry, medicine, education, mathematics, astronomy, psychology, sociology, agriculture and so forth. New schools, universities, clinics and artistic centres have been founded according to Dr Rudolf Steiner's teaching, before the First World War, in many countries.

In times such as ours it is only natural that the spiritual values decline and become hidden from our human eyes. But they themselves ripen and strengthen under the surface of the cruel, noisy and unjust outer life.

The dramatic art of our days, as the most vague and floundering of all arts, shrinking and weakening under the yoke of crude materialism, needs serious consideration. No doubt, in the near future it will greedily absorb into itself all that which may come to it as an exact knowledge both from the realm of science and the spiritual investigations. 'Talent' (this deceiving word of today!), will cease to be a vague general conception for an actor. All accidents will be banished from his profession. The new movement I have mentioned before, will persuade the actor that if the inspirations which he always expects from his 'Talent' have to be incorporated in our concrete, visible and audible world, a proper technique of acting is needed. An exact knowledge has to be acquired for this. The actor will also understand that the talent itself must be regarded by him as a gift from the higher world, in which his creative individuality lives. The actor will learn through personal experience that the growth of his talent depends on his general spiritual development. He will see that sound spiritual thoughts (not vague mysticism) based on concrete spiritual facts (not on theories), profound feelings and strong will-impulses are for his creative individuality what air and food are for his body and his health. He will understand that although his materialistic world-conception may give him certain conveniences in his social life of today, nevertheless it destroys, weakens and consumes his creative powers. Owing to this new movement, (uniting scientific, artistic and spiritual facts and methods), the actor will also realize that one has to be a materialist and a spiritualist at the same time. As an engineer, for instance, has to be a spiritualist while conceiving an idea, an inspiring vision of a new mechanical construction, he has to become a materialist as soon as he is going to incorporate, to materialize his creative idea. The same with the actor. As long as he is creating his character in the realm of his imagination, in his spirit, he cannot deny the spiritual world with its laws and its particular powers shaping in him his visions. But as soon as he starts to incorporate his image and strives to give it flesh and blood, making it visible and audible to others, he needs to 'come down' to earth with its laws, he needs a professional technique, be becomes a 'materialist'. One-sidedness — that is what the movement originated by Dr Rudolf Steiner is going to fight.

The only book on technique for dramatic art is that of Constantin Stanislavski. This book is the first foundation-stone for that great building which can and will be erected in the near future. My aim is to make a humble contribution to the future theatre by bringing another stone for the foundation.

But the task is difficult and I must admit that in re-reading the book, I found, to my great disappointment, that in some places it sounds more theoretical than it should for the nature of the subject. I know this cannot be avoided if one has to <u>write</u> about things which must be <u>demonstrated or discussed in a lively talk</u>. While teaching, I always endeavour to have my students and actors understand by <u>experiencing</u> the things which I wish to convey to them. Sometimes I demonstrate what they are to accomplish in a particular exercise.

That which takes but a few minutes of practical work in the classroom, may require many pages when it is <u>described</u>. A kind of unpleasant 'slow motion' occurs. I am very much averse to theorizing about the theatre, and therefore I must ask my reader to keep in mind that the real content lies behind what is written, and must be understood purely as an <u>inner experience</u>. That which we find in this book is only a hint of the work to be done, and no more. The reader, willing to try the exercises, will soon discover that there is nothing in the book which cannot be <u>experienced practically</u>, and will be able to overcome this theorizing.

I must confess that it is difficult to concentrate one's mind on such a specific theme when our troubled world absorbs one's whole attention, and makes all other things seem small and insignificant in comparison. Nevertheless, through the unshakeable <u>conviction</u> that the victory will be ours, and that freedom-loving people everywhere will have to work creatively in all branches of cultural life after the present catastrophe is over — in this conviction, I have found the strength to finish my task.

I wish to take the opportunity to express my deepest gratitude to Miss Deirdre Hurst, who accumulated the material for this book by means of her patient records. Because of her knowledge of the subject, gained as my associate in the work of teaching, she also assisted in giving the first form to the text.

Great help has been rendered by Professor Paul Marshall Allen. Having worked in the field of college education, and having had constant contact with young people, he knows their needs, doubts and questions from personal experience. Part of his educational work has been devoted to problems of the theatre, and therefore, in revising this book he was able to place himself in the position of my young readers. From this point of view, he has given me innumerable suggestions, and has made many corrections which will undoubtedly serve as a link between the readers and the ideas expressed in this book.

Mr George Shdanoff, co-director of the Chekhov Theatre Studio, since joining in my work of creating a school and a theatre in England in 1937, has taken a close part in the elaboration of the method itself. The many experiments and discussions we have had together have rendered me invaluable assistance in shaping my ideas. It makes me happy to have this opportunity of thanking Mr Shdanoff for his collaboration.

MICHAEL CHEKHOV

Appendix C

An autobiographical note

When I was fourteen, I was rescued from the inarticulate pain of adolescence by the discovery in class of Shakespeare's words. Over the next years, while our peers were dating, my friend Chester and I discovered, after school in a deserted classroom, the wonder and joy of plunging into scenes from *Macbeth*. We wallowed in the permission this gave us to explore depths of feelings which I, at least, had no way to understand in my daily life – or even know that I was feeling. It was always the darker characters that attracted me and along with Lady Macbeth, I spent hours alone in my room at home exploring the emotions of Phaedra or Shylock or Medea. I could not have told anyone what Dawn felt about anything – but I could tell them how Medea felt. Not only that – I could *show* them.

There were times when I astonished my peers and elders with my capacity to enter into such 'mature' roles at such an early age. I was a comedian as well and at school became one of a small group of 'legends' who enjoyed the status of celebrity. Others recognized our powers and bowed in awe. In spite of this so-called recognition, all was not as it appeared. I wanted to perform, yet experienced a pathological terror at being in front of any kind of audience, of any size. I endured the fear of death even to be asked to stand in class and answer a question, let alone to be on stage. As for criticism, any kind of judgement could annihilate me.

To help me with my self-consciousness, my parents sent me first to ballet and then speech and acting classes at The Studio Arts Centre in Adelaide, run by a visionary ballet guru, Joanne Priest. Over many years she became a friend and mentor who inspired in me a vision of art that required willingness to sacrifice oneself by striving for perfection at the altar of truth and beauty. There, too, I felt the wonder of my first acting classes with Gwyneth Ballantyne, who introduced me to the basic principles of Stanislavski.[59] Nevertheless, the terror of 'exposure' remained.

I trained to be a secondary teacher at the University and Teachers College in Adelaide, majoring in history and English literature. There was no professional theatre in Adelaide in those days, the National Institute of Dramatic Art (NIDA) in Sydney had barely come into existence, and the path of an actor was to join a company and learn from one's experience or go overseas and study. I had entertained no ideas of a career in acting.

My first year as a student at the teachers' college coincided with Musgrave Horner's coming to initiate a Speech and Drama training course for teachers. Musgrave had been a teacher and examiner at the Guildhall School of Music and Drama, London, and the London Academy of Music and Dramatic Art. He now wished to pour his rich lifetime of experience into the creation of a training that would enable teachers to bring speech and drama into schools. It was there, he was convinced, that the nurturing of a healthy feeling life through art had to begin. The author of several books on speech and speech in education, he worked with Stanislavski's exercises as a foundation for developing imagination. These, he believed, were the basis not only of an acting technique but also a creative process that would free speech from the straitjacket of *elocution*.

This 'larger than life' human being also became a friend and mentor. He instilled in me the 'British' tendency, sometimes referred to as 'working from the *outside in*', to create an objective form for what one wishes to express. Parallel and, as it proved, completely at odds with Musgrave's teaching, was the work of an American actor who joined the faculty. She was a 'method' advocate who worked strongly out of the American approach to Stanislavski that emphasized the need to work from the *inside out*. Its tendency was psycho-analytical and demanded a relentless probing of one's own unconscious to expose the raw material from which to build a character.

Her intensive work with me resulted in the first of several episodes when I came close to the disintegration of the persona with which I kept up my appearance of 'normality'. Frightened by the consequences of her 'method' and not knowing how to put me back together, the dear woman sent me to a psychologist for counselling. Yet, in spite of this, I found the 'method' of tapping into my own unhealed wounds as a way of accessing a character compelling, and my love of acting turned into a passionate pursuit of those intensities. For a time I longed to make it a career, but teaching was always a calling in its own right and I have continued to do both throughout my life.

When I was nineteen, my American 'method' teacher prepared me to perform a sequence of Lady Macbeth speeches in the Adelaide Eisteddfod. I received such an extended standing ovation from the audience that the adjudicator announced that it was necessary to do something she had never done before and justify to the audience why she could not award me first place. My performance was, she said, compelling and powerful to a degree she had not frequently encountered, but I had ignored the Eisteddfod conventions that provide a frame for such events.

At that same performance I was 'spotted' by Bruno Knez, a Croatian immigrant and innovative director who would eventually set up La Mama in Adelaide. He pounced on me, telling me that for years he had been searching for the right actress to play Medea and, at last, had found ME. Of course, I was hugely flattered. Despite advice that I should wait until I had the maturity to play such great roles, I accepted.

Well into rehearsal and with my vulnerabilities exposed by my method process, I was shattered when Bruno told me that he could not work with me because every slight suggestion made by him was interpreted by my fragile ego as a judgement or criticism that I was not perfect and caused it to fall apart. He asked me to accept instead, the role of messenger, a part that could make use of my intensities but allowed me to be more detached.

I felt humiliated and bewildered. I knew I 'could do it' but now I would never be able to 'show the world my capabilities'. The experience confirmed the emotional fragility that was to plague me through life. On the one hand, my ability to identify with characters whose pathologies resonated with my own gave me emotional intensity and range and on the other, made it challenging or impossible for anyone to work with me. I took increasing refuge in the 'safety' of teaching others, while continuing to search for an artistic form or vessel that could hold me.

My work with Musgrave awakened a deep passion for speech and language and a sense of their potential as a civilizing influence. When rightly nurtured, they cultivate an inner life that is articulate. Without this, Musgrave taught, human beings are sentenced to frustration which cannot express itself except through violence. Certainly the cultivation of objective form, by working on the texts of great poets and dramatists, helped me navigate and balance my chaotic inner life.

My first teaching job gave me unprecedented freedom and creative opportunity for a newly graduated teacher in Adelaide at that time. I was the first teacher in the state system engaged specifically to teach drama as part of the curriculum. I was invited by the Head to develop my own speech and drama syllabus throughout the school with particular focus on a group of students who were guinea pigs in an experimental progressive non-exam-based final year.

Throughout my training and these early years of teaching, I performed in course productions and with various theatre groups in Adelaide. I was directed several times by one of Adelaide's most gifted and respected artists, a terrifying and inspired director. His brutal methods, designed to demolish the ego of the actors so they would be 'putty in his hands', drew out of us remarkable performances. However cruel I felt he was to me, he would always let me know, in his inebriated state at cast parties, I was a 'bloody fine actress' but I 'did it all the wrong way round'.

It took me many years to understand what he meant by this. I had learned through my experience with Lady Macbeth and Medea to create an objective form to contain my intensity, but now, in order to protect myself, I found it safer to begin with form and only then allow myself to *feel*.

After two years of teaching in a secondary school, Musgrave invited me to return to the teachers' college as his colleague. I taught there for five years, lecturing in history of theatre, teaching speech and acting, drama in education and movement styles from different periods of history. I directed students in their course productions. The range of classes meant I could experiment and research my burning questions.

I read Rudolf Steiner's *Speech and Drama* lectures. Although some of the content struck me as outdated and very much coloured by the culture of his time, the early years of the 20th century, there were passages that resonated deeply with dimensions of myself that until then had been only dimly sensed. My earlier studies of broader history and the history of theatre had both fascinated and frustrated me; Steiner's work offered me a way to explore my questions at the deeper level, which until then had eluded me.

His descriptions of the sounds of language also seemed a natural progression from my work with Musgrave. The suggestion that consonants and vowels had objective reality and were not merely abstract noises to which we had ascribed an arbitrary meaning, resonated deeply. Excited by the possibilities, I began experimenting in my classes with the connection between sounds and movement. One approach I found particularly fruitful was between the qualities of consonants and the categories of movement identified by Rudolf Laban as *effort actions*, a technique the speech and drama department at the College was already working with.[60]

I was excited when Musgrave's last book, *Movement, Voice and Speech* was published because what I read seemed to confirm my own instincts and discoveries that the speaking of a poem or text would not merely transmit information infused with feeling but could recreate *the actual experience* embodied in the words. I still remember sharing with him my enthusiasm for what I thought were his ideas — even demonstrating an initial clumsy experiment related to some exercises in his book. It was clear he did not understand what I meant. This bewildering experience would be a stepping stone on a journey I could never have imagined.[*]

It seemed that I was 'talented'. My 'gift' had been acknowledged over and again. Yet, I lacked what was needed to survive the 'real world' of the theatre. I performed less and less. My thwarted ego dealt with its sense of failure by projecting onto mainstream theatre the judgement of 'spiritual shallowness'. I believed I was above the petty ambition of striving after recognition and success in a world which was not 'evolved enough' to recognize my superior capacities. Ha! It would take many years to recognize this self-deception, mingled as it was with my genuine quest for an acting process that would meet my psycho-spiritual needs. Believing such a path did not exist for actors but seeing that it did in Steiner Waldorf education, I decided to abandon theatre and train to teach in such a school.

In 1973, I left my job and went to England to study at Emerson College, an adult training centre based on Rudolf Steiner's work. I felt like someone who having crossed a desert and almost died of thirst, comes to an oasis. I drank deep from the pool for

---

[*] See, *The Art of Speech*, My teacher at the crossroads.

which I had been searching through the years when I had studied history and literature and theatre. I saw that it was possible to research my previously dim and unarticulated sense that behind the appearances of history and culture lay a story of unfolding purpose that cannot be perceived within the framework of effect and cause built from the tiny fragments of material phenomena that still survive and are selected to construct our picture of the past.

And, at last, I could immerse myself in Shakespeare at the level I had always suspected must be there. Francis Edmunds, the inspiring founder of the college, was in his retiring years. In both my years there as a student, he invited me to co-direct with him the annual Shakespeare play which was the culmination of each college year. This opportunity to help translate his vision into a process for my fellow students granted me the privilege to walk beside this great man on his journey into Shakespeare's consciousness. In those years, I also found the path to the experience of speech and language which I had long been searching for.

Yet I was confused. What I experienced in class, and read about 'the Speech' (called Speech Formation from the German *Sprachgestaltung*) answered my deepest questions, but when I heard it performed, my whole artistic instinct was repelled. How could this be? Despite my reaction, I could not quell the sense that Speech Formation was the purpose for which I had been born. But how to let go of those reservations and my other plans to return to Adelaide and help start a Steiner school? Then our painting teacher at the College organized a study tour to Egypt where I met my next great teacher, Maisie Jones, and knew I had to go to London for the four-year training with her in this new approach to Speech.

In performance, Speech Formation often sounded incomprehensible and odd, eliciting a hostile response. Yet always somewhat reckless when I sensed my destiny — and armed with the knowledge that precedents abound in the history of the arts and sciences of the challenges faced by those who plant the seeds for future understanding or capacities, pioneers who threaten the established culture's comfort zones — I worked hard to penetrate and master *Sprachgestaltung*, sensing I had found the vessel that one day would contain and guide my intensities.

I resembled a beginner on the violin who, unable to eradicate the squeaks and wobbles, is only too aware that they offend the listener's ear. Yet, I felt responsible to represent this new technique. As far as I could see, in this life I would never be able to demonstrate more than my *attempts* to do it. I withdrew from performance opportunities and consoled myself that I was planting a seed that would bear fruit in the future.

During the training, I had been invited to return, on its completion, and develop Speech and drama work at Emerson. I was privileged to teach there for the next ten years. In that time, the Speech School moved from London to the neighbourhood of Emerson, enabling me to teach there as well.

During the years of retraining and teaching, compelling questions arose from the necessity to integrate my new experience with the rich methodology I had learned and developed in Australia; to make the bridge between my past and future. I knew that some of the problems with the new approach to Speech that I had faced with my fellow students and now as I taught again myself, would disappear if approached with the drama methodology that freed the soul's relationship to the body. Without such processes to build a bridge on which to step joyfully and freely and into what the Speech work asks we have to will ourselves to overcome resistance as we struggle to find a way between our ordinary mortal consciousness and the sacred mysteries of Speech Formation.

At the same time it was clear that all my former training and experience, so rich in opening the soul, did not reach to the realm of spirit where the Speech work had its source. As always, grace could inspire creative processes that worked in the moment but without them I resorted to the same pedagogy based on imitation by which I had been taught. Now, each successive wave of students increasingly mirrored back to me that human beings of our present time no longer found this method, accepted as normal in the past, was healthy for their present constitution; to be asked to imitate without a process that engaged their own 'creative individuality' forced them to bypass or leap over aspects of themselves which they needed to transform and not exclude from the goal. I needed a reliable, methodical pedagogy that could underpin my inspiration as a teacher; a systematic process, open to but not dependent on the inspiration of the moment and which would make the wonders of Speech accessible.

In addition, although Speech Formation contained the potential for a whole new dimension to the art of acting, this was also in a pioneering stage. I was acutely aware of how inadequate my artistic efforts were and they became increasingly private. Here as well, my search became more urgent. The problem gradually clarified. My old acting methods which opened such a rich path for the soul could not be simply grafted onto an approach to Speech that had its source in realms of spirit. But did what I need exist; an art of acting born out of the same certainties and knowledge as the art of Speech Formation?

Then Diane Caracciolo came to train with me at Emerson. She had experienced the Chekhov work in America and was herself a gifted teacher.[61] I asked her to give some classes for any, like myself, who were interested. Already, in the first I *knew*: a pedagogy that would free me from reliance on imitation, did exist. Chekhov's work held the key to a process which integrated inner life and outer form.

I found myself en route to America. My friend and colleague, Barbara Audley introduced me to Ted Pugh and Fern Sloan, founders of the Actor's Ensemble in New York. Ted and Fern are gifted, professional actors and teachers, devoted for many years to the mastery of Chekhov's work and to understanding it within the context of Rudolf Steiner's Anthroposophy. Both wanted to investigate how their own work of mastering the actor's instrument could extend into Speech and we undertook exploratory workshops together.

These were a revelation. It seemed to me our meeting was a marriage made in heaven; as though we had been always weaving our two streams together. Moving from Chekhov to Speech and back again, I wondered how they ever had been separated. They were two sides of the same coin, two aspects of one reality.

I was shown again, not just how much I needed Chekhov's work in my evolution as a Speech Formation teacher, but also as an actor. I needed a technique that would enable me to access levels of experience outside the range of my instinctive talent. My tiny, tender Chekhov shoots had barely peeped through the earth when, on a visit back to England, I was invited by Portal Productions to play Maria in the third of Steiner's Mystery Dramas.

The acting problem that was now revealed, I had never faced before. I needed to create a character who was both a more mature and consciously developed human being than myself. As I plunged into rehearsals, I met my limitations yet again. How to approach a human being for which I had no basis yet in my experience? I looked with longing at those of my colleagues who could work on characters that acted out their anger, grief or fear; emotions that are given just because we have a soul. But where or how to find those qualities which only manifest when human beings consciously transform that raw material?

I didn't know where to start. Trying to appear as my *idea* of a nice or good person would not support the depth of content needing exploration and expression. Neither my director nor my colleagues (all whom I respected deeply) could help. I was batted back and forth between extremes of being told that I was too emotional or not emotional enough. The problem was, I had no basis in my own experience for objective passion, warmth of soul suffused with consciousness and permeated with intelligent control, achieved not by suppression but by transformation. Such substance cannot be dissembled.

I finished the season of performances knowing I had hardly scratched the surface of Maria's vast complexities, arising as they did from many lifetimes of experience and interaction with the destinies of the other characters with whom she was connected. Once again, the struggle of attempting something unequipped revealed a further missing piece in the jigsaw puzzle of my work that I was seeking to complete. Now I had a Speech technique worthy to contain the depth of substance such a character required, but with no substance to pour into the vessel, it was in danger of becoming 'sounding brass and tinkling cymbals'.[62] I had sampled enough of Chekhov's work to know it could unlock the depth of substance that I longed to access. A taste was not enough. I returned to my teachers in New York to immerse myself for several years in Chekhov's methodology.

Little by little, we invited others to our explorations.

This led to offering through Sunbridge College[63] our first year-long intensive process in the integration of these two streams of work. We team taught; each of us present in each other's classes, continuing to weave, students of each other's work and each of us a teacher of the thread that was our own. That first intensive was followed by a second and advanced work for those who wished to take the journey further. Not every participant connected to the stream of Speech, though many did. As always, I continued to be challenged to move beyond a pedagogy based on imitation. This was my classroom, as much for me as for my students; the opportunity to further research the potential Chekhov offered for my purposes.

After five years, the call back to Australia intensified to a level that outweighed my grief at leaving my two colleagues and I returned in 1995. Invitations to teach workshops in Sydney, Perth and Melbourne led to a request by several participants for a more intensive training in this integrated methodology.

I founded The School of the Living Word in 1998. This provided a four-year full-time training for those who wished to graduate with teaching and performing skills. The first two years were also available for those who wished to do this work for personal growth and development.

I decided not to go ahead with the process required for state accreditation. The size of the school and its finances did not warrant the investment of my energy, capacities and time that would be needed to meet the government criteria. One positive result of this decision was that those who joined the school stayed for as long as the work was meaningful and inspired them to earn the money needed to support themselves throughout the training. The work existed only in the clear energy of those who valued it. I found colleagues I respected and felt would be supportive of my goals who could contribute elements necessary to a comprehensive training, but that I could not provide. The school went through two complete cycles. Each first-year started with twelve students of whom four graduated from each group. In the years since I retired, I have focused on my personal journey of healing and integration, writing these books and freelance teaching.

During my years of intensive work and training in Chekhov's methodology, the world of performance opened unexpectedly again. It seemed only natural to experiment with projects of my own. I searched for opportunities to exercise and stretch my increasingly integrated instrument. So that I could focus on my own agenda of continuing research, I devised a series of solo performances that would test what I could do and challenge how far I could go.

Some of these projects were developed in ensemble with the violinist Perry Hart. We formed 'Voice and Violin' to research the relationship of words and music in performance, beginning with the poetry of Judith Wright and then *The Nightingale and the Rose*, a fairytale by Oscar Wilde. Our most intensive research and collaboration resulted in a chamber presentation of *King Lear*.

After some performances, the unexpected death of my beloved colleague cut short our planned tour with *King Lear*. At the invitation of the Goetheanum,[*] I devised and developed solo versions of Marlowe's *Dr Faustus* and the story of Kaspar Hauser, which was directed by my colleague, Suzanne Kersten. These toured within Australia and New Zealand, the United Kingdom and in Switzerland. Most performances took place within the international circuit of communities devoted to Rudolf Steiner's work.

These solo projects allowed me to experiment in a condensed time/space framework, creating many different characters and contexts. As a teenager and in my early twenties, I had affected audiences with my precocious intensity. Now, for the first time since those years, I could hear people weep or laugh when I performed. I was touching them. And somewhere along the way, I had lost the terror of performing. I began, cautiously, to expose my work to the 'outside world'.

Rosalba Clemente, then artistic director of the South Australian State Theatre Company[†], saw my *Dr Faustus*. She invited me to play the part of Hecuba in Euripides' *The Trojan Women*. This presented an opportunity to work with other actors, trained in different ways, and find out what, if anything, I might contribute in the mainstream context.

The experience and privilege of working with Rosalba and my fellow actors, to practise being present and available to them, required me to let go of my agenda of proving anything to anyone. I know that Chekhov's tools enabled me to build a character that held her own, to inhabit the play in its entirety and drive its action. The artistic substance demonstrated in the Speech and acting of the six third-year students from my school who were also able to participate as soldiers and chorus members was remarked upon by many, in the course of rehearsals and performances.

I missed what I had grown accustomed to in solo work or in my work with students: my evolving and our shared methodology, out of which a scene or play's tapestry of seen and unseen action could be woven; a detailed process that requires commitment

---

[*] The centre for the worldwide movement based on Steiner's work, in Dornach, Switzerland.

[†] Rosalba is now Head of Acting at the Drama Centre, Flinders University.

to as long as necessary (two years in the case of *Lear*). I had been privileged to know the luxury by which I/we could, layer by layer, uncover every nuance and could not expect that in the state theatre context. Nor could I have known that my hope of representing Speech Formation in this context was not to be fulfilled. I did not realize the actors and musicians would be amplified until close to the performance date.[*]

I had believed that such a play and such a role in such a context was an ideal opportunity to demonstrate what the integrated Speech and Chekhov work could do. Instead I learned to serve, in the best way that I could, the play, my director, fellow actors and the audience.

That I received a final nomination by the critics for that year's award for best female performer and achievement of artistic excellence, indicated my performance was, at least, not felt by anyone as 'weird' or inartistic.

I have wanted to share the essential stages of the journey that has resulted in the work described in these three books. I have not wanted to exclude the aspects of myself that are challenging and which belong to the path that we as artists choose to travel. Although the forms they have taken in my life may be unique to me, the themes are not uncommon. There are many, like myself, who have been attracted to a path of art requiring sacrifice upon the altar of an unattainable ideal. Such art is a tyrant whose demands for perfection are merciless, relentless and unachievable. As well, so often the creative process is blocked by unconscious or unresolved emotional dynamics within an individual or between the members of a group.[†]

I am no less grateful for the times of challenge that have taught me than the times of joy in seeing what this work makes possible. Then, like my student in New York, I can only say: *It blows my mind!*

---

[*] The essential qualities of Speech Formation cannot be transmitted by technology. Briefly: an instrument constructed to reproduce or in some way manipulate the wave lengths which are then translated in the brain as sound, cannot record or register dimensions of the sound which are not physical. Without perception of the *life/etheric* and *being* of the sounds, what we hear relates to the living being of the sound as a corpse does to a living human being. It is this 'dead body' of the sound that technology is able to transmit and manipulate.

[†] See endnote 24 for a more detailed consideration of a way of working which includes processes to address these issues.

Appendix D

Colleagues working with Chekhov's Acting Techniques in the context of Anthroposophy and Speech Formation (in English, within established training contexts)

Since 2012, Dawn Langman has been teaching Speech Formation with her integrated Chekhov/Speech methodology to first, second and third-year acting students at the Drama centre, *Flinders University*, South Australia.

Gaity School of Acting, Dublin (GSA). *Michael Chekhov Technique Advanced Training Programme–* Chekhov/Speech Formation stream www.gaietyschool.com. Contact: Joerg Andrees: Coordinator@gaietyschool.com or joerg.andrees@t-online.de

Dr Diane Caracciolo, Associate Professor of Curriculum Instruction, Adelphi University, Garden City, NY. Dr. Caracciolo holds a Goetheanum Diploma in Speech Formation from the London School of Speech Formation (later *Peredur Centre for the Arts* and currently *Artemis School of the Living Word*) and a doctorate in Art and Art Education from Teachers College, Columbia. She currently coordinates a series of interdisciplinary arts education courses and several graduate programmes in Educational Theatre. Her course, *Creative Speech and Storytelling,* is the result of her continuing exploration of the Chekhov method and creative Speech Formation as lively means to animate the imaginative lives and expressive capacities of teachers. Dr Caracciolo also serves on the faculty of the *Winkler Centre for Adult Education* where she teaches speech formation informed by Chekhov methodology to Foundation Year students. Contact Diane: caraccio@adelphi.edu.

Dr Jane Gilmer: Assistant Professor, Department of Visual and Performing Arts/ Drama at the National Institute of Education, Singapore. See her recent article, *Michael Chekhov's Imagination of the Creative Word and the Question of its Integration into his Future Theatre* published in the journal, *Theatre, Dance and Performance Training*, Vol 4, Issue 2, 2013. Contact Jane: jane.gilmer@gmail.com or jane.gilmer@nie.edu.sg

Sarah Kane, teaches speech and acting at various centres in UK, Europe and USA, including the Michael Chekhov Studio UK. Contact Sarah:
www.michaelchekhov.org.uk or sarah@michaelchekhov.org.uk

John McManus: teaches voice, speech, acting and Shakespeare at the Conservatory of the Performing Arts at Point Park University of Pittsburg. Contact John:
shakespearealive@gmail.com or jmcmanus@pointpark.edu

Joanna Panagiotopoulos: teaches Chekhov and Speech Formation within the Steiner teacher-training at Sydney Rudolf Steiner College, Sydney and runs workshops and courses at The Harmony Centre, Mittagong, NSW. The Harmony Centre is a community space integrating artistic, therapeutic and spiritual research and practice. Contact Joanna: joanna@harmonyfoundation.com.au or theartofspeech@harmonyfoundation.com.au

Ted Pugh and Fern Sloan, of the Actors Ensemble, Columbia County, New York — master teachers of Chekhov's methodology who teach regularly at MICHA conferences and in college level courses.

PerformInternational is a new, spirit-inspired training and research initiative in theatre and the performing arts in the UK that is launching a full-time professional training as well as part-time trainings and short courses from Autumn 2014.

The four-year, full-time professional training starting in September 2014 has two main aims:

- To renew for the twenty-first century and integrate the work begun by Rudolf and Marie Steiner in the field of artistic speech and drama with what was further developed by Russian theatre practitioner Michael Chekhov in theatre and acting.
- To create a rigorous training in theatre and the performing arts that enables graduates to both begin an independent professional artistic life in performance and teaching and qualifies them to take up further training in education and therapy at postgraduate level.

PerformInternational's trainings and courses have been set up by Sarah Kane, Gregers Brinch and Geoffrey Norris.

For further information please contact: initiativeperformingarts@gmail.com www.performinternational.org   www.facebook.com/performinternational

In languages other than English

Michael Tschechow Studio, Berlin, (MTSB) www.mtsb.de. Offers 1 and 3 year full-time trainings in Chekhov's methodology from an anthroposophical perspective and including Speech Formation. Contact: Jobst Langhans: jobst.langhans@mtsb.de and Joerg Andrees: Chekhov.training@gmail.com. A number of teachers work there with Speech Formation, including Sarah Kane.

Bibliography

The *Bhagavad Gita*, Bennett, Coleman & Co., Ltd., New Delhi, 2009.

The Tree of Life (the *Bhagavad Gita*), Viking Press, New York, 1942.

A Koestler, *The Act of Creation*, Arkana, London, 1989.

RD Laing, *The Divided Self*, Tavistock Publications, London, 1960.

L Schierse Leonard, *Witness to the Fire: Creativity and the Veil of Addiction*, Shambhala, Boston and London, 2001.

A Miller, *The Drama of Being a Child*, Virago Press, London, 1987.

R Steiner, *The Threshold of the Spiritual World*, Rudolf Steiner Press, London, 1975.

Chekhov on the art of the actor:

M Chekhov, *To the Actor*, Harper & Row, US, 1953. This is the original edition of the English translation. It is now out of print, but is still a rare treasure, if you can find one second-hand.

M Chekhov, *On The Technique of Acting*, Harper Perennial — a division of Harper Collins, New York, 1991. This is the second English publication of Chekhov's original. It contains some material that was missing from *To the Actor* but has lost some that was in the original, so both editions are worth having. It includes a helpful biography of Chekhov and a new preface by Mala Powers.

M Chekhov, *To the Actor*, Routledge, London, 2002. A third edition of the original containing additional material on psychological gesture and a new preface by Simon Callow.

M Chekhov, *On Theatre and the Art of Acting*, Applause Theatre Books, New York, 1992. This is a series of four tapes. They have been edited from an original series of twelve lectures taped by Chekhov just before he died. Included is a *Guide to Discovery* and *Exercises* by Mala Powers. A wonderful opportunity to hear the voice of Chekhov.

D Hurst du Prey, *Lessons for the Professional Actor*, Performing Arts Journal Publications, New York, 1985. A collection of transcribed notes arranged by D Hurst du Prey.

M Chekhov, *The Path of the Actor*, Routledge, Taylor and Francis Group, London and New York, 2005. These are the first English translations of Chekhov's autobiographical writings.

Additional reading

Other related works:

Explorations of Chekhov's work by other practitioners:

Cynthia Ashperger, *The Rhythm of Space and the Sound of Time: Michael Chekhov's Acting Technique in the 21st Century. Consciousness Literature and the Arts*, Rodopi Press, 2008. This book acknowledges Chekhov's relationship with Anthroposophy and the part played by the MICHA organisation in the current renaissance of Chekhov's work.

Franc Chamberlain, *Michael Chekhov, Routledge Performance Practitioners Series*, Routledge, 2004.

Mel Gordon, *The Stanislavsky Technique: Russia. A Workbook for Actors*, Applause Theater Book Publishers, 1988. (This puts Chekhov's techniques clearly in the context of the contributions of Stanilavsky, Vachtangov and the Moscow Arts Experiment.)

Charles Marowitz, *The Other Chekhov, A Biography of Michael Chekhov, the Legendary Actor, Director and Theorist*, Applause Theater and Cinema Books, New York, 2004.

Leonard Petit, *The Michael Chekhov Handbook*, Routledge, 2010.

DVDs: Master Classes in the Michael Chekhov Technique at the Spencertown Academy presented by the Michael Chekhov Association.

Rudolf Steiner, *Speech and Drama*, Anthroposophical Publishing Company, London, 1959. A series of 19 lectures given by Rudolf Steiner in 1924. Chekhov was invited but unable to attend. However, his subsequent profound study of Rudolf Steiner's Anthroposophy became the foundation of Chekhov's own spiritual path.

B Bates, *The Way of the Actor*, Century Hutchinson Ltd., London, 1986. This is the only other book I am aware of that explores, in any systematic way, psychological and spiritual aspects of the actor's work. It offers a comprehensive picture of many differing approaches and draws on the experience of many well-known and respected actors of the last century. It differs from *The Art of Acting* in that my exploration is connected largely to one specific methodology and the world-view from which it springs.

M Langman, *Drama, Myth and Psyche*, Griffin Press, Australia, 2007. This book is the result both of profound, meticulous research and an intense personal quest to penetrate the mysteries of drama. It includes an inspiring exploration of Isis and Osiris, Persephone and Dionysus, and Oedipus, three of the myths seminal to our theatrical tradition and to which I frequently refer in *The Art of Acting*. Contact Michele Langman: langmancentre@gmail.com

Original artworks that serve as a basis for Raphaela Mazzone's illustrations

Isis enfolds us in her wings: based on the representation of Isis from the sarcophagus of Ramses III, reproduced by Arthur Cotterell and Rachel Storm in *The Ultimate Encyclopaedia of Mythology*, Hermes House, 1999.

Anubis leads the human soul: based on the representation from the funeral papyrus in the tomb of Hunefer, now in the British Museum, and published in *Egyptian Painting* by TGH James, British Museum Press, 1986.

Nike of Samothrace: based on the sculpture called 'Winged Victory' or the 'Nike of Samothrace', the original of which is in the Louvre Museum, Paris.

The discus thrower: based on Myron's sculpture of the Discus Thrower. The original sculpture is in the British Museum.

The spear thrower: based on the sculpture thought to represent Zeus or Poseidon. The original sculpture is in the National Archaeological Museum of Athens.

Heart-centre based on the sculpture of Apollo: the original sculpture is in the National Archaeological Museum of Athens.

Will-centre based on a warrior 1: based on the depiction of a Trojan warrior from a Grecian frieze.

Will-centre based on a warrior 2: based on the depiction of a Trojan warrior from a Grecian frieze.

Head-centre based on the charioteer 1: based on the sculpture of the Charioteer. The original sculpture is in the Delphi Archaeological Museum.

The charioteer: based on the sculpture of the Charioteer. The original sculpture is in the Delphi Archaeological Museum.

Head-centre based on the charioteer 2: based on the sculpture of the Charioteer. The original sculpture is in the Delphi Archaeological Museum.

Hermes/Mercury and the baby Dionysus: based on the sculpture of Hermes and Dionysus by Praxiteles. Original sculpture is in the Archaeological Museum in Olympia.

Bacchus/John the Baptist: based on a painting of Bacchus/Dionysus. The original was of John the Baptist painted from an original drawing of the Baptist by Leonardo da Vinci. Although the exact authorship of the first painting is not established scholars think it was painted in Leonardo's workshop by one of his followers. In the 17th century it was painted over and altered by an unknown artist to represent Bacchus/Dionysus.

Priests enact the trope within the Easter mass: based on the 12th century AD ivory carving in Cologne (original drawing by Gerda Becker With from *Die Deutsche Dichtung des Mittelalters*) depicting the scene of the first enactment of the *Quem Quaeritis* during the celebration of the Easter Sunday morning mass, taken from a drawing from Macgowan and Melnitz, *The Living Stage*, Prentice-Hall, 1955. The *Quem Quaeritis* was a fragment of liturgical text (called a *trope*) inserted into the mass and which it is generally acknowledged was the seed from which sprang the rebirth of the drama in Western Europe in the 10th century AD.

Our Western theatre lineage: composite of the five images depicting part of the lineage out of which Western theatre has emerged and revealing the mystery stream which lies at its source and has flowed through the centuries.

The human form divine: based on the sketch by Leonardo da Vinci depicting the 'Human Being Standing in a Circle'.

Wheat sprouting from the body of Osiris: based on a bas-relief of Osiris-Nepra at Philae, Egypt.

Demeter bestows upon Triptolemus and ear of wheat: based on the 5th century BC relief, National Archaeological Museum of Athens.

Other artworks

Van Gogh, *Boots with Laces* (A Pair of Shoes). Original is at the Van Gogh Museum, Amsterdam.

Notes

1. I write *The Art of Acting* with the assumption that if the reader is not already familiar with Michael Chekhov's own written work, they will wish to be. The basic texts which Chekhov wrote himself are listed in the bibliography. Should Chekhov's work be limited to that original and discrete body of content, it would be in danger of becoming a stale dogma. It is testimony to its living power that the capacities gained through the mastery of that original content lead to its becoming an *investigative methodology* through which the work continues to evolve. The growing number of books in recent years by practitioners of Chekhov's work bears witness to this. A list of these is included in the Additional Reading list.

2. There need no longer be a separation between speech and acting because Chekhov's methodology provides this bridge. In my experience, the psycho-physical basis of the Chekhov work will naturally extend itself into the voice if that is encouraged in the ways I have indicated. Likewise, this path to Speech Formation can be the more holistically experienced if it is grounded in Chekhov's psycho-physical approach.

3. *A Spiritual Path for the Actor* is presented as a trilogy. *The Art of Acting* begins with an introductory overview and then focuses on a practical exploration of Michael Chekhov's approach to the art of acting. *The Art of Speech* explores the spiritual foundations of the art of Speech Formation in relation to the English Language, and *The Integrated Actor* deals with the further artistic application made possible by integrating these two streams of work. *The Integrated Actor* deals with the artistic possibilities that arise from integrating these two streams of work, in particular how they enable the investigation of many of the indications Steiner gave for actors in the *Speech and Drama* lectures in the last year of his life.

   For those who seek connection with the art of spoken language, the approach explored in *The Art of Speech* (investigating the speech technique arising from the indications of Rudolf Steiner and the work of his wife, Marie) is complementary to *The Art of Acting*, springing as it does from the same universal realities. Much that will be described in *The Integrated Actor* will not be possible to understand or access without a certain mastery of both the speech and acting work as outlined in *The Art of Acting* and *The Art of Speech*.

4. See Appendix B.

5. Deidre Hurst du Prey; excerpt from *The Actor is the Theatre: A Collection of Michael Chekhov's Unpublished Notes and Manuscripts on the Art of Acting and the Theatre*, 1977.

6. Rainer Maria Rilke, *Gesammelte Briefe in sechs Bänden* (*Collected Letters in Six Volumes*), Ruth Sieber-Rilke and Carl Sieber, Leipzig, 1936–1939.

   In *Witness to the Fire: Creativity and the Veil of Addiction*, Linda Schierse Leonard explores the relationship between the dysfunctional dynamics of addiction and creative gifts in the lives of famous writers. Artists recognizing the addictive aspects of their creativity have developed Arts Anonymous; a programme of recovery based on the 12 step process pioneered by Alcoholics Anonymous. In *Touched with Fire: Manic Depressive Illness and the Artistic Temperament*, Dr. Kay Redfield Jamison, explores the connection that the title indicates.

7. Sophocles translated by E F Watling, *King Oedipus* from *The Theban Plays* published by Penguin Classics, 1977.

8. Sophocles, *Oedipus at Colonus* from *The Theban Plays* translated by E F Watling, Penguin Classics, 1977.

9. From *Ode: Intimations of Immortality* by William Wordsworth. Wordsworth described the process by which the consciousness of supersensible reality many human beings still retain into childhood and adolescence gradually fades until it disappears completely. He likens the fading to 'the shades of the prison house' descending.

10. One source for this description is *The Mahabharata Vana Parva*, section CLXXXIX.

11. Rudolf Steiner, *Occult Science*, Rudolf Steiner Press, Forest Row, 2005 (first printed 1914), (chapters 4 & 6).

12. From *The Selected Poetry and Prose of William Wordsworth* The Signet Classic Poetry Series. Copywrite 1970. William H Hartman.

13. TS Eliot, *Four Quartets*.

14. Virginia Woolf, *Carlyle's House and other Sketches* (entry 29 February 1909), edited by David Bradshaw, Hesperus Press Ltd, London, 2003.

15. Euripides, *The Bacchae*, Penguin Books Ltd, Great Britain, 1960.

16. *Old Testament*, First Book of Kings, chapter 19, verse 12 and Shakespeare, *Macbeth*, Act 1, scene 7. Shakespeare, who understood the language of the Mysteries, reveals through his poetry that at some level both Macbeth and his wife know that the choice they make is between the power that is not of 'this world' and the power that is.

17. Shakespeare, *Macbeth*, Act 1, scene 7.

18. From the *Bhagavad-Gita* quoted from *The Tree of Life: selections from the literature of the world's religions* edited by Ruth Smith, Viking Press, New York, 1942.

19. Christopher Fry, *A Sleep of Prisoners* from *Collected Plays*, Oxford University Press, 1950 (reprinted 1986), p 29.

20. I have borrowed this way of naming the extremes from the title of the novel by Irving Stone based on the life of Michelangelo: *The Agony and the Ecstasy*, Doubleday & Company, Inc., USA, 1961.

21. Shakespeare's *King Lear*: Act 1, scene 1.

22. Rudolf Steiner, 'The Threshold of the Spiritual World', chapters 9 and 10 from *A Road to Self Knowledge and the Threshold of the Spiritual World*, Rudolf Steiner Press, London, 1975.

23. Rudolf Steiner, *Mystery Dramas* translated by Adam Bittleston, *First Mystery Play*, scene 3, Rudolf Steiner Press, London, 1982.

24. **The role of healing processes in artistic work**

    I do not suggest that everyone engaged in practising their art will want or need specific personal developmental/therapeutic work to be included. Nevertheless, experience shows that many now are frustrated with the split between the necessary hours we devote to understand and express at the highest level of our art the processes within characters and scenes while the dramas in ourselves and our interactions which affect our work together, go unacknowledged or we are powerless to deal with them.

These are some of the issues I have found in my years of teaching and rehearsing, can block a group's or individual's creative process:

- The serious illness or death of someone's close relative or friend.
- The breakup of significant relationships, especially if both individuals need to work together in the same class or group.
- Loss of confidence resulting from a struggle with some aspect of the work that cannot be grasped or understood.
- Fear of being judged.
- The need to be 'perfect' or 'brilliant'.
- Need to establish a consensual procedure to healthily receive and give feedback or criticism.
- Addiction.
- Ambition, jealousy and rivalry.
- Necessity to face our limitations.

I have witnessed how unresolved, dysfunctional emotions and behaviour, both of myself or colleagues, can block the free flow of creative energy. This happens whether we express our reactions or suppress them in order to 'get on with the work'. Either way disrupts the harmony of the artistic process, resulting in anxiety or stress in class or the rehearsal space. Not every issue necessarily requires conscious therapeutic intervention. Often it suffices simply to acknowledge what is there and offer compassionate support for what a friend or colleague undergoes.

Some object that taking the lid off 'Pandora's box' will result in a loss of boundaries and 'therapy' will swamp artistic work. I felt wary of this possibility myself. In practice, I found that once permission had been given to honour the personal dimension in our work, the necessity to do so was occasional and could be precisely targeted. Just acknowledging a member of the class or ensemble was struggling or a dynamic between some or all members of the group was impacting the group's capacity to focus healthily on the creative task in hand, would often be enough.

When such occasions would occur, I found it helpful to suggest these options to the individual or individuals concerned:

- Leave the group, process what is happening and return when ready to engage creatively again within the group.
- Acknowledge what's taking place within the group and assess if it can be put on hold until the task in hand has been completed; generally this implies commitment to create another time and space in which to deal with the problem.

- If dealing with it cannot be postponed, share within the group what is occurring and ask for their support to deal with it.
- Invite the group's permission to engage in a process to release what's blocking the artistic work.

In every case in which the process had integrity, I found that once the block was dealt with in one or other of these ways, the problem in our work together disappeared. The individual or group was revitalized and the artistic task resumed with new energy.

My first attempts to consciously address these issues in the evolution of the quest to help create a healthy working culture exposed some problems in this pioneering phase. These served to clarify the conditions needed if such attempts are to succeed.

(a) For therapeutic processes to be included someone in the group must have the necessary skills and training and the trust of the group to guide them.
(b) Such work must be 100% consensual.
(c) There must be recognition when the healing needed by an individual may lie outside what is appropriate within the group. The class or ensemble then is not the place for this to be addressed. The group, however, can encourage and support a colleague's need to seek appropriate assistance. As we become more skilful and the processes evolve to meet this need, we may expect that individuals who seek this integrated work will find their way to groups and trainings that can offer this.

THE PRACTICE

Chapter 1

25. *The Timaeus of Plato*, translated by Benjamin Jowett and published by William Benton for *Encyclopaedia Britannica Inc.*, Chicago, 1969.
26. For Chekhov's own descriptions of these qualities-of-movement, see pages 10–13 of *To the Actor*, and pages 45–51 of *On the Technique of Acting*.
27. From the adaptation by Rosalba Clemente and Dawn Langman, 2004.
28. Shakespeare, *Hamlet*, Act 2, scene 2. Because this is a text that gives us opportunity to practise and apply many of the tools to be described in coming chapters, you can find it in Appendix A for easy reference.

    Although the detailed exploration of the art of speech and language is the subject of *The Art of Speech*, even at this simple level we can experience intuitively how certain consonants seem to naturally integrate with the qualities-of-movement connected with the four elements or states of being. The previous examples are based on images strongly connected to these elements.
29. Translation not known. (Possibly Owen Barfield or Cecil Harwood.)

Chapter 2

30. Martin Buber (1878–1965). The Austrian born Jewish philosopher, who eventually became a professor at Hebrew University in Jerusalem. He is most well-known for his book

Ich und Du, published in 1923. Here he characterizes true dialogue, as a level of encounter that takes place when two beings recognize each other at the level of their *beingness*. In English, this has been most commonly translated as an *I–Thou* relationship, as opposed to *Ich–Es* or *I–It*, in which each experiences the other as an object. Any meeting — human to human, human to nature, human to the divine — can be raised to the level of an *I–Thou* encounter or remain at the level of *I–It*.

31. In his *Speech and Drama* lectures Rudolf Steiner connected the Greek gymnastic exercises to capacities an actor needs. In my experience of being taught the Chekhov work, I found extensive use was made of the connection between running and overall *presence in the body*, particularly legs and feet. As well, we worked with the psycho-physical relationship between projection of the javelin and of the actor's presence. I am not aware of whether Chekhov explored the connections with the other three Greek gymnastic exercises. I would be grateful, if anyone has any information or experience of this, to be informed. In general, the specific exploration of the indications Steiner gave in his *Speech and Drama* lectures is the subject of *The Integrated Actor*. I have chosen to include the exploration of the Greek Gymnastic exercises in Book 1 because they lie at the foundation of the actor's work.

32. A detailed exploration of what I mean will be found in the chapter 'Masculine and Feminine' in *The Integrated Actor*, chapter, The tension of opposites.

33. See chapter 4 and *The Integrated Actor*, chapter, The tension of opposites.

34. The practice of gymnastics as developed by Count von Bothmer, also cultivates this sense. It arose in response to Steiner's promptings that the principles of the ancient art of Greek gymnastics should be re-interpreted for people of today. A branch that has evolved from this and is now practised widely is known as Spatial Dynamics. The practice of these principles in either form and also through the art of Eurythmy strengthens our perception of the 'human form divine'.

35. From the poem *The Divine Image* from William Blake's *Songs of Innocence*.

Chapter 3

36. As we evolve we become more conscious in our will. It requires an investigation of Anthroposophy that is beyond the scope of this book to understand the complex nature and evolution of the will. The interested reader can make a start with the series of lectures Steiner gave to teachers which have been published as *The Foundations of Human Experience* (formerly *The Study of Man*), particularly lecture 4.

37. The relationship between the feeling-centre in our chest and speech is explored in *The Art of Speech*, chapter 3 and *The Integrated Actor*, chapter 3.

38. The relationship between the will-centre in our belly and speech, is explored in *The Art of Speech*, chapter 3 and in *The Integrated Actor*, chapter 3.

39. Chekhov describes working with the will in *To the Actor* on page 6, and *On the Technique of Acting*, pages 52–54.

40. For Steiner's description of a conscious development of the chakras see Rudolf Steiner, *Knowledge of Higher Worlds and its Attainment*, Rudolf Steiner Press, UK, 1963.

41. A detailed exploration of these polarities, their connection to gesture and patterns of voice and speech is included in the chapter entitled Building the bridge between gesture, voice and speech, in *The Integrated Actor*.

42. For Chekhov's own description of this tool, see page 59 of *To The Actor*, and pages 36–38 of *On the Technique of Acting*.

43. The relationship between left and right brain and its implications for our work with language is considered in the chapter on grammar in *The Art of Speech*.

44. Bertolt Brecht (1898–1956): the founder of the Berlin Ensemble and author of several of the twentieth century's great plays (including *Mother Courage, The Caucasian Chalk Circle*). He was dedicated to achieving an Epic theatre that would be the instrument of social change. Central to his quest was the need to find a style of acting and production that would stimulate an audience to think actively about their experience. His theories and methods he encapsulated in the term 'alienation' (from the German: *Verfremdungseffekt*). The emotional power of his plays make it clear that Brecht did not intend his audiences not to feel but to go beyond emotion to a critical engagement with ideas.

Chapter 4

45. This theme, explored in relation to the content of drama, is also explored in *Drama, Myth and Psyche* by Michele Langman.

46. For example: Duerr, *The Length and Depth of Acting*, Holt, Rinehart and Winston, inc, 1962, and Macgowan and Melnitz, *The Living Stage*, Prentice-Hall, inc., 1955.

47. *The Stela of Ikhernofret* was a stone column erected by Ikhernofret somewhere circa 1887–1849 BC (BCE) during the reign of Pharaoh Sesostris. Ikhernofret was a high priest or official ordered by Sesostris to arrange the public processions and rituals connected with the festival. The *Stela* records details of the five day event honouring the passion of Osiris, which Ikhernofret organized. It took place at Abydos annually from circa 2500 BC (BCE) until 550 BC (BCE).

48. Macgowan and Melnitz, *The Living Stage*, Prentice-Hall. Inc., 1955, page 109.

49. Edouard Schuré, *The Genesis of Tragedy and The Sacred Drama of Eleusis*, Rudolf Steiner Publishing Company, London, 1936.

Chapter 5

50. See chapter 5, *The Art of Speech*.

51. Rilke, *Duino Elegies*, University of California press, 1961. Translated into English by CF MacIntyre.

Epilogue

52. For further exploration of the significance of Dionysus to the artist see *The Integrated Actor*, chapter, The tension of opposites.

53. Steiner explored the significance of Dionysus represented as a baby in his lecture series on the Greek mythology, entitled: *Wonders of the World, Ordeals of the Soul and Revelations of the Spirit.* (10 lectures given in Munich, 18–27 August, 1911, first published by Rudolf Steiner Press, London, 1963.)

54. An alternative to Before Christ (BC), is the abbreviation Before the Common/Current/ Christian Era, (BCE) . Common/Current/Christian Era (CE) is an alternative naming of the traditional calendar era, *Anno Domini* (AD).

55. J Gassner ed, *Mediaeval and Tudor Drama*, Applause Theatre Book Publishers, 1963.

56. Marlowe's *Dr Faustus*.

57. Aeschylus, *Prometheus Bound* (translation uncertain: probably Owen Barfield).

58. From the letters of Seneca quoted from *The Plays of Seneca*. In this letter, Seneca quotes from Virgil's *Aeneid*, VIII, 352.

Appendix C

59. Konstantin Stanislavski (1863–1938) was the founder of the Moscow Arts Theatre. His explorations led to a systematic path of training for the actor based on 'truthfulness' of the emotions, which revolutionized the art of acting and continues to be a major influence. He was also a teacher, friend and mentor to the young Michael Chekhov, supporting him to follow the creative impulse of his own genius.

60. Rudolf Laban (1879–1958) was a Hungarian dance artist who worked for many years in Germany. Finally, after World War 2, he taught at Dartington Hall in the UK, where he spent his final years. His explorations into movement have left a system of notation that has deeply influenced twentieth century dance and movement theory.

61. Diane studied the Michael Chekhov acting method and history for many years with her mentor, Deirdre Hurst du Prey, a founding member of the Chekhov Theatre Studio of Dartington Hall, England. Ms du Prey was Chekhov's assistant and author of several studies of Chekhov, including *The Actor is the Theatre: A Collection of Michael Chekhov's Unpublished Notes & Manuscripts on the Art of Acting and the Theatre.* Dr. Caracciolo's oral history of her mentor, *The pencil: Memories of Dartington Hall and the English Origin of the Michael Chekhov Acting Method*, is included in du Prey's *The Actor is the Theatre.* Dr Caracciolo's published works include an article about teaching Chekhov methods to prospective teachers — *Strengthening the imagination through theater: The contributions of Michael Chekhov*, published in 2008 in *Encounter: Education for Meaning and Social Justice.*

62. St Paul, chapter 13 of the second letter to the Corinthians.

63. An adult training centre dedicated to Rudolf Steiner's work, in Spring Valley, New York.